Dynamics of Watershed Development and Livelihood in India

S.S.P. Sharma

U.H. Kumar

SERIALS PUBLICATIONS
NEW DELHI (INDIA)

First Published - 2010

ISBN: 978-81-8387-346-8

Published by

SERIALS PUBLICATIONS
4830/24, 1st Floor, Ansari Road
Darya Ganj, New Delhi-110002 (India)
Phone : 23245225. Fax : 91-11-23272135
E-mail: serials@satyam.net.in

CONTENTS

FOREWORD

Dynamics of 'Watershed Development and Livelihood in India' is a highly suggestive title for the instant volume for it combines within itself twin concepts that need to seen in unison-cost-effective democratic management of the natural water resources in the watershed area and the sustenance that it provides to the crops, vegetation, trees, livestock including wild life, human beings including the people who live within the watershed and beyond on sustainable basis. Each of these words has a loaded connotation. The primary requirement of Watershed is that it should be within a geographic area having a common outlet. The management is required to focus on the management of the natural flow of water and the sub-soil water but not the reserve aquifer. This will lead to conservation of water and its utilisation in a democratic and equitable manner. Water rights are not included amongst the basic rights; they does not belong to the landowners alone but to the entire community and to each individual from that community. There are experiments where the water rights have been made transferable, of the rightsholder is not in a position to use the same. In the Chakriya Vikas system developed by the late PR Mishra the individual water rightsholder is compensated for his non-use. However, there is no commodification of the water rights and the ultimate power of arbitration resides in the community as a whole. This management has to be practised in such a way that the water resources are conserved at a minimum threshold level and should continue to grow.

The second aspect of watershed relates to the technological issues. Technology and knowledge base are important for both planning the watershed and for their implementation. To begin, with there are the traditional technologies which have grown over the course of last several millennia. These technologies vary regionally, are seeped into the soil and are time tested. There is no problem of absorption in the region. However, problems begin once there is an attempt to transplant these technologies to other regions. There have to be adopted to the local conditions.

In addition there are the exotic technologies either developed within the country or imported. There is a process of contestation in the realm of watershed. The bureaucratically driven part of the programme would like to see single unified watershed programme from the micro-watershed onwards. This, however, appears unlikely. Watershed has traditionally twin aspects-the process and the technology. The process would depend largely on the process of social mobilisation of the community. A watershed programme normally takes years to get off the ground. This is because the process of social mobilisation of the community over the question of sharing the water resources is the most difficult, complex and time taking part of it. Contrary to the popular understanding, a village society is far from being a monolithic structure; it is fractured into caste and associations of other nature usually at war with one another. This fragmentation is efficiency reducing and cost enhancing and slows down the process of social mobilization. Mobilisation is a process reverse to fragmentation for it brings fragmented communities together on specific issues and later produces greater homogenisation. The process of mobilisation, hence, is also equated to empowerment of the village society for it is both efficiency enhancing and cost reducing. A well done mobilisation is more than half the work done. Dr SSP Sharma and Dr UH Kumar rightly argue for social mobilisation as the first step in the direction. They have, however, their limitations for within the Government programme structure delivery have to be time bound. One fails to understand how a quarrel going generations back could be reconciled within a matter of days. It may take years. However, within a Government programme structure one does not have the luxury of time. Hurry in social mobilization, hence, is the biggest enemy of watershed and a point of reconciliation could be evolved by taking a longer perspective of the programme. Instead of an annual programme it could be a five- yearly programme

It is still possible to have the watershed without undergoing the process of mobilisation. That would, however, be only formalism and not the watershed. It would have little sustainability. It is possible for a good engineer to design and execute the structures within the watershed within a few months. In the absence of the social mobilisation the watershed would degenerate into a contractor driven programme. It is the social mobilisation which provides the nectar to the programme and everything else is a by product. The objective of the Watershed should be that the villages get together on the issue of water and also on the issue as to what to do with the water. Nothing could be more handy than the four-point talisman of Padmabibhushan Anna Saheb Hazare-Charaibandi (not leaving the animals open); Kulharbabdi (not felling the trees), Nashabandi (prohibition) and Nasbandi (family planning). These are the pre-requisites on which the programme would stand.

This brings us to the second aspect of the programme i.e., that of utilisation of the water so resourced. Here the village has to lay down rules. The fundamental rule of Ralegaon Sidhi or for that matter Hiraware Bazaar in Ahmednagar district is that every drop of water is to be utilised; there should be no sowing of water intensive crops like sugarcane, rationing of crop cycle and four point mantra of the Anna. Where these needs are fulfilled and resources continue to regenerate, the watershed is a success. This demands equity in labour contribution and participative sharing of resources, democracy in decision making and value addition through processing. Where the base of social mobilisation has taken place, technology becomes an important question. The watershed must fulfill five basic needs of the rural society-drinking water. water for irrigation. food, fuel and fodder for the animals. The biggest gains of the community lie in their new found confidence and their willingness to co operate on the livelihood issues. Watersheds are known to have transforming effect upon the village economy. Sustainability is a key ingredient of this programme and using this sustainable base it is quite possible to take off on the path of rapid growth and launch into non-farm activities.

Yet, the programme has run into difficulties. In order to overcome these difficulties the Government of India issues guidelines- there have been nine of them altogether. The last three of them, i.e the Neeranchal and the GoI 2006 and 1994 are similar in many respects and at times the differences are more a matter of semantics. The crux, therefore, lies in better implementation rather than changes in the organisational structure of the programme. It has to be realised that developing a watershed is a slow and painful process and the Government agencies have little patience for it. Now a separate agency the NRAA has been put in place and the task before the new agency is to pool together all programmes of watershed and rainfed agriculture presently in existence. Water Management is the first of the tasks. Livelihood priority or social engineering is usually taken for granted and the social scientists and the agricultural and particularly the dryland agriculture experts are usually missing from the team. Thanks to the evolution of technologies extraordinary agricultural yields are possible without overtaxing the soil or the water resources. N Narasimha Raju Yadav, a farmer from the Gudru village in Andhra Pradesh became the first farmer to win a Padmasri award. He is capable of taking extraordinary yields without the use of much chemical fertilisers and with sustainable results. The Raju type of agriculture gels with the watershed. This is what the book tells and one must read it in order to grasp the essence of a sustainable viable watershed. The instant volume is worth reading because it is precisely such questions that it has taken up for discussions and is not a mere repetition of the guidelines.

A.K. Sinha
Director General, 19.8.09
National Institute of Rural Development,
Hyderabad-500030

PREFACE

Watershed development has been conceived not only as a strategy for natural resource conservation but also as institutional instrument for protecting the livelihoods of the people inhabiting the fragile ecosystems experiencing soil erosion and moisture stress. Closely related to this is the problem of continued drought, degradation of land in the rain fed or dry land areas. As it is, the rate of degradation of land in such areas in the 90s is likely to have proceeded at more than twice the rate observed in the 1980s, basically on account of soil erosion from run-off. This is happening despite the interventions for soil and moisture conservation through watershed development that may not have covered more than 10 percent of rain fed area-needing treatment. The acute scarcity of drinking water experienced in several parts of the country during the last many summers, despite a series of favourable monsoons preceding it, shows that droughts are becoming increasingly severe in the recent period. Clearly, the existing interventions for drought proofing have failed to neutralize the overall processes of degradation of natural resources underway in the rural areas.

Initially watershed projects were concentrating on soil and water conservation issues. A decade later, it became apparent that technical and physical works alone would not lead to the desired objectives of watershed development and it must also take into account the social, financial and institutional aspects of rural development. Livelihood generation under watershed is having strong thrust today or poverty alleviation under watershed programmes.

This book is based on the Papers presented in National Workshop on Watershed organized at NIRD. Authors have modified and incorporated the comments and suggestions received on the papers during the presentation before the final submission. Many papers have been developed on watershed-specific study that made dent in improvement of rural livelihood in different parts of the country. Some papers are theoretical in nature but authors tried to relooked into the emerging situations in watershed development and their impacts on livelihood.

We express our sincere gratitude to our beloved Director General, Mr. B K Sinha, IAS who took pain not only in writing the foreword of the book but also advising for updating of the manuscripts written by NIRD faculty. The Deputy Director General, Mr. K N Kumar, IAS was a source of inspiration in the preparation of the book. We feel grateful to him also. The staff of the Centre for Water and Land Resources helped me a lot in giving final touch to the manuscript. We would like to put on record of the help extended to us during the workshop, particularly the library and accounts section of NIRD. We are grateful to all of them who are directly and indirectly involved in the finalization of the manuscript. Further, we may not miss to express our gratitude to the Publisher of this book who took pain in publishing the manuscript. Finally, we must express sincere gratitude to our family members who raised all efforts to complete this work within time.

S.S.P. Sharma
U.H. Kumar

INTRODUCTION

Watershed development programmes are implemented by different Departments at the Centre, and in the States. The Department of Agriculture and Cooperation implements the National Watershed Development Projects for Rainfed Areas (NWDPRA). The watershed approach has been adopted in other schemes like development of catchment areas of River Valley Projects and flood prone areas and control of shifting cultivation in North-Eastern Regions. The Ministry of Rural Development implements DPAP and DDP as also the Integrated Wasteland Development Programme (IWDP). Besides, several externally aided projects are also under implementation. The Ministry of Environment and Forest is implementing an Integrated Afforestation and Eco-development Scheme to promote the development of degraded forests. The Planning Commission also follows a similar approach to implementing special area development programmes like Western Ghats Development Programme (WGDP) and Hill Area Development. In addition to the above Centrally Sponsored Schemes several State Governments are also implementing schemes for soil and moisture conservation on watershed lines. Maharashtra, Karnataka, Andhra Pradesh and Madhya Pradesh have made great strides in this regard. Orissa and Rajasthan have also taken the initiative.

From the above, it is clear that the watershed approach has been accepted as a means to increase agricultural production while arresting ecological degradation in rainfed and resource poor areas. It would, at the same time, improve the level of living of the poor by providing more sustainable employment. Yet, the implementation of this programme by different departments/agencies has been based on different approaches. This has resulted in problems at the field level. The need for 'a Single National Initiative' has been felt for some time, and was also articulated in the 1999-2000 budget speech of the Union Finance Minister.

The objective of all land based intervention should be, "To enable rural people in rainfed regions to prevent, arrest and reverse degradation of life support systems, particularly land and water, so as to produce biomass in a sustainable and equitable manner'. It is important to look at forest lands, non-forest wastelands and crop lands in an integrated manner. This is often not done as treatment upstream to reduce soil movement does not benefit large farmers who are downstream. They see no advantage and are indifferent or opposed to this strategy. They would prefer to conserve and harvest water in the drainage line so that it can be used directly for irrigation or to replenish groundwater. However, lands in the upper catchment should be rehabilitated first for at least three reasons: First, the landless and the poor who depend on upper slopes can benefit; second, groundwater recharge begins at the earliest; and third, by the time the lower catchment is treated any debris and erosion running down from the upper catchment will have been minimized.

However, upper slopes typically are under the control of Forest Department (FD) and it does not permit other departments to operate on its lands. The Ministry of Rural Development recently permitted its funds to be used in watershed schemes by FD, but a similar initiative is needed from the Ministry of Agriculture too. Between forests and agriculture, the complementarity needs to be strengthened; that way, the local community will get to develop a stake in the preservation of forests, which in turn can deter individual attempts at encroachments or degradation. For now, then, three life support systems — land, water and forests — remain unintegrated administratively and management-wise. Therefore, the government would strive to do integrated planning at the village level through peoples' participation.

Linking the future of forests and uncultivated lands with crop lands and groundwater recharge alone will ensure sustainability of the government efforts.

Watershed programmes are by definition gender friendly. Water, fodder and fuel have been the responsibility of women in the rural areas. Instances of women walking miles to collect these have been documented. A watershed project, which harvests and conserves water, therefore, necessarily lessens the burden of women. Even those watershed projects that do not address the concerns of women in terms of their role in the decision-making and employment opportunities, alleviate the burden on women. Successful completion of watershed projects increases the availability of water, fuel and fodder in the vicinity of the villages. Women have to spend less time on their collection. The time available to them needs to be productively utilized. It is, therefore, necessary to think of creative employment opportunities for women in which they can be fruitfully employed. Training programmes, which impart skills to women, access to credit and marketing and other service support should be clearly spelt out in the watershed project and provided for.Government guidelines have indicated that watershed projects may be saturated on priority basis by ensuring convergence with other Government programmes. However, this convergence is rarely been seen on the ground.

Evaluation reports of watershed projects have very clearly brought out the fact that successful watershed projects which have sustained over the years were designed in such a way that every individual residing in the watershed area came to have a stake in the successful completion and maintenance of the watershed project. This is an important area, which many watershed projects have tended to neglect. Gains from a watershed project largely accrue to the landholders. Marginal farmers and agricultural labourers only benefit from the project on account of increased agricultural activity, which increases opportunities for employment. If flow of benefits from the watershed is not specifically channelised to these groups in terms of greater access to Common Property

Resources (CPRs), fodder for their cattle and fuel requirements, little incentive remains for these groups to cooperate in rejuvenation of the CPRs through the mechanisms of social fencing or any other method which the community might choose for regeneration of non-agricultural land.

The issue of equitable distribution of gains, therefore, is crucial to the sustainability the project in the long run. In this regard, providing access to land to the marginal and landless agricultural labourers through the mechanism of rights on harvested water could be one alternative. It may be desirable to incorporate sharing of water by all residents in a watershed project as one of the preconditions for selecting a village for watershed development project.

Many success stories have emerged in the course of last 10-15 years in regard to development of a particular area on watershed basis. However, the cases of failures of such initiatives are many times more than the instances of success. Apart from the off-cited reasons of lack of people's participation, lack of technical expertise at ground level, corruption and apathy of implementing agencies, many a times, the programmes have floundered because of lack of technical inputs which should have flown to the area once the basic infrastructure of a watershed development project had been put in place. Lack of agricultural extension facilities and the institutions that could supply inputs for a changed cropping pattern would not generate the expected incomes, which would have been projected as one of the outcomes on the successful implementation of the project. Such failures have a snowballing effect and adversely affect people's enthusiasm for taking up developmental projects. The adoption of water conservation technologies for irrigation purposes assumes added importance for agricultural practices in watersheds, which experience low or scanty rainfall. Investments in drip irrigation, sprinkler irrigation and investments on research for crop varieties specifically suited to such areas and such irrigation systems are of particular importance and need to provide for at the planning stage itself (Johnson et al 2001). The areas with extensive wastelands and lands under stress strongly correlate to lack of banking and insurance facilities, lack of veterinary services and other related services. Unless these services are provided to these areas, the expected benefits of watershed development will not materialise.

Management of watershed development in India evolved significantly over the past there decades. During the 1970s to early 1980s, the main concentration was largely on biophysical criteria. In late 1980s there were some significant changes looking beyond soil and water conservation to include improving the productivity of natural resources. In

1994-95 Ministry of Rural Areas and Employment, Government of India came up with strict guidelines to achieve multiple objectives including productive, social, ecological/ environmental and equity issues to achieve optimum utilization of the watershed's natural resources; employment generation and development of other economic resources in the village; easy and affordable solutions and social condition of the resource poor, respectively. The present guidelines outline the various implementation stages of the watershed development projects, the operational procedures and provide sufficient operational flexibility at State, District and Project levels to enable them to respond to differing situations and aspirations of the village community.

Watershed development projects have greater potential to generate employment opportunities to the rural people. This was due to the increased availability of water resources, diversified cropping pattern including cultivation of labor intensive vegetable crops and other horticultural crops. This additional employment generation from a watershed program varies across regions depending on the cropping intensity, and the labor intensive crops grown in that region. This additional employment generation in the villages led to minimizing migration of landless and other labor. Thus watershed programs also contributed towards checking migration of rural people to the urban areas. This migration has greater concern for planning and devising rural development strategies.

The first chapter starts with the historical background of the watershed in the country with an emphasis on the achievements of enshrined goals. The author of this chapter a well acclaimed natural resource specialist K G Tejwani died while the manuscript is in the process of publication. He was a doyen of natural resource management. Based on past and present performance of watershed, he did make a meticulous presentation of the watershed future in the country. For any successful project/programme a synergy among Policy (& legislation)-Institutions-Programmes and People is needed. This system is anthropocentric and of the people – for the people-by the people. Any food producing land use system can support some level of population beyond which it will break down, unless the technology is upgraded or innovated. Now we are at a level where water use efficiency has to be increased to support the expanding population. Population is a key issue. In spite of many policies, good R&D, good HRD and many promises made, the implementation in WSM/NRM has been fair. The targeted goals have never been achieved and the promises never kept. Author therefore concluded that the future of WSM/NRM is full of worry and is "Imperfect". The causes for such a state of affairs are left with a question mark (?). What are the causes and solutions? Dr. Barbora in his paper puts forth that Participatory management is of crucial importance in watershed development projects in order to achieve desired objectives and sustainability. The system of management is an integrated approach to rural development and poverty alleviation, which can be seen, from different evaluation studies. Over the years, the system has undergone a desirable change and today it is recognized that community participation is central to watershed development, which lead to greater success by enhancing livelihood in an equitable manner.

In the third captor, the author Govind Dhaske highlights Gender equity is challenge due to social and institutionalized web of attitudes. The intended gender equity definitely will take some time as it has to happen through social processes. Assuring the change process in the community through programmatic interventions is primary duty of the planners. Immediate concerns and strategic concerns in gender equity in rural livelihoods should be objectively outlined and incorporates in the planned approach. Increased awareness of gender has led to establishment of self help groups (SHGs) that have helped women save, obtain credit, and become more active and visible. But this activity has not become an integral part of the watershed development and has had little impact on traditional gender roles. Ensuring the social processes through structural spaces is challenging task and needs policy inclusion. Regulating the benefits distribution process for assuring not only gender equity but also social equity will create collective understanding about livelihoods sustainability in correlation with gender and social equity. Bharat Patel argues that we are deviating from basic concept of watershed due to need of time, complex developmental issues, various agencies involved in implementation of programmes, to cover more area under treatment in short time span (considering size of the problem of protection and production both). Satpriya Raut is of the view that where participation has been acknowledged as the pre-condition to success or otherwise, it is apt to have a detailed analysis of the concept and its position in the whole debate of sustainable watershed development. The recent government guidelines are expected to institutionalise community participation in watershed development as one of the very important condition of the successes of watershed projects. A K Mishra et al discussed in their paper that Sustainable development in watersheds can only be achieved through optimum utilization of its natural resources. Livestock interventions in watersheds need to be comprehensively planned with the people directly concerned with the problem's of livestock. There is tremendous scope of increasing productivity of existing livestock resources by making appropriate provisions for fodder, water and health services within the watershed. Participation of farmers and village based institution proved to be an effective and efficient mechanism for faster technology diffusion. A favorable policy environment in terms of access to micro-credit, key inputs, assured market and veterinary services will have to be provided and socio-economic and technical constraints needs to be addressed in order to enable the farmers for livestock development. In his paper, M Mishra demonstrates that a livelihoods perspective can be used to encourage a more explicit analysis of the ways in which WSD directly and indirectly affect people's livelihoods. It encourages a broader and more structured assessment of impacts relevant to the poor. Case studies from tribal belts in Orissa particularly from the KBK region support the study. This can help practitioners and policy-makers to adjust their approaches and so enhance poverty impacts. In her paper, J Nirmala opines that the strategy adopted by the government in the rural areas despite being backbone of the village economy, to increase women welfare doing the past decade has not yielded adequate results. Hence a more dynamic proposal has to be made ready on the basis of the suitability and applicability the area of study concerned. The researcher will assure that this paper will add to the available literature and will come out successfully with a suitable watershed project for the women Tirunelveli Revenue Division.

S R Padhi in his contribution explains the initiatives taken through Watershed Development Programme has helped to ecological stabilization of Malkarbandha Watershed area with increased ground water level which in turn has breathed a new life in natural resources of the project area. The programme should be upgraded so that whole community participates and the benefits are equally distributed. For strengthening this approach concerted efforts are urgently required to develop and adopt integrated approach through appropriate technological interventions in participatory mode to offset the looming crisis of natural resource degradation and increased demand of food for sustainable livelihoods. P Banerjee tries to highlight the deeper understanding of both formal and informal networks, norms, values, and trust systems across gender lines is very crucial before implementing any programme meant to accomplish anything for women. These gender analyses likely hold the key to resolving the problem of equity and sustainability in WMP. A community may not ready to accept any developmental change for women and so needs to be sensitized very carefully, so that the informal value chains do not break up and proper vertical and horizontal integration is possible. The solution to WMP inability to sustain improvements for women is to create a more congenial environment where women emancipation is not viewed by the male as threat to the society but a benevolent helping hand ready to share the responsibilities of eradicating poverty and attaining sustainable livelihood. WMP can only succeed in its stated goals by taking into account women's accessibility to social capital.

Vijay Laxmi presents in her paper the Bihar state's study-based results in relation to the watershed and its symptomatic problems with land. Land is one of the most important components of watershed development. Ownership of and access to productive land is very important resource for promoting economic well being and socio-cultural identity. Land resources in India are under heavy pressure due to increase in human and livestock population, poverty and economic policies. Approximately, 57% of total geographical area is degraded to varying degree. Among the different categories of land, the land under cultivation faces the highest problem. Therefore, there is a need to take urgent care of land degradation in crop cultivation. S C Srivastava discusses the project has been instrumental in bringing about socio economic changes in the village society. Through its impact on migration and through formation of seven Self Help Groups (five women groups, one Shepard group and one landless group) involving exclusively the people below poverty line, it has affected the status of the poor also. Most of these groups are involved into livestock activities. Yet the prime question remains- in view of any formal or informal understanding on the right to use the water, what should be next step so that right of the poor are protected. As we have seen, prima facies no inequality is noticed in the water use pattern as such.

Whatever, inequalities are noticed are because of the inequalities in land holdings. C Sekar says that the field level experiences also indicated that the cropping intensity of the sample farms in watershed treated area (WTA) was higher. The financial measures of water harvesting structures also indicated a favourable trend with IRRs ranging from 14.3 to 35. The water conservation works extend the beneficial effects on recharge of ground water, control soil erosion, and alters the cropping pattern and cropping intensity with positive effects on productivity of the crops. Hence the water harvesting structures may be scaled up and implemented in dry lands on large scale to reap the real benefits of the rainwater harvesting, sustainability of natural resource base and strengthening of economic prosperity of our country.

In his paper, D Kumar is of the view that watershed development has more potential to generate employment opportunities for rural poor. This is due to the increased availability of water resources, diversified cropping pattern including cultivation of labour intensive vegetable and other horticultural crops. The additional employment generation from watershed programme varry across regions depending on the crop-intensity. The employment generation potential has got impetus from National Rural Employment Guarantee Act in those areas where the act is being implemented.

S S P Sharma focuses on the role of participatory approach in sustainability of watershed projects. He is of the view that the participatory watershed management is a critical area of rural development that could support rural people in many ways. India's watershed development project is seen as flagship project of Ministry of Rural development, Government of India. Watershed management in India has undergone dramatic change to include greater stake holder's participation for management of natural resources in a sustainable way. It is increasingly recognized that community participation was central to watershed development (Joshi, P.K et al 2003). More participatory approaches have achieved greater success in enhancing livelihoods in an equitable fashion (Kerr and Pangare, 2002).

It has been noted that participatory watershed management projects have been raising income, agricultural productivity, generating employment and conserving soil and water resources (Renfro, R. Z. 2005). Evidence from the three case studies and other general impact studies suggests that watershed development brought several positive trends including diversification of the rural economy, development of new institutions, increasing cropping intensity, Increasing cropping intensity, improved fodder production, increased availability of drinking water with rising ground water table, capacity development of the community etc. Based on the evidence found, it has been suggested that participatory watershed management could be a viable strategy of rural development for achieving sustainable rural livelihoods in India.

In his paper, U H Kumar gives emphasis on the stakeholders' participation in watershed projects. His analysis of seven selective watersheds in two states of Andhra Pradesh and Rajasthan though indicates the potential of watershed development in enhancing livelihoods; it brings out clearly the importance of different stakeholders involvement in the processes of watershed implementation. Based on the preceding analysis coupled with our wider field observations, we discuss here some of the emerging important issues regarding the role of different stakeholders viz., Watershed Committee, User Groups, Self-help Groups, Sarpanch, Gram Panchayat, Gram Sabha, Multi-disciplinary Team/Watershed Development Team and PIA to achieve effective and sustainable implementation of the watershed development programme.

D Ghosh argues that the panchayats in West Bengal are not that much interested in development of watersheds in the drought prone districts like Purulia, Bankura and some parts of Paschim Medinipore, even if there acute crisis of water. The simple fact that more irrigation water has meant greater output and income at the household level does not get the appropriate priority in the action plans designed at the gram panchayats. Primary reason is that everybody is interested in immediate benefits but not in long term benefits. Attitudinal change is urgent; but this requires training of the panchayat office bearers on sustained basis. This is not coming up, however. In the training curricula of the Department of Panchayats and Rural Development, Government of West Bengal, the matters of watershed development do not receive adequate attention.

Finally, it can be discerned that the watershed is now the pivotal force where the rural development revolves. Reasons are quite obvious. Rural development depends upon the availability of two major natural resources-land and water. Development drive in rural areas has no optimization of resources due to resource-limitation on the one hand and to protect the interest of the teaming millions of population, on the other. Watershed serves the strong and larger interest of urban elite also who consumes thousand liters of water a day which certainly comes to meet from the conservation of water in or around of the rural area near by the city. Urban settlement just pays for the services provided in term of tax or interest of what the rural commune serves through the development of watershed. Urban elite should now pay the principal amount of value they get through the support from rural resource-resilience created through the watershed development. Simultaneously, there is not given priority to value addition by processing of rural resource. Consequently, the player of rural development plays without creating the level of playing ground. This requires a lot of exercise in terms of investment. Watershed is now accepted as one of the strong means of resource conservation and also of livelihood generation. Livelihood generation under watershed doesn't pay much attention on value addition of the produce in the hands of rural people nor giving opportunity to explore market accessibility of the rural products. Consequently, the sustainability of rural livelihood is in question. Thus the watershed should be taken as an instrument of change not in terms of resource harnessing but also in investment and also of their effectiveness on livelihood sustainability.

REFERENCES

Johnson, N, Ravnborg, H.M, Westerman, O, and Probst, K. (2001), "User Participation in Watershed Management and Research", working paper No.19, CAPRi, IFPRI, Washington, D.C.

Joshi, P.K., Tewari, L., Jha, A.K. and Shiyani, R.L. (2003), "Impact of Watershed Program and People's Participation". National Centre for Agricultural Economics and Policy Research, (NCAP), New Delhi, India.

Kerr, J.,G. Pangare and V.L. Pangare (2002), Watershed Development Projects in India: An Evaluation. Washington, DC: International Food Policy Research Institute (IFPRI).

Kumar U H and Sharma, S S P (2009), Emerging Issues in the Process of Watershed Implementation: A Comparative Analysis of A.P. and Rajasthan, Journal of Social and Economic Development,Vol. 11, No. 2.

Renfro, R. Z. (2005), "The Value of Participation in Development-relevance to Soil and Water Conservation".

LIST OF CONTRIBUTORS

K.G.Tejwani, Land Use Consultants International, New Delhi-110060.

Saundarjya Borbora, Associate Professor, Department of Humanities and Social Sciences IIT Guwahati, Guwahati-781039, Assam.

Govind Dhaske, Research and Publications Department, *ICFAI University Press, ICFAI Business School, #72, Nirlon Complex,* Goregaon, Mumbai-400063 India.

Bharat Patel, Sr. Faculty, SPIPA, Ahmedabad.

Satyapriya Rout, Lecturer in Sociology, University of Hydera-bad, Hyderabad.

A.K. Misra[1*], B. Shivarudrappa[2], B. Venkatesuralu[1,] K.V. Subrahmanyam[1] and **Y.S. Ramakrishna**, 1 Central Research Institute for Dryland Agriculture, Santoshnagar, Hyderabad 500 059, India 2 BAIF Institute for Rural Development–Karnataka, Jadcherla, Mahabubnagar, AP, India.

M. Mishra, Reader in Environmental Economics, Department of Economics, Faculty of Social Sciences, Banaras Hindu University, VARANASI

J. Nirmala, Reader & Research Guide in Economics, Sarah Tucker College, (Autonomous) Perumalpuram, Tirunelveli.

S.R. Padhi, Deptt. of Socilogy, AERONAUTICS COLLEGE, (SUNABEDA) DIST- KORAPUT (ORISSA).

Poulmi Banarjee, Research Scholor, J N U, New Delhi

Vijay Laxmi, IGIDR, Mumbai

S.C. Srivastava, Professor and Head, Dept. of RDAP, North eastern Hill University

C.Sekar, Professor (Agril. Economics), PHTC, Agricultural Engineering College and Research Institute, Tamil Nadu Agricultural University, Coimbatore.

Dalip Kumar, Manager (Projects), National Council of Applied Economic Research, New Delhi

S.S.P. Sharma, Professor & Head (CWLR), NIRD, Hyderabad

U. Hemanth Kumar, Assistant Professor (CWLR) NIRD, Hyderabad

Dalip Ghosh, Sr. Faculty, SIPRD, Kalyani (WB)

CHAPTER–1

INDIA 60: YESTERDAY-TODAY-TOMORROW OF WATERSHED MANAGEMENT

K.G. Tejwani

PREAMBLE

Watershed Management (WSM) involves Management of Natural Resources (NR) like Land (& Soil), Water, Forest (including Grasses, Vegetation), Livestock (including Wild life, Fauna) and Humans. WSM includes management of all NR by humans for economic-ecological-social (EES) considerations on sustainable basis. The paper attempts a panoramic view-spanning from Civilizational-Historical to Today and to a peak at Future.

CIVILIZATIONAL-HISTORICAL PERSPECTIVE

Natural Resources Management (NRM) for subsistence & sustainance is historical & civilizational as evidenced by

(a) Worship of trees, fruits, grasses, plants, animals, rivers, environment etc.

(b) Hymns & other records in: *VEDAS*, EPICS etc.

(c) Development of medicines from plants & minerals

The ancient Atharva Veda has as many as 115 verses devoted to "Water" & "Earth" resources through 8 out of its 18 books. Only a sample is quoted here (Whitney, 1905; Tejwani, 1997).

EARTH

Ancient Aryans glorified Earth recognizing its bounty for food, cattle etc.

- *"Since ye became foundations of good things, ye much increased, divine, fortunate, wide-extended ones, O heaven and earth, be pleasant to me: do ye free us from distress." (Book IV, Hymn 26, Verse 2).*
- *"Ye who bear the ruddy (kine), who the forest-trees; ye within whom (are) all beings; O heaven and earth, be pleasant to me: do ye free us from distress." (Book IV, Hymn 26, Verse 5).*
- *"On whom the circulating waters flow the same, night and day, without failure-let that earth, of many streams yield us milk; then let her sprinkle (us) with splendour." (Book XII, Hymn 1, Verse 9).*

WATER

Ancient Aryans glorified Water recognizing its utility for life, food, etc. They also recognized different sources of water.

"Weal to thee (be) the waters from the snowy mountains and weal be to thee those from the fountains, weal to thee the running waters, and weal to thee be those of the rains." (Book XIX, Hymn 2, Verse 1).

"Weal to thee (be) the waters of the wastes, weal be to thee those of the marshes; weal to thee the waters of the canals, weal those brought with vessels." (Book XIX, Hymn 2, Verse 2).

"Within the waters is ambrosia, in the waters is remedy; and by the praises of the waters ye become vigorous horses, ye become vigorous kine." (Book I, Hymn 4, Verse 4).

"Be the divine waters weal for us in order to assistance to drink; weal (and) health flow they into us." (Book I, Hymn 6, Verse 1).

AGRICULTURE

When the ancient Indians recognized the utility of earth & water, and then learnt to grow food, they sang hymns of agriculture.

"Harness ye the plows, extend the yokes; scatter the seed here in the prepared womb; may the bunch (?) of Viraj be burdened for us; may the sickles draw in the ripe (grain) yet closer." (Book III, Hymn 17, Verse 2).

"Successfully let the good plow shares thrust apart the earth; successfully let the plowmen follow the beast of draft; O Cunasira, de ye (two), dripping (?) with oblation, make the herbs rich in berries for this man." (Book III, Hymn 17, Verse 5).

CONSERVATION

The ancients were very conscious of need of preservation and conservation

"She the earth, whom the gods, sleepless, defend all the time without failure-let her yield to us honey, what is dear; then let her sprinkle us with splendour." (Book XII, Hymn 1, Verse 7).

"What of thee, O earth, I dig out, let that quickly grow over; let me not hit thy vitals nor thy heart, O cleansing one." (Book XII, Hymn 1, Verse 35).

YESTERDAY (LEADING TO TODAY)

Finally while in the 21st century we are seeking peace, tranquility and splendour by nature conservation, let us seviour this gem from the Atharva Veda of the Ancient Aryans.

"Tranquil, fragrant, pleasant, with sweet drink in her udder, rich in milk, let earth bless me, earth together with milk." (Book XII, Hymn 1, Verse 59).

This attitude of reverence and knowledge about the importance of land, water and vegetation for the life supporting systems of humans, has led to the development of practices and techniques which are in harmony with nature and are sustainable.

CIVILIZATION-HISTORICAL TECHNOLOGY

Indians (in fact humans) have been the most innovative and ingenious in responding to adverse, degrading edaphic & geomorphologic conditions. For example in :

The humid, tropical/subtropical, high-rainfall, nutrient poor soils they developed shifting cultivation. The practice of shifting cultivation requires knowledge of landscape, the soils, the rainfall, sustainable site selection, technique of selective/ clear felling and burning of trees, technique of soil management, crop cultivation, inter/mixed cropping, plant protection, harvesting, storing and processing, the length of the cropping cycle, ensuring sustainability, conservation, knowledge of forest and its products, and finally the rotation cycle (Tejwani, 1994, 1997). Under the similar conditions they have developed the "home gardens" system of farming. Home gardens is a response of people who practice sedentary agriculture. The practice is sustainable, highly evolved, and rumunerative (Tejwani, 1994). Those who have "home gardens" are considered to be "affluent subsistence" farmers.

In arid/semi-arid conditions the ancient Indians have come up with agro-sivilculture & silvopastoral systems combining *Prosopis cineraria* trees with crops on agricultural fields & with grasses in grass lands. (Shankarnarayan, 1984; Tejwani, 1994). The edaphic conditions are very stressed, with 200-500mm annual rainfall, medium to coarse textured desert soils-low in organic matter, soil fertility, low water holding capacity, yet the practices are bio-physically sound, economically viable and socially acceptable. References to *Prosopis cineraria* occur in Rigveda, Atharvaveda and many other ancient scriptures (Shankar, 1980; Purohit & Wajid Khan, 1980).

In hilly & mountain situations the ancient Indians developed land management system of bench terracing; whole hill sides are bench terraced, fed with water tapped from springs and streams. The bench terraces have different designs for irrigated and rainfed conditions; these are marvels of engineering, land physiography, soil science, water management and capital development. No government can support investment of capital of such a large scale of development. All this is achieved through simple tools like spades, sickles and wood choppers by "illiterate" and "unskilled" farmers. They not only grow appropriate agricultural crops, but have also developed appropriate farming practices which integrate trees and animals. Again in hilly and mountain situations the ancient Indians developed water management systems which are marvels of ingenuity. To develop a flowing water resource one needs to tap a spring (or a stream), to transport water along the hill sides at non-scouring velocities in "channels" of appropriate cross sections, applying water to individual terraces, taking down water from one terrace to another and disposing it safely. In fact elsewhere they have transported water through bamboo pipes of different diameters over long distances and applied water in the form of "trickle" irrigation in North Eastern Hill Regions.

Development of water resource through tanks in arid/semi-arid regions by the ancients is a perfect example of "watershed management". It called for managing the "catchments" for yield of "silt free" water, designing a tank for storage of water for multiple uses, desilting the tank periodically, and using the tank silt as a "fertilizer" and to restore the soil which might have been lost by erosion. This was an extensively practiced system with involvement of the communities & religio-political system. However with the planned construction of large reservoirs the whole system of tanks has been going down in use and maintenance (Anonymos, 1984; Randhawa 1980).

Development of grazing–systems in hills, mountains, plains in different climatic zones by the ancients is also unique (Tejwani, 1994). Grazing system *"Kharak"* in Himalaya in Uttar Pradesh & Uttar Anchal states, and *"GOL"* system of Rajasthan are the best examples of methods of grazing. In this case when the grass gets thin/or gets finished, the herd is moved and a new *"Kharak"* or *"GOL"* is built. Total nomadism/semi-nomadism/partial nomadism/transhumans are four migratory grazing systems. Silvipastoral system of grazing in Himalayas is an outstanding example of silvi-pastoral practice of the farmers & nomadic communities.

MODERN PERSPECTIVE

Soil & water conservation (NRM/WSM) are historical/ civilizational in India as indicated above. The modern perspective can be started with the British rule in India. When the British established their rule in India they "got" problems of NR degradation. For example, Problem of *Raos, Chos* (Hill torrents) in Siwalik Hills; problem of gullies & ravines in the alluvial plains; problem of severe deforestation. The causes of these problems were partly non-anthropogenic and mainly anthropogenic (wars, development activities, political changes). The Britishers tried to address these problems. The first step they took was to pay attention to forests which were deforested & degraded due to wars but much more they were interested in extracting timber for railways & other development activities concerning their empire. They also addressed the issue of agriculture more for raw materials for export. Forest Research Institute, Forest Colleges, Agriculture Research & Colleges were established. They addressed the issues of *Raos* & torrents in Punjab (year 1900), ravines & gullies in UP province (year 1920) and SWC & dry farming in south India (year 1930). Thus a beginning had been made-the seeds had been sown.

The second phase of the modern issue of NRM & WSM started with the independence of India. Within one year of independence (1948) Damodar Valley Corporation act was passed to establish an inter-state system to undertake integrated WSM in the catchment of Damoder river. The project was comprehensive-addressing flood control, water storage, hydro-power generation, irrigation, fisheries, industrialization etc. It concerned cooperation between two states Bihar & West Bengal and had research & development components. The project is considered a great success having converted a "River of Sorrow" into a "River of Happiness". This was a good model but has not been repeated again. It may be noted that "Tanks" were smaller historical models of WSM. With adoption of new policy on "Planned Development" of natural resources emphasis was laid on large reservoirs, big dams, irrigation of large areas, hydropower etc. Hence soil & water conservation, afforestation became essential for silt free water yield. WSM was not the term used then. It was used much later in the 1970s. The ecological consideration was implied and economic consideration for the people was ignored. The economic and social upliftment came much later.

When the above programmes were initiated it was realized that while the problems were broadly known and traditional technologies were available yet answers to them backed by scientific investigations were not available. Consequently a chain of nine Soil & Water Conservation Research and Training Centers was established (1951-56). This process continued and India at present has many research institutes/coordinated research projects/national research centers where research on WSM is carried out directly and indirectly. These are Central Soil & Water Conservation Research and Training Institutes (CSWCRTI) (along with its regional centres), Central Arid Zone Research Institute, Central Research Institutes for Dryland Irrigation, ICAR Research Complex for North East Hills Region. Central Agricultural Research Institute for A&N Islands, Central Soil Salinity Research Institute, National Research Centre for Agroforestry (with its centres), State Agricultural Universities, Indian Council of Forestry Research and Education, Indian Grassland and Fodder Research Institute etc. CSWRTI is a unique institute and it along with other institutions, has addressed all the physical parameters of WSM, and has demonstrated very positive aspects of WSM, through many Operational Research Projects. It has contributed to the acceptance of integrated multidisciplinary approach to WSM. The Research achievements and their application in a smaller scale are many yet the issues of transfer of technology remain unsolved. Gradually many other research institutes have taken many operational research projects many line development departments have implemented WSM projects.

While in the beginning the approach was for integrated working together as evidenced by D.V.C. and Bhakra Project and during the early three five years plans ,gradually the concerned departments have drifted away and they do not work together in various components of a watershed. In early years, CSWCRTI had regional committees for each of its centers, where all the concerned departments heads/ representatives used to participate to tell what their problems were, what they needed, discuss about human resource development (HRD) needs, and the centers used to tell what they can offer and what they will do. At present the system has broken down and the linkages between the concerned departments and the developments agencies at "regional level" are not existent due to changes in "policy" at higher level, or administrative restrictions on the initiative of the centers. For example ICAR now says that they will only do the research and training and will inform the departments of the availability of technology at zonal levels in India. Very large sums of money have been spent on WSM research and development during the last 55 years. However, the technology developed either lies in the files or is not valid for socio-economic conditions, or break down of institutional mechanisms.

Table 1
Physical Parameters & Cumulative Achievements in WSM/D in India. Since the Start of the First Five Year Plan

Total Geographical Area (m.ha)	328.6
Degraded/Eroded Land (m.ha)	146.8
Rainfed Area (m ha)	85.2
Land Treated under WSM/D Programmes (m.ha)	50.8.

Cost of land treated under WSM/D Programmes since start of the first plan. (Rs. m. 192036.9)Projects: National Watershed Development Programme in Rainfed Areas (NWDPRA); River Valley Programme & Flood Prone Rivers Programme (RVP & FPR); Watershed Development Programme for Shifting Cultivation Areas (WDPSCA); Drought Prone Areas Programme (DPAP), Watershed Development. Fund (WDF); Integrated Watershed Development Programme (IWDP); etc. (Pandey and Singh, 2007).

WSM/D projects have reported increase in production and productivity of agricultural crops, ground water recharge (in operational/small watersheds), increase in cropping intensity (about 1.1 m.ha), reduction in sediment yield, creation of new-land areas, creation of supplementary/life saving irrigation, creation of forest area (about 2 m. ha). (Pandey & Singh, 2007), and positive b:c ratios have been observed in successful projects.

Forests are an importants land use (comprising 20.6% of land area of India in 2003, (MOEF, 2006). Other 2.4% of land area is under tree cover (comprising orchards, coffee/tea/rubber plantations, public parks etc.) in 2001 (FSI, 2003). Forest planting and reforestation were and are important components of WSM since the first five year plan. In the 1950's "VANA MAHAUTSAV" (festival of trees/forests) was promoted and is now regularly and ritually observed in August every year. However one wonders how many trees have grown or how much tree cover has been achieved in India!

In 1950's it used to be said that 33% of land area of India should be under forest. After over five decades of plantations of trees by forest departments, only 20.6% of the geographical area is under forest in 2003. Only 3.75 million ha have been recorded as additional forest, between 1987 to 2003 which works out to 0.24 m. ha per year (or increase of additional forest by 1.15%) (Table 2).

Table 2
Forest Cover (1987 to 2003) in India

			*Forests & Tree Cover**	
Year	*Forest Cover (m. ha)*	*% of Land Under Forest*	*(m.ha)*	*% of Land Under Forest*
1987**	64.1	19.49	–	–
1997	63.3	19.27	–	–
2001	67.6	20.55	75.7	23.03
2003	67.8	20.64	–	–

* Forest cover is in recorded forest area. Tree cover is in orchards, plantations, agroforestry, public parks etc.

** Forest cover & Tree cover 1987 to 2001 (FSI, 2003, Forest cover, 2003 (MOEF, 2006)

If one looks to forestry statistics, they refer to area under forest cover, out turn and value of forest produce and employment of labour. The component of grasses and tree leaf is extremely insignificant, and the statistics are silent on how much area is grazed. The issue of the inputs of tree leaf fodder and grasses needed by the grazing animals in the forests, as a NTFP, remains in the realm of unknown (Table 3). Yet the foresters continue to complain that forests are degraded./destroyed by overgrazing.

Table 3
Non-timber Forest Products (Tonnes)* in India

Food	*Fodder*	*Medicines & Aromatic Plants*	*Color & Dyes*	*Utensils & Crafts*	*Exudates*	*Others*
61000	46000	63000	4900	1315000	3000	547000

* FAO. 2006

Table 4
Modern Leading to Future

Yesterday to Today	Today to Tomorrow
Not importing food	Now importing food
We were worshipping rivers/ having a lot of water	Now fighting for water at interstate/ intercity/inter colony levels for water
We had plenty of wood products	Now importing
We had small individual fights for land	Now we are having roits/law order problems for land (e.g. sez)
We had reasonable per capita share of NR	Now we have ever diminishing per capita NR

It is obvious that we are slipping on all fronts-more specifically natural resources management, food, water, timber, grasses etc. production. It is difficult to accept this situation since we have in place the frame-work of policies (and legislation)/institutions/plans/programmes (Fig. 1) and intentions. What are the causes of our slipping down ward?

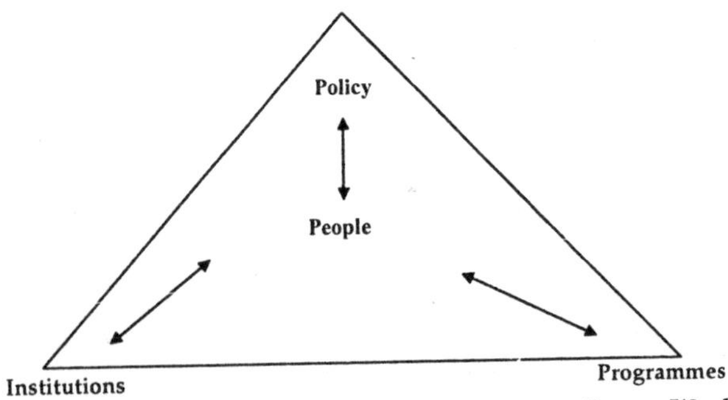

Figure 1: Policy-Institutions-Programmes Frame Work

For any successful project/programme a synergy among Policy (& legislation)-Institutions-Programmes and People is needed. This system is anthropocentric and of the people – for the people-by the people.

Not only the success of programmes is anthropocentric, but also any land use system is anthropocentric and dependant on the number of humans and also animals (Fig. 2).

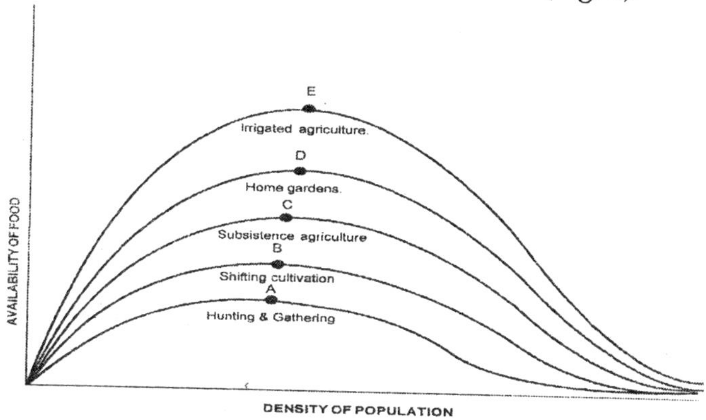

Figure 2: Population–Land Use Technology and Availability of Food

It is obvious from Fig. 2, that any food producing land use system can support some level of population beyond which it will break down, unless the technology is upgraded or innovated. Now we are at a level where water use efficiency has to be increased to support the expanding population. (There are other options, which are not discussed here). Population is a key issue.

Table 5
Modern Leading to Future

Activity	*Today*	*Tomorrow*	*Causes*
Polices	Many and workable	Will be more and more	?
Policies (Implementation)	Imperfect but workable	Will be more imperfect	?
Institutions	Plenty	Will increase	–
R & D	Good & useful	Will be more difficult	?
Programmes formulation	Plenty	Will be more and more	?
Programme implementation	Fair	Will be poorer	?
Future	Many promises but not kept	Imperfect	Let us decide

This table is judgmental. We must see if we accept it and let us decide what to do.

FUTURE PERSPECTIVE

If WSM/D is anthropocentric the stake holders need to be identified. They are people at large, farmers, graziers, landless; peoples representatives; (legislators-national, state); people working in institutions research/ development/programmes: agriculture/forest/animal husbandry/SAUs etc.), any one and every one. Role of stakeholders is defined and determined by concerted, concerned and united action. For example one and one does not make two but it make eleven. Each finger is weak by itself but five put together make a punch. So each finger has to contribute. Each stake holder has a role. Those of us who are discussing these issues are concerned with the full operational frame work articulated in Fig. 1 above. We of the institutions are very important *stake holders-infact according to Indian civilization terminology Rishis & Maharishis*-who can help by correct and powerful contribution.

POLICIES-PROGRAMMES-PROMISES

Inspite of many policies, good R&D, good HRD and many promises made, the implementation in WSM/NRM has been fair. The targeted goals have never been achieved and the promises never kept. It is therefore concluded that the future of WSM/NRM is full of worry and is "Imperfect". The causes for such a state of affairs are left with a question mark (?). What are the causes and solutions?

There are a number of national and international seminars/ symposia/conferences to be followed by a set of recommendations which are forgotten immediately and later the same or different people have a similar gathering with a different title (dictated by the sponsor). We will take one example.

"Poverty Reduction" was included in the soil and water conservation programmes in the third five year plan (1961-66), and India re-inforced it with the slogan of "*Garibi Hatao*" in 1977, and has accepted the Millinium Development Goal (MDG) of UN, yet poverty does not seem to be leaving us? Why?

The causes of concern are many-Institutional and socio-economic. One institutional issue for WSM/NRM and some socio-economic issues which are running as a thread in the garlaland of beads will be cited as an example.

INSTITUTIONAL ISSUE: LACK OF COORDINATION AND SYNERGY

At some stage there used to be one ministry dealing with land use (Agriculture, Forest, Animal Husbandry, Irrigation etc.). Over a period of time it "Fissioned" and got divided into separate ministries such as Land, Forest, Water etc. This was a response to increasing activities. Thus the fission was not the problem, but the problem was created due to lack of coordination and synergy, starting with the top right leading upto bottom. Each ministry got busy defending its turf. Better coordination & synergy is a solution. For transfer of technology the mechanisms created earlier need to be revived and re-enforced. For example, there is much more need for achieving coordination and synergy by reviving regional committees which were provided for WSM/NRM at CSWCRTI, Research Centers, comprising of the ICAR, Central & State depts. of the region. They used to exchange technology, discuss needs of problem solutions, review the achievements, needs of actions taken and to be taken and HRD. This lacuna is true of all agencies concerned with WSM/NRD at all level.

Table 6
Per Captia Availability of Natural Resources

	Year			
Item	*1951*	*1996*	*2025*	*2050*
Total land area (ha)	0.91	0.35	0.23	0.19
Total cropped area (ha)	0.33	0.15	0.11	0.09
Irrigated area (ha)	0.06	0.07	0.08	0.06
Forest area (ha)	0.11	0.08	0.05	0.04
Total green area (ha)	0.19	0.09	0.08	0.07
Total area for biomass production (ha)	0.75	0.29	0.19	0.15
Utilizable water (m3)/year	–	778	571	470
Land needed for non-agricultural Use (mha)	9.40	22.69	22.50	43.00

The problem of decreasing per capita availability of natural resources is to continue, and the NR will be ever insufficient for life supporting and soio-economic conditions (Table 6).

Technology improvement in future has limited scope. Possibilities of improvement are:

- Agriculture - Increased water use efficiency and hence increased productivity.
- Forest-Afforestation will not solve the problem. Reforestation may help mitigate or solve the problem. (Tejwani, 2001)
- Agroforestry -May solve some problem. One ha of waste (d) land given to a landless labour may help to grow ten goats.
- Grassland-Limited scope

Role of forests, agroforestry and grasses has all of a sudden acquired urgency for carbon sequestration (Bhatt, 2007).

As mentioned above there has been a concern about poverty alleviation/reduction since the third five year plan (1961-66).

GARIBI HATAO-POVERTY REDUCTION-EMPLOYMENT GENERATION

Achievements in Poverty Reduction can be listed as under:

Awareness was initiated in India 1960 onward and has been much enhanced by MDG of UN. Policies, strategies, legislation on NRM are comprehensive-intra-sector as well as inter-sector. Institutions to carry out research, develop technology, transferring mechanisms etc. are in plenty, and there is a plethora of programmes.

The projections made in the Table 7 indicate very interesting trends, namely (i) in the year 2018 India will still have the same number of poor as in 1950; (ii) it will be the year 2030 that we will have 2.9% of the population still poor, but it will not be possible to achieve it, since it will be a utopian condition. Any society will have to carry 5-10% poor for various social & political reasons, natural disasters, and human behaviour reasons etc. Keeping this in view we will be having at least 163 million poor in the year 2020; (iii) in the year 2015, the MDG will not be achieved; (iv) the total population of India by the year 2030 will be 1822.6 million (it will be 2012 million in 2035) causing tremendous and explosive pressures on natural resources and production systems. Further WSM/ NRM programmes provide employment (in the name of poverty reduction) only. No poverty reduction is expected from WSM/D, NRM, forest Sector, agroforesty or grassland.

Table 7
Actual (Estimated), and Projected Number of People Below the Poverty Line in India

Year	*Population (million)*	*Poverty (%)*	*Number of Poor (million)*	*Remarks*
2001	1027*	26.1*	269.0*	*Official figures
2002	1047.6#	25.3**	265.0	# Population of 2002 and thereafter is projected @2% of natural growth.** Poverty reduced at the rate of.8% per annum. This is official figure
2005#	1111.7	22.9	254.6	#Projected (2005-2030) by author
2010	1227.4	18.9	232.0	
2015##	1355.1	14.9	201.9	## MDG Year
2018	1438.1	12.5	179.8***	*** Same number of poor as in 1950.
2020	1495.2	10.9	163.0	
2030	1822.6	2.9	52.8###	### This is utopian figure since this level is not reached any where in the world.

We have not achieved poverty, reduction due to serious social-economic reasons. Two exaple are given. One is governance.

Often we been witness to non-delivery of goods and services in quantity, quality, space and time. This explains why demonstrations succeed (due to proper management), and a project/programme fails (due to poor management). If the programme does not take off on its own steam (after the project withdraws) how is it expected that poverty reduction wili take place?

The second serious social-economic issue is syphoning of programme funds (Late) Rajiv Gandhi, PM of India-articulated that only 15% of the funds reach the field. Dr. Manmohan Singh the current PM of India has articulated that only 1% of the funds development funds reaches the field.

With this scenario it appears provision of basic needs of life, reducing poverty and upgradation of ecology & environment are not probable. This view is succinctly capsulated by R.K. Laxman, Cartoonist of Times of India taken from the TOI, Archives (Fig. 3). One could say that the principles of good economics and social growth are consistently ignored. It has to be recognized that "Good Economics does not tolerate waste and inefficiency" and good sociology means zero tolerance of greed and unequality". Keeping in view the issues of ever expanding human population, poor delivery of goods and services, syphoning of funds, one could presume that the promises will not be kept. It can concluded that the future seems imperfect unless the issues are addressed.

REFERENCES

——(1994), Anonymous. Indian Agriculture in Brief. Ministry of Agriculture, Govt. of India, New Delhi, India. 465 pp.

Bhatt, R.K. (2007), Impact of Climatic Change on Agriculture and Carbon Sequestration. Presented at the National Symposium on Rangeland and Forage Resources in Changing Socio-Economic Scenario. Range Management Society of India and Indian Grassland & Fodder Research Instiute, Jhansi, India.

——FAO, (2006), Global Forest. Resources. FAO Forestry Paper 147. Food & Agriculture Organisation of the United Nations, Rome, Italy. pp. 320.

——FSI, (2005), State of Forest Report, 2003. Forest Survey of India (MOEF), Dehradun, India. pp. 134.

——MOEF, (2006), Annual Report, 2005-2006. Executive Summary. Ministry of Environment and Forest Govt. of India, New Delhi, India. pp. 49.

Pandey C.M., and Jagat Veer Singh (2007), Watershed Development under River Valley Project and Flood Prone River Programmes.

Future Strategies and Guide Lines. J. Soil Water Conserv. 6(2): 88-100.

Purohit. M.L. and Wajid Khan (1980), Socio-Economic Dimensions of *Khejri*. In H.S. Mann & S.K. Saxena (eds). Khejri in the Indian Desert. Monograph No. 11 CAZRI. p. 1-3.

Randhawa, M.S. (1980), A History of Agriculture in India . Indian Council of Agri. Res., New Delhi, India. Vol.I. 541 pp.

Shankar, V. (1980), *Khejri* in Scriptures in H.S. Mann & S.K. Saxena (eds.) *Khejri* in the Indian Desert. Monograph No. 11 CAZRI. p. 1-3.

Shankaranarayan, K.A. (1984), (ed-in-chief). Agroforestry in Arid and Semi-arid Zones. Pub. No. 24. Central Arid Zone Research Institute. Jodhpur, India. pp. 295.

Tejwani, K.G. (1994), Agroforestry in India. Oxford & IBH Publishing Co. Pt. Ltd. New Delhi, India. pp. 233.

Tejwani, K.G. (1997), Indigenous Knowledge in Soil, Water & Forest Management. Proc. Intnl. Seminar: Local Knowledge of Forests and Forest Uses Among Tribal Communities in India. Eds. Klaus Seeland and Franz Schmithusen. Eidgenossische Technische Hoch scheule, Zurich,. Switzerland p. 57-76.

Tejwani, K.G. (1998), R&D in Watershed Management in Asia, Africa and the Pacific Sepcial Lectures & Recommendations, Central Board of Irrigation and Power, New Delhi, India. p. 27-34.

Tejwani, K.G. (2001), Natures Nurture: Greening of Wastelands and Biodiversity Perspectives. Wastelands News. New Delhi, India Aug. Oct. p.15-20.

Tejwani, K.G. (2005), Power, Policies and People. Wastelands News. New Delhi India. 20 (2): 36-38.

Tejwani, K.G. (2005), Policy Issues in Watershed Management. Lead Papers, National Conference on Watershed Management, Sustainable Production, Livelihood and Environmental Security. Soil Conservation Society India, New Delhi, India. p. 148-153.

Tejwani, K.G. (2006), Issues in Grassland Management in India. Range Mgmt. & Agroforestry. 26(1): 32-36.

Tejwani, K.G. (2006), Ecology, Economy and Employment. Wastelands News. New Delhi. India. 22 (1); 39-41.

Tejwani, K.G. (2007), Gaining Grazing Grounds Wastelands News. New Delhi. India. 21(3): 33-36.

Tejwani, K.G. (2007), Strained Subsistence : Agroforestry, Agricutlure and Poverty Alleviation. Wastelands News. New Delhi. India. 22 (3): 34-37.

Whitney, W.D. (1905), Atharva Veda Samhita. Harvard Oriental Series. Authorized Indian Reprint. Motilal Banarasidas, 1984. Delhi, India.

CHAPTER–2

WATERSHED DEVELOPMENT: PARTICIPATORY MANAGEMENT AND RURAL LIVELIHOOD ISSUES IN INDIA

Saundarjya Borbora

INTRODUCTION

Watershed Development is a composite concept in which the management of soil, water, and plantations is integrated with the development of people around them. It is a concept, which aims to establish an enabling environment for the integrated use, regulation and treatment of water, and land resources of a watershed based ecosystem to accomplish resource conservation and biomass production objectives (Jensen, 1996).

There is a greater emphasis today on sustainable development and as such emphasis is to check the exploitation of natural resource base. Soil erosion, land degradation coupled with declining per capita availability of land and water are posing threats to environment. With increased population, these problems are becoming acute and may cause food security problems especially in developing countries. Hence concerted efforts are necessary for effective management of natural resources for increased productivity.

The Working Group on Watershed Development, Rain fed farming and Natural Resource Management also recognized the strong co-relation of poverty with degradation of land and was of the view that different programmes implemented on a watershed basis should be strengthened. The watershed development programme has to become a people's movement if it has to be a sustainable programme. A number of Watershed Development Projects were taken up by several government and non-government agencies in different parts of the country to tackle some of the problems like soil conservation, improving land productivity, sustainable use of natural resources etc. But world over, many projects have not performed well because of lack of people's participation (Johnson et al., 2001). The same had been echoed by the Expert Group also in their report. As such in order to achieve the desired objectives of Watershed Development projects and its sustainability, participation of people, the community organizations and stakeholders are important. Local people's participation from the conception to implementation is also crucial. As such participatory management is essential in order to have a positive impact on the lives of people around the catchments areas. These changes are being incorporated in India in an integrated way to have better results.

On the background of the above, the paper tries to highlight some of these issues and try to provide some impact assessment as case studies on the basis of literature review including watershed development project for shifting cultivation area in the North Eastern Region of India.

A BROAD OUTLOOK OF WATERSHED DEVELOPMENT IN INDIA

India embarked on watershed development project in the 1970s for controlling land degradation and increasing productivity with emphasis on soil and water conservation. By 1980s, the situation changed as it became apparent that technical and physical works alone would not lead to achieve the objectives of watershed development. It has to take into account several aspects of rural development such as social, financial and institutional. In India, watershed development programme are being implemented over a diverse range of agro-climatic zones and due to the inherent heterogeneity of agro-climatic characteristics, they have different potentials and opportunities. Depending upon the size of the watersheds, there are micro and macro watersheds. Watersheds with areas upto 1250 hectares were classified as micro-watersheds and beyond that these are macro-watersheds. As micro-watersheds projects are gaining ground from Government and non-government agencies, the concept of management of such programmes also getting changed with more emphasis on community participation. In 1994, the Ministry of Rural Development of the Government of India came out with a set of guidelines for watershed development programmes, which is basically a people's centered policy, which incorporated good practices. As such, it is noted that there is a change in perception regarding management of watershed projects. Community participation in such projects is desirable to make them objective oriented and sustainable.

In the early 1970s, watershed management was depended on biophysical framework which is mostly based on top-down approach (Rhoades and Elliot, 2000). In such a system, the local people were not consulted which lead to lack of participation and failure of the project to have a desired impact. Watershed projects are more effectives if local people are given a role to manage their own water resources (Johnson et. al., 2001). In the traditional system, which was based on capacity of land rather than the needs and capacities of local people creates a situation where there is gap between outside project people and the local population and there was no flow of information. This may be due to the fact that such programme were based on technology transfer and not on development of technology on local people's land and their surroundings. There was also weak linkage with varies aspects of social sciences like capacity building, links with non-farm sector etc. If there would have been more coordination between engineer's, scientists, local people, adoption of technology and thereby the impact would have been immense.

But there is a paradigm shift in the conception of watershed development and management in India today. Previously it was supply driven and there was a mismatch between the needs of the stakeholders and project objectives, which often lead to failure. As such, participatory watershed management has emerged which is based on the concept of decentralized governance. Participatory watershed management emphasizes inter-sectoral and multi-institutional mechanism. It can be defined as a process "which aims to create a self-supporting system, which is essential for sustainability"(Wani et al, 2005). This system of management provides opportunities to stakeholders to participate in the watershed project from conception to implementation and managements. This has been widely practiced since late 1980s with decentralized institutions and peoples groups. Over the years with more emphasis in micro watershed projects, several NGOs are also involved.

IMPACT OF PARTICIPATORY WATERSHED MANAGEMENT

Many developing countries including India have adopted watershed development as a part of their rural development strategy. It focused on achieving sustainable rural development for reducing the incidence of poverty. Most of such projects have some common purposes like:-

- Increasing agricultural productivity
- Raising income
- Soil and water conservation
- Generating employment
- Etc.

Several studies revealed that participatory management of watershed projects had a positive impact on agricultural productivity. Due to increased irrigated area, the increase in crop production was possible (Shah, 2001). Productivity gains were reported to be greater in the case of rain-fed crops (e.g. soybeans, legumes), which had increased by 280% (Renfro, 2004). This increased in productivity have an impact on income of the poor and their livelihood also. Many farmers in watershed area have reported an increase in soil moisture level (Shah, 2001), which open new opportunities for diversifying farm activities. The cropping intensity has also increased to an extent of 13-25 %, which was observed by Renfro in 2004. Some other studies pointed out that such projects were successful in controlling soil erosion (Kerr et. al, 2002). Besides, soil and water conservation measures adopted in watershed development projects were helpful in increasing water storage capacity and improving local water resources (Butterworth et. al, 2001)

Table 1
Watershed Management Impact on Productivity of Arable Lands, Employment and Economic Viability

Wasteland	*State*	*% Increase in Cropping Intensity*	*% Increase in Productivity*	*% Increase in Employment*	*B/C Ratio*
Sukhomajri	Haryana	82	210	29.40	2.06
Nada	Haryana	78	165	18.60	1.97
Bunga	Haryana	110	170	28.20	2.05
Rel Maira	Punjab	32	52	24	
Behdala	H P	17	12	Neg.	
Bajra-Ganiyar	Haryana	21	58	16	1.58
Siha	Haryana	23	67	27	
Kharkhan Kalan	Rajasthan	17	15	Neg.	6.07
Kishangarh	Rajasthan	10	12	Neg.	2.35
Chhajawa	Rajasthan	32	45	36	2.24
Mandvarsa	Rajasthan	31	13	3	1.90
Matatila	U P	41	21	4	3.80
Tejpura	U P	97	180	40	3.40
Gomti (Gyij)	U P	68	52	18	3.90
Gomti (GK3a)	U P	41	24	6	2.00
Rebari	Gujarat	20	56	3	2.60
Joladarasi	Karnataka	18	56	5	1.50
Chinnatekur	A P	25	62	7	1.80
GR Halli	Karnataka	12	42	3	1.50
Shankarpura	Gujarat	60	82	14	
Ralegaon-Siddhi	Maharastra	62	185	21	

Note: Neg.= negligible
Source: Sarma and Dhyani (1998), adopted from Common Property Resource Management –Reflections on Theory and the Indian Experience by Gopal K. Kadekodi, page-182

Watershed development projects have potential to generate employment opportunities also. Due to increased availability of water resources, diversified cropping pattern, extensive and intensive cultivation, employment opportunities could be created in rural areas. This may lead to minimizing the migration of labour from rural areas. A sample outcome from watershed management programmes in India is provided in Table-1, which shows remarkable changes in various states.

A case study is also provided below on the basis of literature review, which will show the impact of watershed development projects in rural livelihood and poverty alleviation (directly and indirectly):

CASE STUDY

CASE1: WATERSHED DEVELOPMENT PROJECT FOR SHIFTING CULTIVATION AREA IN THE NORTH EASTERN REGION OF INDIA

Shifting cultivation (Jhum cultivation) is toady a serious threat to land degradation and ecological problem. In the N. E. Region, an area of 14.66-lakh hectare of land is affected involving 4.433 lakh Jhumia families. The main objectives of watershed development project for shifting cultivation areas are:

(a) To protect the hill slopes of jhum areas through soil and water conservation measures and to reduce further land degradation.

(b) Encourage relocation of jhumia families by providing developed productive land and improved cultivation package

(c) To improve the socio-economic status of jhumia families through land/household based activities.

(d) To mitigate the ill effects of shifting cultivation by introducing appropriate land use.

This programme is being implemented in several N E States through government and non-government organizations, with 100 % central grant. The achievement of this programme is provided in Table 2, which is self-explanatory.

Table 2

State-wise Area of Shifting Cultivation, Achievement Upto IX Plan, During Four Years od X Plan (2002-06) and Programme for 2006-07

(Phy. In lakh ha. & Fin. In Rs. crores)

State & No. of Jhumia Family in Lakh	Extended Shifting Cultivation Area*	Achievement Since Inception upto IX Plan		Achievement in Four Years of X Plan		Achievement Since Inception upto 200-06		Allocation 2006-07	
		Phy.	Fin.	Phy.	Fin.	Phy.	Fin.	Phy.	Fin.
Arunachal Pradesh(0.540)	2.10	0.199	12.46	0.043	4.29	0.242	16.75	0.035	3.50
Assam(0.580)	1.39	0.139	10.75	0.147	13.20	0.286	23.95	0.055	5.50
Manipur(0.700)	3.60	0.513	26.53	0.106	9.41	0.619	35.94	0.060	6.00
Meghalaya(0.523)	2.65	0.256	17.92	0.220	13.50	0.467	31.42	0.055	5.50
Mizoram(0.500)	1.89	0.660	39.01	0.176	20.20	0.836	59.21	0.055	5.50
Nagaland(1.161)	1.91	0.602	45.12	0.152	18.00	0.754	63.12	0.105	10.50
Tripura(0.430)	1.12	0.208	14.48	0.108	10.71	0.316	25.19	0.035	3.50
Grand total(4.433)	14.66	2.577	166.27	0.952	89.31	3.529	255.58	0.400	40.00

* As per ICAR Research Complex for NEH Region

Source: NEC Hand Book 2001.

IMPACT STUDY

Number of evaluation studies has been conducted and some of the outcome is summarized below, which provides the positive impacts of watershed programme as mentioned above. Some of these are:

(1) There is a significant decrease in shifting cultivation area due to adoption of permanent/settled cultivation.

(2) About 27% jhumias have abandoned the practice.

(3) Jhum area per family has been reduced from 0.84 ha. To 0.56 ha.

(4) Sustainable increase in productivity of agricultural crops, horticultural crops, inland fisheries etc were observed. In case of paddy cultivation 13% increase in productivity is reported.

(5) Overall income increased by 25% to Jhumia families.

(6) Cropping intensity increased by 40 %.

(7) Participatory management lead to sustainability of the project and effective maintenance of the capital assets created, which also lead to capacity building of the local people.

CONCLUSION

Participatory management is of crucial importance in watershed development projects in order to achieve desired objectives and sustainability. The system of management is an integrated approach to rural development and poverty alleviation, which can be seen, from different evaluation studies. Over the years, the system has undergone a desirable change and today it is recognized that community participation is central to watershed development, which lead to greater success by enhancing livelihood in an equitable manner. It is also noted that such projects have been effective in raising income, agricultural productivity, generating employment and conserving soil and water resources. In the case study in N E Region also, such positive impact could be found from watershed development projects. As such, this participatory watershed management can be seen as a viable strategy for rural development for achieving sustainable rural livelihoods in India.

REFERENCES

——(2007), Brief on Watershed Development Project for Shifting Cultivation Area (WDPSCA) from: http://www.agricoop.nic.in/dacdivision/WDPSCA.pdf.

Butterworth, J, Reddy, M.Y.V, and Batchelor, C. (2007), "Addressing Water needs of the Poor in Watershed Management" from: http://www. nri.org/WSSIWRM/Reports/water%20needs%20in% 20 watershed%20management.doc.

——(2001), Govt. of India, Planning Commission, " Report of the Steering Group on Rural Poverty alleviation, Watershed Development, Decentralized Planning and Panchayat Raj Institutions" for the Tenth Five Year Plan 2002-2007, November.

Jensen, J, "Watershed Development:Concepts and Issues' in J. Jensen, S. Seth, T. Sawney, and P. Kumar, Watershed Development: Proceeding^ of Danida's Internal Workshop on Wtershed Development, New Delhi, 1996.

Johnson, N, Ravnborg, H. M.,Westerman, O and Probst, K.,User (2001), Participation in Watershed Management and Research", Working Paper No.19, IFPRI, Washington D.C..

Kerr, J.,G. Pangare and V.L. Pangare "Watershed Development Projects in India: An Evaluation, 2002, IFPRI, Washington D.C. from: http://www.ifpri.org/pubs/abstract/abstr127.htm, accessed on 08/12/2007

Renfro, R. Z. (2007), "The Value of Participation in Development – Relevance to Soil and Water Conservation" 27 November 2004. From: http://www.adbi.org/speeches/2004/11/27/828. soil. water. conservation.

Rhoades, R. E., and Elliot, T. S. (2000), "Participatory Watershed Research and Management: Where the Shadow falls"., Gatekeeper Series No.81, London, International Institute for Economic Development (IIHD).

Shah, A., (2001), "Who Benefits from Participatory Watershed Development? Lessons from Gujarat, India". Gatekeeper Series No. 97, IIHD .

Wani, S. P., Singh, H. P., Sreedevi, T. K., Pathak, P., Rego,T. J., Shiferaw, B., and Iyer, S. R. (2005), "Farmer- Participatory Integrated Watershed Management: Adarsha Watershed, Kothapally India. An Innovative and Upscalable Approach", ICRISAT, India.

Vaidyanathan, A., (2006), India's Water Resources – Contemporary Issues on Irrigation, OUP.

Kadekodi, G. K., (2004), Common Property Resource Management-Reflections on Theory and the Indian Experiences, OUP.

CHAPTER–3

THE QUEST FOR GENDER EQUITY IN RURAL LIVELIHOODS: SOME EXPLORATIONS

Govind Dhaske

INTRODUCTION

Rural livelihoods have been the core focus of planning bodies in India since independence. With village based development planning, as prescribed by Mahatma Gandhi, development programmes in India have followed considerable focus on rural livelihoods. Watershed being an integral part of village environment in agrarian livelihood systems it has became a significant factor in overall development. Despite policy attention for sustenance of rural livelihoods, migration and poverty among various social sections has remained distressful reality of rural hinterland. The threatening environmental degradation and decline in agricultural productivity are the prominent features of this failure at macro level of policy and planning and micro level of rural livelihoods and rural poverty. The transition observed in Indian economy with shift from agriculture sector to services and manufacturing sector clearly indicates considerable impact on the populace in terms of change in sources of livelihoods and income generation. As the industry centered urban planning gained momentum in post reform period, rural based agricultural livelihoods have come under pressure due to decline in production, migration of human capital as well as various other social, political, and environmental factors. Various researches have demonstrated that dependency on agriculture for employment and livelihood will remain more or less same though there is decline in share of agriculture in GDP (see Hashim 2004).Environmental, social and economical quality of watershed determines farm based as well as other allied income generation activities and also fulfills various other survival needs like drinking water and fodder etc. Although there is uniform pattern of watershed projects, impact varies based on various factors in local contexts. The inclusion and exclusion within the development programmes has been predominantly advocated by voluntary organizations and internalized to great extent in the planning system. Gender has become central theme of impact analysis of watershed development project in recent times for several reasons. The most obvious and researched out reason is the differential impact of watershed development project on men counterparts compared to women. Watershed programmes hold the best potential to serve women not only due to their multiple resource provision but also because of its potential for income generation in the light of microfinance movement in India. The correlation of women's role and participation in watershed with livelihood sustainability is one of the motivations for same. Considering the vulnerability of women in normative society like India it is imperative to discuss the equitable distribution of benefits of livelihoods projects intended at collective welfare.

RURAL LIVELIHOODS, EMPLOYMENT AND WOMEN

Rural livelihoods are having peculiar characteristics in terms of dependence on the natural resources. There is visible existence of non farm income generation activities but considering infrastructural and human capital issues, speed of growth of same is gradually increasing but it will take more years to show a concrete existence in the form of percent share in the rural economy. Rural livelihoods projects are well-known for there differential impact on various sections of the society as well as the rampant rural poverty. The impact of the programmatic interventions differs on various social, economic, and environmental aspects. The existing source of livelihood in rural India is primarily agriculture sector. According to Results of 60th round of NSSO survey on employment and unemployment situation conducted in January-June 2004, in the rural areas, about 66 per cent of usually employed males and 84 per cent of usually employed females were engaged in the agricultural sector; on an average, per day, a male casual labourers earned Rs. 56.53, Rs. 20.38 more than a female causal labourers who earned Rs.36.15.Further the NSSO survey reports that unemployment rate for females increased from 5.6 per cent in 1993-94 to 9.3 per cent in 2004 in rural areas and from 10.5 per cent to 11.7 per cent in urban areas. It is logical to say that the existing differences in the wage structure that reflect in all livelihood activities is clear example of gender discrimination. The increase in the rural unemployment is significant for rural female due to the socio-economic constrains on their mobility and lack of social opportunity. This signifies an enquiry into the gender differentials in the rural livelihoods. It is also very important to explore the various strategies and tools which can be used for enhancing the impact of rural livelihoods project on women. Watershed being core programmatic development activity, strategically planned for promotion sustainable rural livelihoods needs a specific attention for gender equity. The concept of equity does not remain within the programmatic boundaries of watershed projects but also guides us to other domains of social and political spaces in the broader rights based approaches to development as there is multiplier effect incorporated while programme formulation.

WHY GENDER EQUITY IS IMPORTANT?

Gender equity appeared on global front after the Beijing Declaration in Fourth World Conference on Women in 1995[1].The importance of gender equity remains prominent to mankind for various reasons. In an agrarian country like India this fact has special significance as more than 70% of the population lives in rural areas. Mapping of all activities carried out by rural women indicates the interface of women with the watershed ecology. Right from fodder, fuel to drinking water and other economic activities, women rely on natural resources which require planned recreational engineering through various environmental and biodiversity conservation activities. Watershed projects include such recreational approach in its programmes. The direct impact on the livelihood and income generation through watershed is visible in the form of livestock and various other agricultural labour activities based on same. Women rely on watershed not just for livelihood and various other domestic and occupational needs but for there personal use they need watershed ecology for various medicinal and other nutritional herbs. The knowledge about various techniques pooled from traditional informal sciences also lack practice interface with environment this fractures knowledge production and transmission due to gender based discriminatory practices. The fracturing of human development status of women due to normative structure and cultural rigidities is serious issues surfaced by outcomes of various development projects.

GENDER EQUITY IN RURAL LIVELIHOODS: CONCEPTUAL FRAMEWORK

Gender equity is outcome of long term social change induced by communities themselves with or without external facilitation. The processes integrating such civilizational change must be participatory. The non occurrence of gender equity in outcomes of livelihood projects is result of social reality of gender discrimination among rural households since time immemorial. The correlation of women with various segments of watershed/livelihoods projects has been emphasized by various researchers and committees since the inception of the nationwide programme. Agriculture being the predominant source of livelihood women depends on it for income generation. With agriculture becoming cost and labour intensive, incidences of male migration towards towns for earning money through other development work are prevalent.

Women without much of technical skills are exposed greatly to agriculture and allied activities (Gangwar R 2005).This hapless picture of rural women in India is largely been controlled by watershed projects by making available additional labour opportunity based on the skills as well as provision of natural resources for nutrition, medication, fuel and fodder and various other resources for individual as well as household. Considering the dependency and role in sustaining the watershed projects there is need of assuring gender equity in watershed and allied livelihood project. The equity and sustainability linkages are obvious in case of watershed projects. Participation being key for achieving social sustainability and in turn total sustainability is an important aspect to be reviewed in the watershed projects. The normative structures in the Indian society restrict women's participation in various platforms. This hampers the sustainability aspect of watershed inducted livelihood projects in many ways and at many levels mainly the social, economic and environmental. Assuring gender participation right from the programme formulation stage seems the most feasible approach to cover the gender deficit. This approach becomes prominent because of the paradigm shift in rural women development due to the microfinance movement in India. The slowdown in the rural economy due to stagnant investment in agriculture can be addressed by viable diversification methods especially on the non farm and farm based front. Women being the core recipient of micro credit have major role to sustain rural household in this diversification. This slight but considerable and countrywide uniform shift in the rural economy signifies need of integrating the microfinance boom in the traditional watershed based livelihoods. The economic aspect of the sustainability as result of the microfinance portfolio in rural India, gender equity has become the watchword due to interlinked nature of rural livelihoods primarily rooted in watersheds and agriculture. The development score achieved in the microfinance movement by majority of the rural women can be extended to the watershed based livelihood to achieve the long awaited goal of gender equity.

INSTITUTIONAL ARRANGMENT FOR GENDER EQUITY

Establishment of mechanism and processes as well as institutional arrangement for assuring gender equity still remains the quest of the watershed programmes as the external variables influencing the process of equity are rooted in the institutional as well as social domains. The overlapping rural development projects needs to be reworked to streamline to achieve the broad intended objectives. The programmatic interventions ranging from social, economic, and environmental aspects of rural life overlap with the watershed projects. As reported by NABARD, the existing major developmental intervention of micro credit with SHG-Bank Linkages programme has reached cumulative achievement up to 31st March 2007 of Rs 1584340 Lac and number of self help groups linked up to 2711016.It is worth noticing that almost 90% SHGs are of women members. The institutional arrangement in this context should involve self help groups as major representative group. It is obvious that SHG related activities are primarily of non farm nature and require skill up gradation. Considering the need of diversification in watershed based livelihoods and the seasonality of the employment in watershed based livelihoods, there is immediate need of programmatic internalization of integrated approach demonstrated by SHGs. Report of the steering group on rural poverty alleviation, watershed development, decentralized planning and Panchayati Raj Institutions for the tenth five year plan 2002-2007 suggested that Training programmes, which impart skills to women, access to credit and marketing and other service support should be clearly spelt out in the watershed project and provided for. The credit needs of the women self helps groups should also get reflected in the district credit plan of the commercial banks. Interdepartmental coordination between the government units, participation of community members with equal representation of women members, involvement of representatives of private players and various other significant stakeholders identified collectively should systemize an institutional arrangement for assuring gender equity. The role of Grampanchayat is significant in this process hence assuring the participation of political representatives of women will play a major role to extend the economic empowerment to political empowerment. It has been found that the marginal farmers and landless laborers receive less benefits of the watershed based livelihoods project. In this case it is an imperative to accelerate the programme impact on these weaker sections. Considering the feminization of poverty in rural India and likelihood of male migration from such households to urban areas women from such household should be given priority in decentralized programme for sustainable livelihood generation. Thrust on economic activities may spoil the recreational cycles of ecology hence conservation should be the major objective of the livelihoods programme and economic gains should be made secondary. For applying this understanding in field, the portfolio approach will be helpful strategy as it also provides concrete direction for gender equity. By using portfolio approach, interlocking of the institutions, inter-sectoral benefits could be so designed that unequal distribution of resources in each sector could generate equitable distribution at the portfolio level. Organizing inequity at the sectoral level may thus be a key to organize equity at the portfolio level (Gupta, Chokkakula 1999).Integrating the microfinance based livelihoods activities falling in the domain of watershed should be the major action in this regard for enhancing women's participation and structural spaces in rural livelihoods.

TOOLS AND STRATEGIES FOR GENDER EQUITY

Apart from the institutional arrangement, it is very important to adopt certain tools for designing, monitoring and evaluation of gender equity in rural livelihoods project. There are various agencies working with development mandate including NGOs, government departments, Private Banks and various other collaborations. The programme implementation processes establish an interface with communities which last till the end of the programme period. Some tools and strategies can be suggested. The frontline workers being the core motivators and guides for the community needs frequent *gender sensitization training*. This can be ensured in separate training programmes or can be incorporated in the exiting training programmes. *The assertiveness and advocacy skills for gender equity* should be one of the objectives of this training. The other major tool which can play significant role is *gender screening of development projects* by various implementing bodies. This should primarily on the aspects like participation, economic and environmental benefits in programme from formulation stage to final stage. *Use of questionnaires by the field workers* as well as planners will be very useful. Use of *pictorial tools for participatory impact assessment* with illiterate women will enhance the participation of rural women and will ensure gender impact of livelihoods programme. The core strategy should be *identifying the equitable roles of women in programme processes and assuring the performance of the same* by executives as well as community. Ensuring participation in decision making and using *gender quorum*[2] as criteria for validation of decisions taken is one more programmatic arrangement. *Gender budgeting* is another but very important tool which will guide the equitable budgetary allocation at macro and micro level. Assuring adequate spending on women focused activities for larger impact accelerates the women development. *Assuring spaces for women* and deliberate attempt of development of such platforms at various social and institutional levels is very important. The knowledge development and dissemination processes in rural livelihoods are mainly looked after by women due to the vicinity to the watershed econ logy for various purposes. *Creating platforms for knowledge production and knowledge sharing* is an important task. This will make the invisible contribution of women more visible. Developing more tools and strategies by including the programme staff as well as community will enhance the gender equity approaches.

CONCLUDING REMARKS

Gender equity is challenge due to social and institutionalized web of attitudes. The intended gender equity definitely will take some time as it has to happen through social processes. Assuring the change process in the community through programmatic interventions is primary duty of the planners. Immediate concerns and strategic concerns in gender equity in rural livelihoods should be objectively outlined and incorporates in the planned approach. Increased awareness of gender has led to establishment of self help groups (SHGs) that have helped women save, obtain credit, and become more active and visible. But this activity has not become an integral part of the watershed development and has had little impact on traditional gender roles (Joy et al 2004).Ensuring the social processes through structural spaces is challenging task and needs policy inclusion. Regulating the benefits distribution process for assuring not only gender equity but also social equity will create collective understanding about livelihoods sustainability in correlation with gender and social equity.

REFERNECS

Hashim S R (2004),"Indian Agriculture-The Need for a New Direction" Agricultural Economics Research Review Vol 17 January June 2004 pp 1-10.

——(2007), NSSO's 60th Round Survey on Employment and Unemployment conducted in January-June 2004 accessed from http://indiabudget.nic.in/es2005-06/chapt2006/chap104.pdf on 5th December.

——(2001), Planning Commission Government of India November- Report of the Steering Group on Rural Poverty Alleviation, Watershed Development, Decentralized Planning and Panchayati Raj institutions for the Tenth Five Year Plan 2002-2007.

Gangwar Rashmi (2005), "Empowering Self-Help Groups to Address Gender Inequity" paper presented at International Conference on Education for a sustainable future at CEE Ahmedabad.

——www.nabard.org

Gupta Anil K. & Chokkakula Srinivas (1999), 'The Status of Formal Watershed Management in Asia (Ed. Prem N Sharma and Mohan P. Wagley), pp.14-18.

Joy, K.J., Suhas Paranjape, A.K. Kiran Kumar, Rohini Lele, and Raju Adagale (2004), "Watershed Development Review: Issues and

Prospects", Centre for Interdisciplinary Studies in Environment and Development, Bangalore.

NOTES

1. Beijing declaration in Fourth World Conference on Women in 1995 can be accesses at *http://www.un.org/womenwatch/daw/beijing/platform/declar.htm*
2. Gender quorum is an innovative suggestion came forward during author's interaction with community about participation of women in common property resources management related intervention in Udaipur.The qualitative interaction about the same revealed that many meetings happen in some central place in the village but in rural parts with tribal and non tribal population, it becomes difficult to reach to the meeting place in time. In most of the cases women, burdened with household as well as occupational responsibilities find it difficult to leave the work and attend the meetings in time while important decisions are taking place.

CHAPTER–4

WATERSHED IMPLIMENTATION IN GUJARAT: SOME ISSUES OF EVALUATION

Bharat Patel

INTRODUCTION

India is the second largest country in the world having over 100 crore population. Around 70 percent of its population engaged in agriculture or allied agricultural activities. The declining per capita land and fresh water availability coupled with soil erosion and depleting/degrading land and water resources are posing serious threat to food, environmental, social and economic security in the country. The total geographical area of the country is 328 million hectares. Rainfed areas, that constitute about two-thirds of nation's 142 M ha cultivated area, are the resource poor areas with low levels of productivity and suffer most from such degradation and vagaries of nature. It is estimated that these Rainfed areas contribute only 45 percent to total food grain production whereas irrigated areas which account for 37 percent of the cultivated area contribute 55 percent to total food grain production. With the projections made that about 20 M ha additional area is likely to be brought under irrigation, nearly 69 M ha will still be left under rainfed condition.

Land and water go together and their development cannot be considered independent of each other for sustainable agriculture in rainfed areas. Conservation and management of rainwater holds key for sustainable agriculture in Rainfed areas. It has also been amply demonstrated in India and elsewhere that it is impossible to envisage or implement sustainable solutions for land and water resource development and management without active and full participation of local community. Development of land and water together with sustainable production system when confined to small natural drainage unit such as watershed leads to sustainable development. Watershed Management (WSM) has, therefore, emerged as a new paradigm for planning, development and management of land, water and biomass resources with a focus on social and institutional aspects apart from bio-physical aspects following a participatory "bottom-up" approach. A large number of projects for productivity enhancement are being implemented on the watershed approach.

Soil and water conservation including micro-scale water resource development is the foundation of any watershed development programme supported by number of other protection, production and livelihood support interventions. This is so, because water is the most crucial input and acts as a catalyst to bring in ecological, social and economical revolution. Sustainable production depends considerably upon proper development, conservation, management and use of watershed resources at micro-level. Watershed management becomes increasingly important as a system approach to improve livelihood of people while conserving and regenerating their natural resources. The role and importance of community participation in ensuring the success and sustainability of watershed management is now widely accepted.

NEED

Presently, the Government has accorded very high priority to the holistic and sustainable development of rainfed areas on the 'Watershed Approach'. It is being considered as the principal vehicle for transfer of rainfed agricultural technology and to bring in ever green revolution. The National Agriculture Policy seeks to promote the integrated and holistic development of rainfed areas through conservation of rain water and augmentation of biomass production through agro forestry with active involvement of the watershed community. Such system based approach distinguishes watershed development from earlier plot/field based approach to soil and water management.

Watershed development being a multi-disciplinary approach, it has to integrate technical and scientific aspects of various disciplines.

WATERSHED MANAGEMENT: AN OVERVIEW

WATERSHED APPROACH/CONCEPT

In most parts of the country water is the chief agent causing erosion, catchments degradation, including loss of protective cover, and also transporting the eroded materials to far away places such as reservoirs. However, in considerable areas, particularly in the Western and Southern arid and semi-arid regions, besides wind, water which is continuously in short supply but on occasions also comes in torrential rains followed by flash floods. Again, loss of proper cover and productivity of land surfaces are due to inability in optimizing the use of available rain water through conservation and re-use, particularly to tie over the dry spells. Therefore, it would be seen that in the ultimate analysis in most parts it is the management of rainfall and resultant runoff, both for control measures as well as productive land management systems. The action of rainfall or flowing water is best understood with the attributes of physiography and management practices in vogue in a particular area. The factors which influence runoff, erosion and resultant flood and sedimentation, range from climate to physiography. Similarly, production potential, for optimum use of available resources of water and soil, is also affected by such factors. The inter-action of these factors, in the context of degradation and production potential, is best understood when examined on the basis of a natural unit. Watershed happens to be such a natural hydrologic or physiographic unit and, therefore, offers a very good unit for planning and implementing the soil conservation programmes. Watershed also satisfies the area concept which is considered a rational base for economic development of available resources.

Over the last 60 years, there have been many variations in conceptual models, objectives and implementation models of watershed programmes. The initial protection oriented approach got enlarged to restoration of degraded areas then to protection-cum- production oriented objectives of related natural resources and eco-restoration. Watershed management is a single window, integrated, participatory and sustainable area development programme. Watershed concept is an integrated approach to harmonize use of natural resources like land, water, vegetation, livestock, fisheries and human resources.

Watershed, a hydrological unit of an area draining to a common outlet point, is recognized as an ideal unit for planning and development of land, water and vegetation resources. Watershed concept has been used extensively because of importance of water balance in the study of ecosystems. Watershed also allows accurate measurements and monitoring of components of water balance on hydrologic cycle, sediment, energy, heat, carbon and nutrients balances in a watershed ecosystem. This can provide a network of monitoring stations on sites within a basin in a nested form or otherwise to track down the status of pollutants at different points. The monitoring at the level of watersheds or sub–watersheds in a basin will help in analyzing impacts of current and future activities and accordingly plan area specific management options or alternatives based on the priorities as per the intended project objectives.

The concept of watershed is not a new concept. Its level of concern is evident by the wide variety of programmes and institutions involved in the study and management of watersheds. However, the traditional top down approach of watershed management has not paid dividends, partly because of entire stress on biophysical aspects without proper regard for socio-economic aspects any community participation. Watershed management programmes should, therefore, be intimately linked with the people, whose socio-economic and cultural background play a decisive role in meaningful planning, implementation and operation of watershed programmes. Integrated watershed management covering the area from the highest point (ridge line) to the outlet is, therefore, the process of formulating, implementing and managing a course of actions involving natural and human resources in a watershed, taking account of all the factors operating within the watershed.

WATERSHED PROGRAMMES: GROWTH & DEVELOPMENT

DEVELOPMENT AT NATIONAL LEVEL

Pre-Independence Development: As early as in 1920s severe soil erosion in hilly regions and frequent droughts in the region of rainfed farming drew attention of the Government. Research programmes were taken primarily in the old Bombay State to prevent erosion and to provide a viable technology for the region practicing dry land farming. The government carried out pioneering work in controlling and stabilizing torrents which was a serious problem in the foothills of Punjab and disrupted communication system. Legislation had also been enacted in some of the State to enforce closure of areas to grazing and regulating indiscriminate grazing, exploitation of forest etc. Some of the Princely States also took up programmes for afforesting denuded areas, controlling gullies and ravines, particularly in the State of Uttar Pradesh, Madhya Pradesh, Rajasthan and Gujarat.

Post-Independence Development: Soil Conservation Progammes received attention during the *First Five Year Plan* itself. During the period, a Central Soil Conservation Board was set up and a chain of 9 Research Demonstration and Training Centers, with multidisciplinary expertise, were established in representative areas under the control of the Ministry of Agriculture. For tacking the problems of desert and their control, Desert Afforestation Station was established at Jodhpur.

At the State level initial steps were taken by the old Bombay State by adopting intensive programme of contour bunding to combat erosion and moisture stress conditions and also resultant famine in the Deccan Plateau. Similar programmes for conservation of soil and moisture, particularly to support Rainfed agriculture and that of afforestation on the foothills and hill slopes to control erosion, got extended in small way in other states as well.

During the *Second Five Year Plan* All India Soil and Land use Survey (AISLUS) Organization with its 4 Regional Centers was established particularly to meet the soil survey requirements of the programmes in the catchments of river valley projects. Under the centrally sponsored scheme, 43 Dry Farming Demonstration were launched in eleven states, union territory of Delhi and Damodar valley. In 1959 a Model Soil Conservation Bill was circulated to the States for enacting suitable legislation for effective implementation of the soil & water conservation programmes.

In the *Third Five Year Plan,* a working group reviewed the problems and facilities vis–a–vis new programmes to be taken up in the field of soil & water conservation. Besides, strengthening existing programmes and organization, a national scheme for treating the catchments of selected multipurpose river valley projects was launched in 13 catchments. Another programme for survey and categorization of waste lands was taken up in 17 States in order to ascertain areas which could be reclaimed and through a third scheme landless agricultural laborers were resettled. Similarly a Centrally Sponsored Scheme was launched for identification and categorization of ravenous areas in the four states. The programme content, both for agricultural and non-agricultural lands, got diversified to include practices like nalla bunding, reclamation of ravines and alkaline land, stabilization of shifting sand dunes by afforestation. Treatment of coastal areas subject to a limited extent, the problem of salinity, was taken up. State Soil Conservation Boards were also established in a number of States.

During the period from 1966 to 1969 (*Annual Plan Period*) the centrally sponsored scheme of Soil Conservation was launched in five intensive Agricultural Development Programme Districts whereas the scheme for survey and categorization of Waste Lands for re-settlement of the landless labourers as well as the scheme for identification & categorization of ravines areas were transferred to the State Sector, During this period a separate inter-ministerial Working Group was set up to go into the problems of ravines in the state of Uttar Pradesh, Rajasthan and Madhya Pradesh. With the transfer of agricultural research to the Indian Council of Agricultural Research (ICAR) all the Central Research Demonstration & Training centres (Expect the Centres located at Chatara, Nepal and Hazaribagh, D.V.C.)were placed under the control of the I.C.A.R. and re-organized into a Central Soil and Water Conservation Research & Training Institute. While All India Soil and Land Use Survey continued to function under the Ministry of Agriculture a part of it was taken out and strengthened to form the National Bureau of Land use Planning under I.C.A.R., an attached office namely Resource Inventory Centre was set up in the Soil and Water Conservation Division of the Ministry of agriculture.

During the *Fourth Five Year Plan,* the concept of taking integrated programme planning on the basis of watershed with a multi-disciplinary approach was strongly advocated while serious attempts were made to initiate collection of hydrologic and sediment data from small watersheds and tributaries particularly from those covered under the Centrally Sponsored Scheme. Manuals for collecting hydrologic and sedimentation data and handbooks for estimation of runoff and sediment production were brought out.

By 1974 the Model Bill was re-circulated among the 14 States and 2 Union Territories enacted suitable legislations to facilitate implementation of Soil & Water Conservation Programmes with greater involvement of the people.

Watershed approach got wide acceptance during *Fifth Five Year Plan* period. Three new Central programmes of diverse objectives namely, (i) Pilot Project of Amendment of Alkali and Acid Soil in Compact Areas & (ii) Strengthening/ Creation of State Soil and Land use Survey Organization and (iii) Pilot Project for Control of Shifting Cultivation were launched. The All India Soil and Land use Survey Organization extended its activities to three more sub-regions and also started works on remote sensing in collaboration with Indian Space Research Organization and National Remote Sensing Agency.

Recognizing the seriousness of the problem of *Jhuming* (shifting cultivation) on the economy of North–Eastern India and the production potential of the alkali soil in Indo-Gangetic Basin, two National Boards have been set up to deal with these problems moiré effectively. The States were requested to set up State Land Use Boards to provide policy framework for matters relating to land use including soil survey. 22 states and 4 Union Territories have by now established such Boards.

Watershed management, though less focused earlier, has a history of about 60 years in India. Multiple agencies have been involved in the growth and development of watershed programmes.

DEVELOPMENT AT STATE LEVEL

Early Efforts: During pre-independence period sporadic efforts were made with regard to contour bunding, field bunding and moisture conservation measures in some of the southern states based upon the results of dry land farming research work carried out during 1930s. Some afforestation and gully control works were taken up in Himalayan region of Punjab and ravinous areas of Uttar Pradesh. Reclamation of deteriorated lands in a few other cases was taken up.

Planned Programmes: Planning of soil conservation in the States started with the implementation of Five Year Plans. Targeted programmes of bunding, afforestation of deteriorated areas, gully plugging, ect. were taken up. In addition to training, facilities were created under Central Government for training of officers & Assistants. Training courses were started under State sector also for sub-assistants and in some cases assistants also. Research and demonstration stations were established in some of the states to investigate local problems and for development of suitable soil and moisture techniques.

Table 1
Growth of Nationally and Internationally Funded Organized Watershed Management Programmes in India

Schemes/ Projects	*Year of Launch*	*Watershed Numbers/Area*	*Sponsoring Agencies*
Research watersheds	1956	42 Nos.	MoAgril,GOI/CSWCRTI.ICAR
Soil Conservation in RVP Catchments	1961-62	29 catchments in 9 States	Ministry of Agriculture, GOI
Operational Research Watersheds	1974	4 Nos.	CSWCRTI,ICAR
Watershed Management in Catchments of Flood Prone Rivers	1980-81	10 catchments in 8 States	Ministry of Agriculture, GOI
Model Watersheds	1983	47 Nos.	CSWCRTI & CRIDA,ICAR
Watershed Development in Rainfed Areas	1984	28 Nos.(3.47 lakh ha)	World Bank (A.P., Karnataka, M.P.& M.S)
Watershed Development in Ravines Area	1987	0.62 lakh ha	EEC
Drought Prone Area Programme(DPAP)	1987*	91 districts 615 blocks	MRAE,GOI
Desert Development Programme(DDP)	1987*	21 districts131 blocks	MRAE, GOI
Western Ghats Development Programme (WGDP)	1987*	158 blocks5 States	Union Planning Commission
Indo-German Watershed Project	1990-91	Maharashtra	Germany
Indo-German Bilateral Project	1990-91	Monitoring	Germany
NWDPRA	1991	2497 Nos.	Ministry of Agri.,GOI
IWDP(Hills & Plains)	1991	1.12 lakh ha	World Bank
Comprehensive Watershed Development Project	1991	1.13 lakh ha	DANIDA(Karnataka,Tamil Nadu and Orissa)
Rel Majra Watershed Project	1991	1 No.	CSWCRTI, ICAR/Ministry of Environment, GOI

Contd.

Schemes/ Projects	*Year of Launch*	*Watershed Numbers/Area*	*Sponsoring Agencies*
Doon Valley Project, UP	1993	1.72 lakh	EEC
Integrated Wasteland Development Project/IWDP	1994	25 States	MRAE,GOI
Indo-Swiss Participatory Watershed Development	1995	0.35 lakh	Swiss Government
Attapadi Wasteland Comprehensive Environment Conservation Project. Agali, Kerala	1996	507 Km^2	OECF,Japan

MRAE - Ministry of Rural Areas & Employment
*Since Programmes adopted on watershed approach
Source: pSoil Conservation Problem Approach and Progress in Indiap by Ministry of Agriculture, Government of India.

Organization: Separate divisions and wings for soil conservation have been established in most of the States under the State Departments of Agriculture. Separate Directorates of Soil Conservation have also been established in some of the States namely, Punjab, Bihar, Assam, Nagaland, Meghalaya, Kerala & Orissa. In Tamil Nadu, the Department of Agriculture Engineering look after soil conservation, while in Arunachal Pradesh the Department of Rural Works is Responsible for such works.

In addition to the Department of Agriculture, soil conservation programme are undertaken by the State Forest Departments also, which in a few cases have established separate Project Directorate/Division. In Gujarat, Maharashtra and West Bengal, Public Works Departments and Irrigation Departments undertake Special Soil conservation activities like reclamation of coastal saline, stream bank erosion control, landslide treatment ect. Land Development Corporations have also been established in a few states such as Gujarat, Haryana, Uttar Pradesh ect. to draw funds from Banks.

Boards and Acts: As a follow up to the establishment of the Central Soil Conservation Board, the number of States have set up similar Boards at State level to achieve better coordination amongst the concerned Departments. Similarly the States of Gujarat, Madhya Pradesh, Rajasthan and Uttar Pradesh set up State level Boards corresponding to the Central Ravine Reclamation Board. Later 20 States and 6 Union Territories have also set up the State Land Use Boards to provide high level policy direction. Consequent to the circulation of the model bill 14 States and 2 Union territories have so far enacted suitable legislation for taking up soil conservation programmes collectively and on scientific lines.

Programme Contents: Over a period of time the State have diversified the soil and moisture conservation programmes from bunding and terracting alone to an integrated multi-treatment approach consisting of nalla bunding, check dames, gully plugging, land shaping, percolation tanks, pounds, improvement of water conveyance system and development of irrigated lands. On non-agriculture lands afforestation, grassland development with enclosures and moisture conservation measures such as trenching besides other erosion control structures are also undertaken. Since IV and V Plans, special programmes of reclamation of problem lands, like ravine lands, alkali soils, water logged areas and other kinds of waste lands have also been included under soil conservation activities. The soil conservation programmes have been progressively oriented on watershed basis for an integrated development of whole watershed. The progressively trained soil conservation organization in the State have been able to take up special development programmes under the area development approaches, like Drought Prone Area Programme (DPAP), Small Farmers Development Agency (SFDA), Integrated Tribal Development (ITD) and Command Area Development (CAD) etc, by the State Soil Conservation Wings/ Departments.

WATERSHED MANAGEMENT IN GUJARAT STATE

PROFILE OF THE GUJARAT STATE

Gujarat state has 19.50 million hectares of land ,of which 12.8 million hectares of land is cultivable and only 9.5 million hectares were actually under cultivation. The irrigated land is only 2.8 million hectares, which is nearly 30 percent only. The average yield in Gujarat is low as compared to various other states. As the irrigation is limited around 30% only, there is a need to conserve soil and moisture in rainfed areas to obtain sustainable agricultural production.

The total geographical area of the state, according to area classification, admeasures 196.00 lakh hectares of which the area reported for land use is about 188.25 lakh hectares.

Excluding area under permanent forests and the area under non-agricultural use, an area of 158.58 lakh hectares requires soil and moisture conservation measures. These areas can be classified into following three major categories:

(a) Agricultural land predominantly rainfed.

(b) Agricultural lands in the command areas of irrigation projects.

(c) The problems soils affected by salinity or alkalinity.

Table 2
The Ownership and Land Use Pattern of Gujarat State

Particulars	*Physical Area in Lakh Hectare*	*Percentage of Reporting Area*
Cultivated land of Private ownership	103.40	54.93
Panchayat Land	8.46	4.49
Government Land		
a. Cultivable Land	19.50	10.36
b. Non-Cultivable Land	27.22	14.46
Sub-Total of (a+b)	46.72	
Forests Land	18.78	9.98
Area under non–agriculture	10.89	5.78
Total	188.25	100.00

Source: "Annual Report of 2006-07" of GSLDC, Gandhinagar, Gujarat.

The Agricultural land covered by various command area development schemes including Narmada Dam, would be about 38.34 lakh hectares. Areas affected by salinity and alkalinity and requiring special treatment will be 12.16 lakhs hectares. After deducting these two areas, area of 106.78 lakh hectares require treatment for soil and moisture conservation, under the programme of watershed management.

Out of this area, an area of 32.78 lakh hectares had already been treated till last year and an area of 51.22 lakh hectares remain to be treated. It is expected that about 30% of this area i.e. 15.36 lakh hectares would be treated by farmers themselves. Thus an area of 35.86 lakh hectares still require soil and moisture conservation treatments. Looking to the present pace about one lakh hectares per year, it would require perhaps more than 50 years to be completed unless the pace of watershed development activity is accelerated substantially.

GROWTH AND DEVELOPMENT IN THE STATE OF GUJARAT

Soil and water conservation activities with watershed approach were started in the state very late but it was adopted gradually and various agencies were involved in this process of development and growth.

- During Pre-Independence period some of the Princely ruled areas of the State took up programmes for afforesting denuded areas, controlling gullies and ravines.

Table 3
Area Treated Through Watershed Approach in the State
(Year 1978 -79 to 2006-2007)

Year	*Area Treated in Ha.*	*Expenditure Rs. in Lakh*
1978-79	15848	371.13
1979-80	16683	354.08
1980-81	14619	558.17
1981-82	19292	794.99
1982-83	19611	1179.74
1983-84	36327	1769.01
1984-85	17377	1161.52
1985-86	11420	966.13
1986-87	16953	1105.78
1987-88	49282	2052.01
1988-89	67558	2654.43
1989-90	40242	1972.49
1990-91	45974	2602.38
1991-92	104715	3752.41
1992-93	104528	3763.63
1993-94	82558	1932.20
1994-95	102673	3713.99
1995-96	121486	4755.86
1996-97	116459	3750.50
1997-98	74108	4026.39
1998-99	136115	5063.11
1999-2000	130328	4643.13
2000-2001	82103	10243.74
2001-2002	80069	8110.76
2002-2003	26974	4229.81
2003-2004	63294	8098.53
2004-2005	93588	10110.26
2005-2006	127825	14339.21
2006-2007	180698	20874.41
Total	19,98,707	1,28,949.80

Source: "Annual Report of 2006-07" of GSLDC, Gandhinagar, Gujarat.

- During Post-Independence for local problems related to soil and moisture conservation, farmers themselves were taking care in traditional way and with traditional knowledge inspite of insufficient resources with them.

- In fifties, Forest Department was looking after Soil and moisture conservation activities for the purpose of employment generation in the state in scattered manner, but pace of activities were very slow, type of treatments were limited up to protection measures only.
- In sixties, the soil and moisture conservation programmes in the rainfed areas of the state were implemented by the Department of Agriculture as a part of other activities. Watershed Approach for soil and moisture activities were adopted by Department of Agriculture in mid seventies.
- Gujarat State Land Development Corporation (GSLDC) came into existence in the month of March - 1978. GSLDC was started with the purpose of generating funds for watershed programmes through institutional finance to speed up the activities. The objective of creating new and independent organization was to take up full-fledged watershed management programmes with more pace, more financial support, and more technical expertise in watershed management having multidiscipline functionaries. The physical and financial achievements from 1978-79 to 2006-2007 by GSLDC are as follows.

SOME OBSERVATIONS

Looking into this all growth and developments of watershed programmes at national level as well as state level, and involvement of various implementing agencies therein, there are some basic issues which I have observed during my this research work and some practical experiences also. There are certain major problems with the implementing agencies in relation to adoption of basic concept of watershed for basinwise planning and implementation, plus selection of different treatments in watershed area according to land capability classification done in scientific manner. There are some research notes and research comments observed by different researchers, implementers and academicians in the field of watershed management, discussed as under.

"HOW A WATERSHED WORKS"

Mr. JOHN H. WETZEL, Chief, Watershed Planning Research, U. S. Soil Conservation Service, published his paper titled "How A Watershed Works" in the year 1957 , a book compiled by soil conservation society of India. He observes that:

"Many definitions have been developed over the years for the terms watershed, catchment, drainage basin, and river basin. While these definitions employ a wide variety of words and local terminology, they all mean practically the same thing. A very simple definition that can be applied to any of the above terms is that they embrace all of the land and water areas which contribute runoff to a common point. The watershed above any point on a defined drainage channel is, therefore, all of the land and water areas which drain through that point. A watershed may be only a few acres or hundreds of thousands of square miles, such as the watershed at the mouth of the Ganges."

"During this Development Centre, the principal emphasis will be on the small watershed. In order to orient everyone's thinking, a small watershed might be considered as an area of from a few square miles to a maximum about one hundred square miles. This range of size will encompass those watersheds on which local people and local governments can be expected to substantially participate in the planning and development of a watershed program. It is true that some assistance will be required from State, Provincial or Central Governments, but in general the problems of the small watershed are local problems which can best be solved by the action of the local people. For a such program to be successful, the landowners must be able to say "we" are doing this for ourselves rather than feel that some form of governmental organization is coming in and doing the whole job for them."

"Long experience throughout the world has shown that land and water resource can most effectively be considered and treated on a watershed basis because they are interdependent resources. Any alterations in the treatment of either resource within the watershed area usually have a significant effect on other portions of the area. Problems within a watershed generally also have their source or cause within the watershed. To correct the problem, its source must be treated. Since what is done by one landowner within a watershed affects several neighboring landowner within the watershed and vice versa, the watershed provides a basis for group attack on a common problem."

"Watershed management or protection, as an abstract term, implies the wise use of all soil and water resources so as to provide a clean, uniform, water supply for beneficial use, and to control damaging overflows. In the abstract, the term is very nearly synonymous with soil and water conservation with emphasis on water production and control rather than on maximum safe crop production. In general, the types of measures applied for control of erosion also provide a high degree of watershed management or protection. The original concept of watershed management was to apply conservation measures on any land where the need and opportunity existed with little emphasis on the needs and problems of the specific small watershed."

"Watershed management or protection *programmes* as currently defined imply a project-type operation developed and applied to all land and water in a specific watershed, taking into consideration the physical conditions, needs and problems of the watershed, its relationship to a larger watershed, and the facility available to accomplish the project."

"No two watersheds are alike. No general rules can be laid down which will apply to all watersheds. Each watershed must be studied in the light of its problems and individual characteristics before the most desirable corrective programme can be developed and a determination made as to how the specific watershed will operate."

Whatever Mr. JOHN H. WETZEL, Chief, Watershed Planning Research, U. S. Soil Conservation Service, says as above in his paper published in the year 1957 compiled by soil conservation society of India, it is still relevant and necessary to follow conceptually for any programme of watershed management after 50 years. But now a day while implementing the programmes we are facing so many complex developmental issues. So for all programmes in guidelines we are insisting upon adopting basic concept of basin wise planning and implementation but while implementing because of flexible provisions and ground level issues we are deviating from the concept. It is my observation in number of cases.

"ADVANTAGE DECLINED PART III"

Mr. Anil C. Shah, Director, Development Support Centre, (NGO) Ahmedabad, Gujarat, India, Published his research report name, "Advantage Declined Part III of a Longitudinal Study of Sixteen Drought Prone Villages of Gujarat" In the Year April 2004. In the preface and findings of the study, it is mentioned that:

"The severe drought of 1999-2000 in Gujarat provided an opportunity to DSC to find out if watershed programme had any impact on the problems of drought affected villages. A study was carried out in drought–prone districts of Gujarat. Sixteen villages, eight villages where watershed projects were implemented-to be known as watershed villages–and eight villages which did not have watershed projects–to be known as non-watershed villages-were selected. The study examined the impact of drought on these villages in terms of ten critical parameters; like milk yield, Local employment, Migration, and Food Security. The study confirmed the expected outcome; the impact of drought was mitigated in watershed villages."

"In addition to the watershed programme, the role of the rainfall pattern in diluting the severity of drought also needs to be examined. Successive droughts for two to three years are not uncommon in drought–prone areas. How long the drought-mitigating effect of watershed programme lasts in watershed villages when they face serious drought years needs to be looked into."

"Some evidence for this was found when DSC revisited the same villages to ascertain the extent to which watershed villages enjoyed a differential advantage over the non-watershed villages under repeated droughts in 2001-2002. The finding of the study "Advantage Watershed" was that though several watershed villages were better placed than non-watershed villages in the chosen life-saving parameters, the differential was reduced. In 2003, another year of drought, DSC revisited the same villages and found that the differential was almost flattened as shown in" Advantage Declined". The comparison is given in Table-4.

Table 4
Impact of Continuing Drought on Watershed Villages

Parameters	*1999-2000(First Year of Drought)*	*2002-03 (Fourth Year of Drought)*
Tankers for drinking water	1 village	4 villages
Failure of crop	2 villages	4 villages
Fodder available within the village	2 villages	1 village
Local employment available throughout the year	5 villages	2 villages
Migration out of watershed villages	No village had migration for more than 6 months	5 villages had migration for 6 months

Source: "Advantage Declined Part III" 2004, by Anil C. Shah, DSC, Ahmedabad.

The findings of the DSC studies raise a very important issue about the measures required for alleviating the misery of the people who have to suffer drought conditions year after year. There is obviously a need for strengthening and augmenting the current programme of watershed development. This may be in terms of investment, better conservation of vital resources like water and fodder, and a strategy for productivity enhancement and value addition with *Basin Wise Planning*.

While discussing findings of the study the author had insisted upon funding for watershed and in particular *Basin Wise Planning* "Both the scope and the need exist to cover the entire catchments of a local stream that may be serving several villages. This approach will obviate conflicts between upstream and downstream villages and ensure equitable use of available water. In a way this is a localized, small scale application of basin–wise planning that has been recommended as the right approach in the national water policy 2001.

Stream-wise planning and management of watershed has two implications. First, it would mean that the village watershed of 500 ha. may extend to more than 10,000 ha. involving may be 10-12 villages. Secondly, for coordinating several village institutions and their common plan, there would be need for a supporting organization that has competence in community organizing as well as technical competence. NGOs, which have the experience, resources and capacity for innovation, can handle such projects. Fortunately, MoRD's revised guidelines as well as HARIYALI watershed guidelines (2003) envisage that an NGO-Project Implementing Agency (PIA) shall normally be assigned 10-12 watershed projects covering an area ranging from 5000-6000 ha. However, in exceptional and deserving cases, an NGO-PIA may be assigned a maximum of 12000 ha. in a district and a maximum of 25000 ha. in the State."

The study clearly indicates that we are deviating from basin wise planning and implementation and that is why not getting desired results.

"PROVISIONS OF HARIYALI GUIDELINES"

Considering recommendations given by Expert Committee (1994) under chairmanship of Shri C.H. Hanumantrao for DPAP and DDP, The new guidelines for watershed programme were issued by Ministry of Rural Development in the year 1995.

Guidelines were revised in the year 2001 on the basis of experiences of implementation of six years with more liberty and Flexibility at village level.

Once again the Guidelines of watershed programme were revised and issued in the name of "HARIYALI" on 27th January 2003.As per provisions of guidelines para-5, regarding selection of watershed area and criterions thereof – it is clearly indicated that if you have to compromise for selection of area because of area of villages then you have to have treat total watershed area simultaneously. As per provisions of guidelines para-9,

11, and 12, nodal agency will be District Rural Development Agency (DRDA) and for implementation of programme Project Implementation Agency (PIA) will be decided.

CAPART is also one of the PIA for this programme and they are funding for watersheds. CAPART is appointing third party Facilitators CUM Evaluators (FCA), for pre-funding evaluation, mid-term evaluation, and post-funding evaluation to check their different type of works. During my tenure of two years from 2004-05 to 2005-06 as FCA I observed that inspite of clear provisions in guidelines of HARIYALI , so many works were carried out without maintaining criterions for selection of watershed areas. Sequence for carrying out works from top to bottom in terms of slope was also not observed. Means we have very good guidelines with scientific base but fails to implement.

COMMENT BY TECHNICAL EXPERT & IMPLEMENTER

COMMENT BY TECHNICAL EXPERT & IMPLEMENTER

Joint Director (Technical), Gujarat State Land Development Corporation Ltd., Gandhinagar, Gujarat, India, is implementing watershed programmes since last 30 years. He is associated with all most all the central and state Government sponsored programmes. While academic discussions, I observed that-he also feels, - "For all programmes in guidelines we are insisting upon adopting basic concept of basin wise planning and implementation but while implementing because of flexible provisions and ground level issues we are deviating from the concept due to different implementing agencies, of which some do not have technical base and understanding of watershed concept properly."

COMMENT BY LEADING & IMPLEMENTING NGO

Executive Director, Development Support Centre, Ahmedabad, Gujarat, India, is in the field of rural development for various activities like training, research, documentation, policy interventions to government, and implementation of watershed programmes since more than 25 years. While academic discussions with him, he expressed the feelings, "Very few agencies have technical base and understanding of watershed concept properly. For all programmes in guidelines we are insisting upon adopting basic concept of basin wise planning and implementation but while implementing because of different reasons and local issues we are deviating from the concept. It is high time to review our progress in terms of quality and quantity both, and check the track that are we going in right direction for sustainable development or we are playing with our natural resources for sustainability of development."

COMMENT BY STATE ADMINISTRATOR & EXPERT

Deputy Director, Watershed Management, Commissioner of Rural Development, Gandhinagar, Gujarat, India, is in the field of rural development for various activities like training, research, documentation, policy interventions to government, and implementation of watershed programmes since more than 30 years, with core expertise in forestry and training of Watershed Management. While academic discussions with him, he suggested, "So many agencies are involved in implementation of various watershed programmes without sufficient technical manpower. They require fundamental technical training on Watershed Management. They may be expert in any one subject but watershed requires multi disciplinary expertise, at least in basic streams. On other side in guidelines of all programmes we are insisting upon adopting basic concept of basin wise planning and implementation but while implementing because of untrained and unaware implementers we are deviating from the concept due to different implementing agencies."

COMMENT ON LAND CAPABILITY CLASSIFICATION

Optimum protection and production both can be obtained from implementation of watershed programmes through recommendations of various treatments with the help of Land Capability Classification; it is prerequisite for the same. It was observed by me during my service tenure at training institute that Watershed Development Team (WDT) members appointed for implementation of Hariyali programme were absolutely unaware about Land Capability Classification and how it can be used. More than 500 WDT members were trained and interacted with them but most of them were not known to the concept and use of it. These kinds of lacunas with different implementing agencies are leading towards dead end of road of development and growth of watershed programmes and sustainable development.

CONCLUSIONS

As we have seen from different observations and analysis of the same, basic concept of watershed and how we deals in implementation of various watershed programmes at national as well as state level through different agencies with the twin objective of conservation and production. We can draw the conclusions with the help of this study, *that we are deviating from basic concept of watershed due to need of time, complex developmental issues, various agencies involved in implementation of programmes, to cover more area under treatment in short time span (considering size of the problem of protection and production both).*

In guidelines of all programmes we are insisting upon adopting basic concept of basin wise planning and implementation as I have mentioned in the beginning, but while implementing because of flexible provisions and ground level issues as well as many complex developmental issues we are deviating from the concept. Many agencies are involved in implementation of various watershed programmes without sufficient technical manpower. Very few agencies have technical base and understanding of watershed concept properly. Others require fundamental technical training on Watershed Management. They may be expert in any one subject but watershed requires multi disciplinary expertise, at least in basic streams. On other side in guidelines of all programmes we are insisting upon adopting basic concept of basin wise planning and implementation but while implementing because of untrained and unaware implementers we are deviating from the concept due to different implementing agencies. It is high time to review our progress in terms of quality and quantity both, and check the track that are we going in right direction for sustainable development or we are playing with our natural resources for sustainability of development.

REFERENCES

——"Soil Conservation Problem Approach and Progress in India" year- 1982 published by Ministry of Agriculture, Department of Agriculture and Cooperation, Soil and Water Conservation Division, Government of India. New Delhi.

——"Technical Manual for National Watershed Development Programme in Rainfed Areas (NWDPRA)" by Ministry of Agriculture, Department of Agriculture and Cooperation, Soil and Water Conservation Division, Government of India. New Delhi.

——"The Challenge of Our Watersheds" Proceedings of the Development Centre on Watershed Management for Asia & The Far East, Published in the year 1957 by Soil Conservation Society of India, Hazaribagh, Bihar, India.

——"Annual Report for the year 2006-07" of Gujarat State Land Development Corporation Ltd., Gandhinagar, Gujarat, India.

——"Guidelines for Watershed Development Scheme of HARIYALI -1995,2001,2003" issued by Ministry of Rural Development, Government of India, New Delhi.

——"Advantage Declined Part III of A Longitudinal Study of Sixteen Drought Prone Villages of Gujarat." Year April 2004, Study by Anil C. Shah, Development Support Centre, Ahmedabad, Gujarat, India.

CHAPTER–5

WATERSHED MANAGEMENT IN INDIA: ISSUES OF PARTICIPATION AND DECENTRALISATION

Satyapriya Rout

Over the years, watershed development has emerged as a solution to the problems of India's rainfed agriculture in semi-arid areas, which are characterised by low productivity, degraded natural resources and widespread poverty due to livelihood insecurity. Millions of people living in these semi-arid areas rely upon degrading agriculture and natural resources to sustain their livelihood, and struggle to cope-up with the changing agro-climatic conditions. Considering the current rate of land degradation, which has almost doubled itself from that of 1980s, and the associated livelihood difficulties, watershed development has been approached by policy makers, development planners and practitioners, and researchers as an effective mechanism to raise productivity, and ensure environmentally sustainable land and water management system. Watershed development projects are designed to harmonise the use of water, soil, forest and pasture resources in a way that conserves these resources while raising agricultural productivity, by way of moisture conservation and increased irrigation through tank and aquifer-based water harvesting systems. It, thus, involves, capturing rain water in the rainy season, so that soil moisture, surface as well as ground water remain available even when there is scarcity in rainfall. Watershed projects have become widespread in rainfed areas of our country in recent years, with a current annual budget from all sources that exceeds US $500 million (Farrington *et al.*, 1999). Further, it is expected that nearly 63 million hectares of land will be developed under a plan for holistic and integrated development of rainfed areas in the next 25 years (Government of India, 2000).

Watershed development has been approached from a multiple dimensions, given its ability to address a wide array of objectives (see German *et al*, 2007). For example, amongst agronomists, it is seen as a means of scaling out technologies, primarily those for soil and water conservation or environmental protection (Hinchcliffe et al., 1995). For the water resource sector and policy-makers, it is seen as a means for enhancing environmental services and public goods emanating from upper watersheds for the society at large (FAO, 2000; IIED, 2004). Among conservationists, it is viewed as a framework for enabling trans-boundary natural resource management (van der Linde et al., 2001), in which livelihood concerns are often addressed only to the extent that they help to further conservation goals. However, from a social science perspective, the major concerns in a watershed management context are mainly problems of equity of access to natural resources, and issues of livelihood, governance and collective action that cannot be solved at the level of the farm or household (Meinzen-Dick et al., 2002).

Albeit its multiple dimensions and benefits that it offers, implementing a watershed project is much complicated, as it requires collective action among villages, while distributing differential rewards. In a watershed context, benefits mainly go to relatively wealthy landowners in the lower watershed, where the irrigation potentials are increased through water harvesting measures, where as costs fall on the people who rely on land on the upper watershed, either for rainfed agriculture or for grazing and collecting fuelwood from uncultivated lands. This is because protecting water harvesting system at the lower watershed requires investing in soil conservation and afforestation in the upper watershed, thereby limiting access to these lands. Further, a watershed is also an area that contains different administrative and property boundaries, lands that fall under different property right regimes, where farmers' action may affect each other's interests. Therefore, successful implementation of watershed depends upon convincing everyone in a community to support watershed development efforts, resolving inevitable conflicts that arise in the process, and organizing them around watershed development efforts (Farrington *et al.*, 1999; Kolavalli and Kerr, 2002). In other words, one theme that is central to success of the whole process is that of sustained participation of stakeholders in the whole process of watershed development and management.

It has, therefore, been acknowledged that participation is very much critical to success or otherwise of sustainable watershed management. Over the years, there has been no dearth of studies concluding that participation leads to favourable outcomes in watershed development (see for example, Farrington *et al*, 1999; Hinchcliffe *et at.*, 1999; Kolavalli and Kerr, 2002). Participatory approaches, the credit of which in most occasions has gone to efforts made by Non-Governmental Organisation, have now found a place in the government's project implementation measures. In recent times, Government of India has tried to incorporate participatory approaches pioneered by NGOs in its watershed development programmes. Especially, watershed projects under the Ministry of Rural Development have made provisions to involve local people in making decisions about project design and funding (government of India, 1994). Further, the guidelines of Ministry of Agriculture also provide scope for inclusion of local people in watershed development and management (Government of India, 2000).

In the aforesaid context, where participation has been acknowledged as the pre-condition to success or otherwise, it is apt to have a detailed analysis of the concept and its position in the whole debate of sustainable watershed development. The recent government guidelines are expected to institutionalise community participation in watershed development. In the background of this, the present paper, therefore, aims to explore the manner in which community participation has been approached and preceded in watershed debate. *The main objective of the paper is to analyse the very process of community participation in the watershed context, and to suggest ways and means to mainstream participation in the whole process.* The paper will review various approaches of working with communities that enhance participation, and various incentives (and dis-incentives) that generate enabling environment for development of institutions or organisations required for community participation. Another related objective that the paper aims to explore is to consider the role of decentralisation in the process of watershed development. While the new guidelines of watershed development constitute elements, that itself talk about decentralised natural resource management, through devolution and inclusion of people in decision making, the 73rd Constitutional Amendments of 1993, provide constitutional backup and institutional design for development of watershed in semi-arid areas. Article 243 G (3) of the XI Schedule, which accompanies the amendments, talks about watershed development (see, Bauman, 1998). This generates an opportunity to study the linkages between political decentralisation in the form of Panchayats, brought out by the 73rd Amendment Act and the administrative decentralisation, in the form of watershed guidelines, issued by Ministry of Rural Areas and Empowerment of Government of India. The second objective of the paper is, therefore, *to examine the interface between decentralisation efforts and watershed development in India.*

The paper will be based on secondary data source, and will engage with a critical review of published and unpublished documents, government orders and guidelines concerning watershed development and decentralisation.

REFERENCES

Bauman, Pari (1998), *Panchayati Raj and Watershed Management in India: Constraints and Opportunities.* Working paper No. 114. London: Overseas Development Institute.

——(2000), FAO, Land-water Linkages in Rural Watersheds: Introductory Note. Land-Water Linkages in Rural Watersheds Electronic Workshop, 18– 27 October, 2000, FAO, Rome.

Farrington, J., C. Turton and A. J. Adams (eds) (1999), *Participatory Watershed Development: Challenges for Twenty-first Century*. New Delhi: Oxford University Press.

German, L. H. Mansoor, G. Alemu , W. Mazengia, T. Amede, A. Stroud (2007), 'Participatory Integrated Watershed Management: Evolution of Concepts and Methods in an Ecoregional Program of the Eastern African Highlands'. *Agricultural Systems*. 94: 189–204.

——(1994), Government of India, 'Guidelines for Watershed Development'. Ministry of Rural Development, Government of India.

——(2000), Government of India, 'Common Approaches to Watershed Development'. Ministry of Agriculture, Government of India.

Hinchcliffe, F., Guijt, I., Pretty, J.N., Shah, P., (1995), New Horizons: the Economic, Social and Environmental Impacts of Participatory Watershed Development. IIED Gatekeeper Series 50, pp. 3–20.

——(2004), International Institute for Environment and Development (IIED), Developing markets for watershed protection services and improved livelihoods. Report of the Implementation Phase Planning Workshop, January 28–30, 2004, London, IIED.

Kolavalli, S. and J. Kerr (2002), 'Scaling up Participatory Watershed Development in India'. *Development and Change*, 33 (2): 213–35.

Meinzen-Dick, R., Knox, A., Place, F., Swallow, B.,(2002), Innovation in Natural Resource Management: The Role of Property Rights and Collective Action in Developing Countries. IFPRI, Washington, DC, 317 pp.

Van der Linde, H., Oglethorpe, J., Sandwith, T., Snelson, D., Tessema, Y., (2001), Beyond Boundaries: Trans-Boundary Natural Resource Management in Sub-Saharan Africa. Biodiversity Support Program, Washington, DC, 166 pp.

CHAPTER–6

INTEGRATION OF LIVESTOCK AND GENDER CONCERNS IN WATERSHED DEVELOPMENT FOR SUSTAINABLE LIVELIHOOD OF RURAL POOR

A.K. Misra, B. Shivarudrappa, B. Venkatesuralu, K.V. Subrahmanyam, Y.S. Ramakrishna

INTRODUCTION

Livestock are an important asset of the rural poor. About 75% of rural households are small and marginal farmers, who own 56% of the large ruminants and 62% of the small ruminants (World Bank, 1999). In most of the drylands and hill regions, livestock farming is a major player, as more than 70 % of family income is derived from livestock (GOI, 2002). Studies have also found that livestock generally contribute significantly more to the income stream of poor households-particularly the income controlled by women-than to the incomes of those living above the poverty line (*Thornton et al. 2002*). The benefits from livestock can even extend to those who don't own livestock-often the poorest members of the community. These vulnerable groups require special considerations in rural development programmes, as the contribution of livestock will be an important means of alleviating poverty and improving their livelihoods.

Watershed development is a major initiative in the direction of poverty alleviation in arid and semi arid areas in India. The treatment of watershed is expected to improve agricultural as well as livestock productivity. However, several studies show that the benefits are not uniform across the regions, and in many watersheds, ineqaties are increased, since for non-land owning and well owning households access to drinking water, grazing lands and other natural resources (Kerr 2002). It is increasingly being recognised that to increse the equaty of watershed deveolpment, more attention has to be paid to livestock production, which is major livelihood activity in most of the rural areas. Several studies have indicated that in most of the watersheds, the practice and the facilitating mechanisms do not explicitly consider livestock development as an integral part of watershed development. It was observed in the Process Evaluation studies of ANTHRA and WASSAN that the only interventions taken up at large in the mainstream watershed development programs are distribution of livestock assets (or credit) and fodder seeds. These perspectives are limiting the scope of the watershed program itself. The major constraints in promoting livestock and gender concerns in watersheds might be lack of clear methodologies for action planning, good field examples of practice, resource material and appropriate policies-planning, monitoring etc. In order to solve this problem, approaches that guarantee effective linkages among researchers, NGOs, extension workers, decision-makers and farmers, who have a complex knowledge base of production and livelihood systems and widely dispersed expertise, are needed (Misra *et al.*, 2007). However, the challenge is to develop novel mechanism for effective integration of the livestock and gender concerns into the overall watershed development policies and practices.

THE PROCESS

The present study was conducted under DFID-NRSP project entitled "Enabling rural poor for better livelihoods through improved natural resource management in SAT India" in clusters of two/three selected villages in Mahabubnagar and Anantapur districts of Andhra Pradesh and Tumkur district of Karnataka with an aim to improve the livestock productivity under small holder production systems. The project was implemented by the Central Research Institute for Dryalnd Agriculture in collaboration with two State Agricultural Universities (UAS Bangalore and ANGRAU, Hyderabad) and a grassroots NGO, the BAIF Institute of Rural Development. The project introduced a participatory approach to developing livestock production technologies and addressing gender concerns in selected watersheds. It uses many of the principles of Participatory Rural Appraisal, but extends the active participation of farmers well beyond the initial stage of appraisal to technology development and evaluation on farms. The approach begins with in-depth participatory diagnosis by a broad cross section of the farming community, including both men and women and farmers from the different wealth groups. This helps the community to define, group and prioritize their main problems.

After identifying the major problems, various interventions, mostly in the form of observation trials-cum-demonstrations, were planned and discussed in *Salaha Samithi* (farmer advisory committee) meetings. Several interventions were brought to the doorsteps of farmers in the form of a 'basket' of technologies' in order for the farmers to select those interventions they felt could assist them in producing optimal farm management systems. Then, a comprehensive schedule for implementing the technical interventions was discussed and finalised in the *Salaha Samithi* meetings. An 'open door policy' was adopted for the interventions, implying that all interested farmers in the community were free to participate in them. *Salaha Samithi* facilitated implementation and monitoring of interventions. Volunteer farmers served as advisory persons. The evaluation process is monitored and assessed by the *Salaha Samithi* members and necessary changes made to any technology that is being developed or adapted. The core principle of the process is active, decision-making involvement of farmers at all stages of technology development with technical input and facilitation by project staff. Attendance of community members at the SS meetings and the number of farmers willing to introduce the technologies

Table 1
Characteristics and Cropping Systems of Selected Clusters

Particulars	*Cluster 1*	*Cluster 2*	*Cluster 3*
State	Andhra Pradesh	Andhra Pradesh	Karnataka
District	Ananthpur	Mahaboobnagar	Tumkur
Mandal/block	Atmakur	Mahaboobnagar	Tiptur
Villages as a part of the cluster	PampanurPampanur Tanda Y. Kothapalli	Dharmapur Chowdarapalli Zamistapur Bukkalonpalli	Shankaranhalli
Total Geographical area (ha)	2111	15617	711
Rainfall (mm)	520	600	650
Soil	Red sandy loam, patches of black soil; 30-50 cms soil depth, moderate in nutrient content	Red sandy, patches of black clay soil, 30-50 cms soil depth, moderate in nutrient content	Red sandy loam, small pebbles, saline soils; 20-50 cms soil depth; moderate in nutrient content
Climatic zone	Hot arid	Hot semi arid	Hot moist semi arid
Length of growing period (days)	60-90	120-150	120-150
Major Crops			
Kharif (Rainy season)	Groundnut, paddy, pigeonpea, sorghum, castor, cow pea, other pulses-horsegram, redgram and sunflower	Castor, sorghum, maize, paddy, groundnut, pigeonpea, and fingermillet	Fingermillet, sorghum, pulses, groundnut, castor, sesame, niger, paddy, and redgram

Contd.

Particulars	*Cluster 1*	*Cluster 2*	*Cluster 3*
Rabi (Post-rainy season)	Groundnut, paddy, horsegram, and vegetables	Groundnut, chick pea, paddy and vegetables	Fingermillet, sorghum, niger, fieldbean, horsegram,cow pea and blackgram
Intercropping system	Groundnut + redgram Groundnut+cowpea Grounnut+castor	Castor + redgram, Jowar + redgram, Jowar + greengram	Castor + redgram, Jowar + redgram, Jowar + greengram
Perennial crops	Papaya, sweet lime	Mango	Coconut, banana, mango
Major livestock species	Buffaloes, small ruminants, backyard poultry	Local buffaloes and cows, Sheep and goats, backyard poultry	Crossbred cattle and local buffaloes, goats, sheep

into their farming systems were regarded as indicators of acceptability. The characteristics and cropping systems of selected clusters are summarized in Table-1.

TRADITIONAL LIVESTOCK PRODUCTION SYSTEMS

The livestock production systems are complex and generally based on traditional and socio-economic considerations, mainly guided by available feed resources (NRSP Project PRA 2003) and can be described as low input system. These traditional production systems are designed to be self sufficient at the household level and are dependant on the low-cost agro-by-products as nutritional input to animals for producing quality food of high biological value. The characteristics of various kinds of production systems are given below.

CATTLE AND BUFFALO

Predominantly local buffalo and cattle are largely kept for production of milk for direct consumption and occasional sales in rural areas. The animals are maintained mostly on open grazing and locally available feed resource. Few farmers, who involved in small scale dairy enterprise, maintain graded or purebred Murrah buffalo and occasionally high blood crossed Jersey/Holstein Friesian. These farmers procure most of the feed and fodder from outside and the enterprise is profitable because of the closeness of a quality-appreciating market and the resulting high value of milk. Milk production in the selected clusters is a low-input, low-output farm activity with a smallholder production system. The average milk productivity per year per cattle is about 1,124 kg. The available data on milk yield indicate that average productivity of cows went up substantially during last 2 decades. There is an increase in the yield of buffaloes also, but it is less sharp than that of cows. A key factor accounting for the sharper increase in cow milk yield is the increasing proportion of crossbred cows (NRSP Project PRA, 2003) due to government supported AI facilities. In general, buffaloes have higher yields than indigenous cows, but crossbred cows are more productive than either indigenous cows or buffaloes. The average productivity of local cows is

3.08 kg/day. For crossbred cows it is 5.73 kg/day. The average productivity of buffaloes is 4.15 kg/day.

SHEEP AND GOAT

In Anantapur, Nellore sheep are kept in mostly stationary flocks whereas, in Mahabubnagar, mainly Deccani, partly stationary partly migratory flocks are maintained. In Anantapur, farmers purchase lambs for the purpose of fattening for a period of 4 to 5 months and sale for ready cash. Flock size fluctuates from a few to 30 head. In Mahabubnagar, most villagers have few goats that utilise the available fodder trees. The concentration of goats is higher in Mahabubnagar than in Anantapur: farmers of Andhra Pradesh consider sheep and goats as a working capital and opt for a zero input system of production.

BACKYARD POULTRY

Keeping a few chickens for eggs and meat for direct consumption is a widely spread practice in Anantapur and Mahabubnagar. By contrast, in Tumkur cluster poultry is a less preferred species of animal because of the dominance of *Lingayat* community who are mostly vegetarians.

PROBLEMS RELATED TO LIVESTOCK PRODUCTION

In Anantapur, livestock are experiencing serious fodder and water scarcity in summer, accentuated by the drought in the last four years, and leading to a sharp decline in livestock population. Foot and mouth diseases and premature abortions have been mentioned as major diseases among cattle and buffaloes. In the Mahabubnagar cluster a similar situation prevails. Fodder availability was maximum for four months between August and November with acute shortages between March and June. Foot and Mouth Disease (FMD), Black Quarter and Haemorragic Septicemia are the major diseases among cows and buffaloes. Among sheep and goats, FMD and Blue Tongue are common. Livestock diseases occur mostly between November and February. Similarly in Tumkur cluster, heavy morbidity due to FMD was reported with shortage of fodder in summer as the main problem. Thus, low productivity of livestock due to inadequate availability and poor quality of feed and fodder; high incidence of diseases; and inadequate knowledge on appropriate management of livestock was identified as the major problems facing smallholder farmers in the selected cluster villages.

TECHNICAL INTERVENTIONS FOR IMPROVING THE LIVELIHOOD OF POOR

The adoption of livestock-related technologies by smallholder mixed (crop-livestock) farmers is usually slow. Farmers need to be able to test such interventions taking into account their economic viability and social acceptability. The project assisted the farmers to do this, with back up from appropriate specialists. Table 2 presents the suspected causes of low productivity of livestock in selected clusters and strategies adopted to solve the problem by NRSP project. A summary of the technical interventions carried out to address the problems are given below:

Table 2
Identified Constraints to Low Livestock Productivity, Suspected Causes and Adopted Strategies

Problem	*Suspected Causes*	*Adopted Strategies*
Inadequate quantity and poor quality of feed resources	Lack of fodder production efforts and inadequate knowledge on how best to utilise locally available feeds	Promote fodder production and chopping of fodder
Low milk yield in cows and buffaloes	Poor genetic potential of native breeds and imbalanced nutrition	Up-gradation of native animals with improved breeds and supplementary feeding of mineral mixture and urea molasses mineral blocks
Poor health particularly in dry months due to high incidence of infectious diseases	Heavy worm loads, compounded by poor nutrition and irregular deworming/vaccination	Promote regular deworming and timely vaccination
Poor management practices	Inadequate knowledge on appropriate livestock management practices	Reinforce farmer training on all aspects of livestock management

INTEGRATED ANIMAL HEALTH CAMP

Almost 90 % of the farmers in the cluster villages did not follow the deworming and vaccination calendar recommended by the veterinary staff. Most of the farmers lacked confidence in applying the extension advice and cited cash constraints as a compounding problem. This problem was discussed in *Salaha Samithi* meetings along with the local veterinary staff of the respective clusters. As a result and in conjunction with the local Animal Husbandry Department, animal health camps were conducted in Mahabubnagar and Tumkur cluster. Promotional campaigns were also launched in these clusters that encouraged farmers to adopt a regular vaccination and deworming schedule as a preventive measure and to provide mineral supplements to animals to overcome the problem of infertility in case of buffaloes and crossbred cattle. Initially, the cost of medicines was met from the project funds. Afterwards, the *Salaha Samithi* mobilised the funds from the farmers.

Implementation of scheduled prophylactic health measures has reduced mortality from 17 to 8 percent in small ruminants and from 12 to 7 percent in large ruminants. Most of the farmers reported an increase in growth rate of 25-30 percent in the animals between 6 and 12 months of age in their flocks. The treated cows recovered from mastitis. About 30 percent of the animals, which were suffering from the gynaelogical, problems become pregnant after treatment. Further, farmers reported immediate recovery of animals from recurrent attacks of gastro-intestinal parasite infestation. A large gathering of farmers from all livestock owning wealth groups was evidenced during the animal health camps. Camps created awareness among farmers regarding the adoption of better livestock practices. Farmers are demanding more number of such camps in the clusters. The more progressive farmers are following the recommended livestock management practices at their own cost.

ETHNO-VETERINARY TRAINING

From each cluster, 3-4 persons who are already involved in the livestock treatment of diseases were identified and trained at BIRD-K Shankar Lakkihally in order to upgrade their skill and capacity. All the trained persons are doing good service as para vets in their respective clusters. They are helping the farmers in identifying the health problems, providing information on husbandry practices and treating the sick animals. They have become a good link between the Animal Husbandry department and farmers. Even the Animal Husbandry department recognized their talent and seeks help from them during vaccination and deworming camps.

BREED IMPROVEMENT

The project staff encouraged farmers to breed indigenous cows and buffaloes with improved breeds, particularly Jersey and Murrah, through A.I. This was done in order to combine the hardy characteristics of indigenous cattle (namely tolerance to poor nutrition, heat stress and tropical disease challenge) with high milk-producing qualities and hence the higher income potential of the improved breeds. To support this, an artificial insemination (AI) centre was established in Chouderpally village of Mahabubnagar cluster to provide door-to-door artificial insemination service and to serve as a training centre to promote entrepreneurship among the unemployed youths in the project villages.

The performance of the AI centre shows that the conception rate achieved by the centre is considerably higher (70 % in cattle and 50 %in buffaloes) than the usual Veterinary Department AI conception rates (20-45%) (GOI 2005). More than 300 farmers from all sections of the community (Rich/Poor; Forward /Backward caste; SC/ST)/ used the AI service for breeding their cows and buffaloes. Farmers from the surrounding villages (apart from project villages) also used the services of AI centre for up gradation of local cows and buffaloes.

CHOPPING OF CROP RESIDUES

In all the clusters normally the farmers offer fodder without chopping where as in case of sorghum and maize they cut it by sickles into large pieces (50 cm length). In this kind of prevalent practice, wastage of the fodder is very high. In order to reduce the wastage of feed resources, the chaffing of fodder was promoted. Two kinds of chaff cutter: manual and power operated were promoted in all the clusters. By using the chaff cutter wastage of the fodder could be reduced substantially (up to 30%). For personal use, villagers preferred the manual chaff cutter rather than the powered chaff cutter, because of its low cost as well as easy operation. Only two persons are required to cut the fodder by manual chaff cutter, whereas for the power operated chaff cutter, a minimum of three persons are needed to perform the task satisfactorily. The power chaff cutter is generally fixed in one place to which people have to bring their fodder for cutting, which is not preferred by some social groups. However, one advantage is that it can provide a livelihood option: because of its output capacity, the owner or operator charges a cutting fee (Rs. 0.70/crop residue bundle of about 10 kg) to villagers those wishing to cut their fodder.

IMPROVED FEEDING PRACTICES

The farmers were mixing different feed (concentrate) ingredients such as wheat bran, rice bran, cakes, broken grains, *chunies* (broken grains of pigeon pea/black gram) before offering them to their animals as supplements or in a few cases, as complete diets. However, the quantities of individual feed ingredients included in the concentrate mixtures seemed to depend on their relative availability rather than on the farmers' conscious desire to supply better quality feed to their animals. Only lactating cows and bullocks during work were allocated the supplementary feed. This existing farmer practice appears to be a good example of strategic supplementation. Lactating and work animals require extra nutrients to meet the requirement and farmers use their limited available resource (concentrate feed) based on the priority of the animals.

The farmers reported that repeat breeding was a serious problem in their herds particularly in buffaloes and crossbred cows. Probably, this was the major cause of the long calving intervals. Mineral deficiencies were suspected to cause this problem. Use of mineral mixture in concentrate feed was demonstrated to the farmers of Tumkur cluster to overcome this problem. Farmers' response was very encouraging: they observed an improvement of 0.5 to 1.0 litre/animal in milk yield due to supplementation with mineral mixture. They also reported that mineral supplementation was helpful in increasing the appetite of animals. Now farmers from all wealth groups have started purchasing the mineral mixture from the local market and mixing in the concentrate.

In order to improve the productivity of milch animals, supplementary feeding of mineral mixture through urea molasses mineral blocks (UMMB) was demonstrated to the farmers in Mahabubnagar cluster. The main objective of UMMB supplementation is to provide a constant source of degradable nitrogen throughout the day and promote growth of rumen microbes in ruminants fed poor quality forage. The intake of UMMB ranged from 200 to 275 g and the average intake observed was 250 ± 49.5 g/buffalo/day. An average increase in 1.25 litre/day in milk yield was observed due to supplementation of UMMB during summer. Besides the increase in milk production, all the animals of supplemented group showed symptoms of heat at the proper time and conceived at first service. By comparison, in the un-supplemented group, one cow did not conceive even after third service/insemination and on average 1.7 services were needed for conception. No symptoms of mineral deficiency and disease were observed in the supplemented group whereas animals of un-supplemented group showed symptoms of mineral deficiency. The cost benefit ratio was 2.83. Further, farmers reported that by supplementing UMMB, buffaloes consumed more roughage, maintained good health and productivity even during summer months when green fodder scarcity was acute. All the farmers readily accepted the practice of using UMMB supplementation and are willing to purchase UMMB. However, they expressed apprehension about the availability of quality UMMB supplement from the local market.

IMPROVED FORAGE PRODUCTION

The most important constraint prioritized by the farmers in all the cluster villages was the problem of fodder availability.

Various fodder interventions (maize, sorghum PC 23, hybrid napier-Co1/2, guinea grass and Lucerne, etc) were promoted under irrigated conditions in a smaller area alongside the farmer's priority of their stable crop of paddy. Most farmers initially refused to spare their land, as irrigated land possessed by them is very small. However, a women farmer came forward to take up Napier planting in her field. She was supplied with the cuttings for an area of 1/10 of an acre, which she grew successfully and started feeding to her milch animals. This has resulted in increased milk production and also quality of the milk. Seeing this benefit, many farmers realized the economic benefits of feeding green forage to animals and came forward to take the cultivation of improved forage cultivars.

SHEEP REARING

In order to promote sheep rearing as a source of income generation and self employment for the poor and landless households, including widows, two models of sheep rearing, (i) lamb fattening (ii) breed multiplication, were tried to evolve a practical model for replication elsewhere and to identify the potentials and constraints of wider uptake of sheep as a livelihood enterprise. Based on a decision taken in the *Salaha Samithi* meeting, sheep units of 4-5 sheep in Mahabubanagar and Tumkur for breed improvement and multiplication purpose and units of 3 (later reduced to 2) sheep in Anantapur for fattening purpose were given to improve the livelihoods. The project had planned for all sheep units to contain 5 animals but the Anantapur farmers pointed out that they were not certain of accessing sufficient fodder for 5 animals, neither did they have the labour resources to herd the sheep. With three animals, they thought they would be able to take the sheep with them to graze while they were working as daily agricultural wage labour. They later decided that they could not manage more than 2 sheep under this system and this became the size of their fattening unit. The *Salaha Samithi* proposed 10-40% contribution of total cost from the participating farmers, on a sliding scale based on the owner's capacity to pay. In Mahabubnagar and Tumkur the contribution was 10% whereas in Anantapur it was 40%.

In Anantapur cluster, the 16 participants in 2003 increased to 54 in 2004. The individuals are selling the sheep after 4-5 months of rearing/grazing and again purchasing the sheep with the balanced amount after repaying the loan to the *Salaha Samithi*. Three cycles of lamb fattening are completed. It is interesting to mention that in Anantapur cluster, all poor families are covered under this intervention and now every individual in the group has a minimum income of Rs. 4,000/- per year only from lamb rearing as subsidiary livelihood interventions. Results have shown that the contribution of sheep rearing to family income ranges between 20-35 percent with an average of 25 percent.

Performance of the sheep-breeding unit was better in Mahabubnagar cluster than Tumkur. This may be due to the availability of more grazing and common lands in Mahabubnagar. Farmers in both the clusters are selling lambs at an early age due to necessity of money required to meet the household expenditure. Almost all sheep in Tumkur cluster are sold in local market whereas in Mahabubnagar cluster 60 percent farmers sold sheep within the village itself. The location of marketing had significant influence on earnings of the farmers. After realizing the economic benefit, many families from the forward community in Anantapur and Mahabubnagar are coming forward to take a loan from the *Salaha Samithi* to start sheep rearing. Experience showed that support either in the form of funding or stock animals are good tools in starting the livelihood programme. In addition basic knowledge of sheep keeping should be provided directly. Through sheep rearing, the poor increased their income, improved the nutrition of the family, the stability of the households and their self-reliance. Rearing of sheep by women for improving their economic status created an immense interest among other people. The lamb fattening sheep unit represents a very reasonable livelihood option for agricultural labourers as it require less resources and not demand very specialized skills. The breeding unit, which requires the part time involvement of the farmer, or his family member, provides a very stable and attractive source of additional income for small and marginal farmers without affecting their main occupation.

BACKYARD POULTRY

Backyard poultry was promoted through the project as a livelihood option for the landless poor in all the clusters. Improved strains of birds, Giriraja and Vanraja, were provided to landless poor people @ 5 birds/unit to rear in the back yard. The purpose behind this intervention was that the poultry would be a laying unit that could be managed by the landless and poor, and would produce eggs that are sold at three times the price of local eggs and hence generate income. The success rate of poultry was low (10-30%) in most of the clusters. Reasons for failure of poultry reported by the farmers are: the birds died in summer due to high temperature; the chicks were very vulnerable to the heat; the birds are not able to move quickly or fly due to their heavy weight, because of this, the dogs and wild cats caught the birds and ate them; the birds were cut for meat during festivals or also offered when some guests arrived as a part of meals and few people realized how much they could earn from the five birds.

Experience shows that the poultry unit as livelihood intervention did not achieve its purpose in any of the clusters: however, they improved nutrition to the poor families, as in most of the cases, people just preferred to have them in their plate and palate than in their backyards! Some of the causes for the poultry failure might have been avoided if increased attention had been given to planning with the recipients how to manage the birds and protect them from heat, predators, etc. A technical factor, which needs re-examination, is the vulnerability of small chicks during summer. This intervention is an example of where there is a gap between an improved technology and the resources of the (poor) farmers to manage it. An alternative approach might be to work with a group of farmers and an improved management system of looking after the birds.

POLICY RECOMMENDATIONS

Sustainable development in watersheds can only be achieved through optimum utilization of its natural resources. Livestock interventions in watersheds need to be comprehensively planned with the people directly concerned with the problem's of livestock (Puskur et al 2004; ANTHRA 2005). There is tremendous scope of increasing productivity of existing livestock resources by making appropriate provisions for fodder, water and health services within the watershed. Participation of farmers and village based institution (*Salaha samithi*) proved to be an effective and efficient mechanism for faster technology diffusion. A favorable policy environment in terms of access to micro-credit, key inputs, assured market and veterinary services will have to be provided and socio-economic and technical constraints needs to be addressed in order to enable the farmers for livestock development.

The project interventions had an ample effect not only on the farming community but also on the landless livestock keepers and women. The project experiences suggest that a continuous dialogue is essential for promoting the interventions. Animal health camps created awareness among farmers regarding the adoption of better livestock practices like supplementation of mineral mixture in the concentrate ration, chopping of crop-residues, cultivation of improved forage cultivars, etc. The landless and women were benefited in several ways, sheep rearing was found quite beneficial across the clusters while poultry had mixed results. After realizing the economic benefit, many families from the forward community are coming forward to take a loan from the *Salaha Samithi* to start the livestock rearing. Through exposure visits and farmer-to-farmer interaction, many farmers realized that integration of livestock and fodder production within their limited land and water resources provides a better livelihood option in drylands.

REFERENCES

ANTHRA (2005), Impact of Vision 2020 and Other Policy Reforms on Livestock, Peoples' Livelihoods and Related Biodiversity– A Study: www.anthra.org/advocacy/Briefs.htm

——(2002), Government of India, Report of the Working Group on Animal Husbandry and Dairying for the Tenth Five Year Plan (2002-2007). Working Group Sr.No. 42/2001. Planning Commission, Government of India, New Delhi, India.

——(2005), Government of India, Annual Report 2004-05. Department of Animal Husbandry, Dairying and Fisheries. Ministry of Agriculture, Government of India, New Delhi, India. http://www.dahd.nic.in/rep/Annual%20Report%202004-05%20(English).pdf

Kerr J. (2002), Sharing the Benefits of Watershed Management in Sukhomajri, India. Pages 63-76 in Selling Environmental Services: Market-based mechanisms for conservation and development (Pagiola S, Bishop J and Landll-Mills N eds.). London, UK: Earthscan Publication Limited.

Misra, A. K. , Rama Rao, C.A., Subrahmanyam, K.V. Vijay Sankar Babu, M, Shivarudrappa, B. and Ramakrishna, Y.S. (2007), Strategies for Livestock Development in Rainfed Agro-Ecosystem of India. Livestock Research for Rural Development 19 (6) www.cipav.org.co/lrrd/lrrd19/6/cont1906.htm

Puskur, R.; Bouma, J and Scott, C. (2004), Sustainable Livestock Production in Semi-arid Watersheds. Economic and Political Weekly, 31 July 2004:3477-3483.

Thornton P.K., Kruska R.L., Henninger N., Kristjanson P.M., Reid R.S., Atieno F., Odero A. and Ndegwa T. (2002), *Mapping Poverty and Livestock in the Developing World.* ILRI (International Livestock Research Institute), Nairobi, Kenya. 124 pp.

Turner, R.L. (2004), Livestock Production and Rural Poor in Andhra Pradesh and Orissa States, India. Pro-poor Livestock Policy Initiative Working Paper No. 9. FAO, Rome.

——(1999), World Bank, India: Livestock Sector Review: Enhancing Growth and Development. The World Bank and Allied Publishers: New Delhi.

CHAPTER–7

SUSTAINABLE RURAL LIVELIHOOD THROUGH WATERSHED MANAGEMENT: THE INDIAN CONTEXT

M. Mishra

Poor people heavily depend on natural resources for their livelihoods. Open access resources are vital for the subsistence needs of the poor (Jodha, 1990). Open access resources provide an estimated 12% of the income to poor households in India (Beck and Nesmith, 2001). These products are gathered from areas—including village pastures, community forests, wastelands, watershed drainages, village ponds, and small reservoirs and riverbeds—where there may be some limits imposed by communities on access to extractable types of resources but for which no one has exclusive access rights. A growing body of research and policy within the international development literature highlights the multidimensional nature of poverty. One framework, known as the sustainable livelihoods approach, focuses on the livelihoods and assets of the poor in terms of their financial, physical, human, social, and natural capital.

Water is life and livelihood. But the rural water crisis in India exemplifies the lack of sustainability and equity in natural resource access. Drought is a commonplace occurrence in India that continues to affect livelihoods in critical ways. As is evident failed or delayed rains translate into severe hardships.

The standard government response to drought has been to provide immediate relief measures through provisions of food, fodder, and employment and long-term plans for drought protection have focused on building large dams and extensive canal systems to channel water from rainfall rich areas to drought-prone regions, often at a distance of hundreds of miles. The continued incidence of severe water scarcity in rural India however suggests that an alternative is needed to the standard government response.

The alternative is the development and management of watersheds the only solution to ensure drought proofing and to mitigate the distress. The watershed programme envisage a great opportunity for improving the productivity, profitability, equity, improved livelihood opportunities and sustainability through social mobilization, institution-building and, the introduction of a sustainable rural livelihoods approach.

Watershed development is as old as agriculture itself. There are ancient traditions of collective, village-level water harvesting and distribution and water management in every part of India. Shifting the focus of development efforts from resources and products to people and their livelihood outcomes lies at the heart of the sustainable livelihoods approach, as livelihoods have been defined as "comprising the capabilities, assets and activities required for a means of living".

The watershed development programme seeks to improve the quality of the land resources through water and soil conservation measures. The main livelihood impact has been the improvement to household's land assets. Where there is higher concentration in land ownership, benefits to the land-poor and land-less amount to temporary employment opportunities in the water harvesting structures, and the possibility of increased agricultural employment opportunities. With assured availability of water, farmers become motivated to accept more profitable, sustainable and innovative farming systems. The watershed programme envisages a great opportunity for improving the productivity, profitability and sustainability of dry farming areas through social mobilization.

In terms of *livelihood strategies,* WSD can open up new opportunities by supporting agricultural intensification processes. While increases in agricultural productivity might occur as a result of WSD, men usually appropriate on-farm gains and the increased drudgery is disproportionately borne by women. With an increase in land productivity, men frequently choose to increase the production of cash crops such as sugarcane and cotton. WSD can also provide new opportunities for households to diversify their livelihood strategies. NGO projects have paid specific attention to providing opportunities to the poor to diversify, often through the formation of self help groups for women, the landless and other marginal groups.

Overall, it is acknowledged that watershed-based approaches can lead to substantial improvements in rural livelihoods. However, they are not a panacea: productivity gains in pilot projects have not been achieved to the same extent on a wide scale and the links between productivity gains and livelihoods is complex and poorly understood. There is the need of a caution over the potential role that WSD can play in enhancing livelihood opportunities for the poor provided the recently experienced institutional, organisational, and implementation issues that are hindering the effectiveness with watershed programs in India are properly taken care of. Further it is observed that there is a general neglect of local knowledge about indigenous soil taxonomy, biodiversity, soil and water conservation structures and traditions and experimental ethic of the local communities in designing and implementing these schemes which in majority of cases lead to failure of the programme.

In conclusion, this paper demonstrates that a livelihoods perspective can be used to encourage a more explicit analysis of the ways in which WSD directly and indirectly affect people's livelihoods. It encourages a broader and more structured assessment of impacts relevant to the poor. Case studies from tribal belts in Orissa particularly from the KBK region supports the study. This can help practitioners and policy-makers to adjust their approaches and so enhance poverty impacts.

CHAPTER–8

WATERSHED DEVELOPMENT AND WOMEN LIVELIHOOD IN TIRUNELVELI REVENUE DIVISION

J. Nirmala

For overall development of any country, there must be the optimum utilization of natural resources such as land and water. Agriculture is a source of livelihood that has special significance for poor sections of rural people in India. Agriculture is in the hands of millions of peasant households but still remains a key sector providing both employment and livelihood. Indian agriculture has been developed with higher levels of labour and land productivity due to technological and biological improvement. A new phase of agricultural development from 1991 marked a significant departure from the past. The liberalization policy of the government provided new opportunities and raised new challenges also. Agriculture the primary sector increasingly becomes female centered activity. This sector employs 80 per cent of all economically active women in the country as compared to 63% of men. Though five decades have passed since independence still the living standards of the poor have declined, their income has decreased. It is a fact that poverty is gender conscious. Amongst the poor, the poorest are always the women. The farm women, who work hard to survive but contribute to the economy, have every right to its budgetary resources. When a country is poor and its description of poverty country is poor and its description of poverty must be linked with broader concept which is related with the problem of aggregation. (Sen.1981)

To develop the living standard of the people, especially the farm women, it is imperative to bring a revolutionary change in the agriculture sector. From 1980s, the areas better endowed with assured water supply are progressively moving towards production of many food crops and some non-food crops which can withstand short dry spells require less water for production and are amenable for cultivation under drip and sprinkles techniques of irrigation. Under Integrated Wasteland Development programs watershed approach is adopted to achieve the goal. The watershed Development program was implemented first in 1962 in India. (Jeyaraj.2007). Watershed program and its impact on the living conditions of farmers are important areas in a country like India when it has the Prime task of optimum utilization of its natural resources towards conservation regeneration and protection. In the watershed areas, there will be socio-economic transformation in the status of farm workers. Watershed program generate man days of employment during its period. Watershed programs are the alternative for livelihood in agriculture as and when agriculture it fails to provide gainful employment and regular income. Towards sustainable development, it becomes compulsory to-day. Tirunelveli district, in the South Tamilnadu, has the geographical area of 6810 sq.km and a population of 3006467 in which nearly 45 per cent are in rural villages. It has 1271930 women and 871858 are in rural areas. The wok participation ratio for its women comes to 47 percent, in which 38.50 per cent are agricultural workers. The district has 628 revenue villages with 435 village panchayats. The District is divided into 3 Revenue Division—Tirunelveli, Tenkasi and Cheranmahadevi. The Tirunelveli Revenue division had been selected as study area to collect the primary data.

Therefore this is an attempt

- To study the impact of watershed program on the existing living conditions of farm women in Tirunelveli Revenue Division.
- To design a more suitable watershed program for farm women of the area to generate new employment opportunities and income.

In Tirunelveli District, there are 420 big tanks and 1779 small tanks used as water source for irrigation. Besides rainwater, the tanks are fed by the reservoirs of the rivers of the district by means of channels. The average annual rainfall in the district is 853.6 mm. Out of the total available annual average groundwater, 15 percent kept reserved for drinking water supply and the balance 85 percent is taken for irrigation purposes. The network of the irrigation system makes full use of the water resources. Most of the soil types identified one subjected to varying degrees of sheet and gully erosion; thereby the fertile top soil is lost resulting in poor crop growth. Therefore, a bare necessity compelled both the government and others to look after the alternative to agriculture. Without simply wasting the natural resources, watershed program are implemented in order to provide adequate employment and a more regular income to the farm people.

To equip the farm women with modern trends in agriculture, a program called 'Tamilnadu women in Agriculture' (TANWA) was launched during 1986. The Integrated Watershed Development Project funded by the World Bank is implemented in the Nanguneri block with a project outlay of RS. 25 lakh. Another scheme The National Watershed Development Project for Rain fed Areas (NWDPRA) is also implemented in the Melaneelithanallur and Sankarankoil blocks with a project outlay of Rs. 49 lakhs per block. Nearly 350 to 600 ha of dry land are brought for agriculture under the Watershed Development Projects.

Researches are focusing the fact that the strategy adopted by the government in the rural areas despite being backbone of the village economy, to increase women welfare doing the past decade has not yielded adequate results. Hence a more dynamic proposal has to be made ready on the basis of the suitability and applicability the area of study concerned. The researcher will assure that this paper will add to the available literature and will come out successfully with a suitable watershed project for the women Tirunelveli Revenue Division.

REFERENCES

Amerthya Sen (1981), Poverty and Famines Oxform.

M. Jeyaraj (2007), Sustainable Agriculture through Watershed Development Programmes' in K. Dasaratharamaiah and M. Jeyaraj (Ed) 'Sustainable Agriculture in Drought Prone Regions" Serials Publications, New Delhi.

CHAPTER–9

PEOPLE CENTERED HOLISTIC WATERSHED MANAGEMENT FOR SUSTAINABLE LIVELIHOOD OF RURAL POOR: A CASE STUDY OF MALKARBANNDH WATERSHED OF KORAPUT DISTRICT IN ORISSA

Soubhagya Ranjan Padhi

INTRODUCTION

Watershed management programme has emerged as a sustainable strategy to conserve the natural resources i.e. water, soil, and forest in an integrated manner. Since, the inception of human civilization, natural resources continued to provide vital life support system to human being. The symbiotic relation between the human beings and the nature and its vast resources (renewable and non- renewable) has sustained the human existence on earth. But it is unfortunate that, the rapidly growing interventions of human in the state of these rare natural resources, from which they derive their modes of subsistence are depleting rapidly in recent days. This calls for effectively managing the natural resources, with integrated initiatives. Blending the best of modern technologies and some of the Traditional Ecological Knowledge (TEK) of rural community for rain water management, soil conservation and management of common property resources should receive prioritization for sustainable development.

Water is the most vibrant form of the natural resources available on this earth. It constitutes a significant proportion of the food contents of the living organisms like plants and animals. Hence, the need of water is obvious for every living organism for its existence and survival. The growing quest for acquiring water resources in the global level is a matter of great concern in the present scenario. The scarcity of water is greatly realized in recent days. In the context of increasing water scarcity and competitive demands, water resources have become one of the critical imperatives for livelihood, particularly to the vulnerable poor who reside in the rural and tribal areas. Hence watershed management must get the foremost priority among the various objectives, in our National Rural Development policy for the overall development of rural area.

India has traveled a long distance on the road to development since independence and has made significant progress in various sectors. However, the development in rural areas has not kept pace with the overall progress in other aspects of national life. Even today, most of rural poor subsists in poverty and lack of livelihood opportunities. The sustainable development of rural Bharat is essential for the country to realize its potential and unleash the process of all round growth, based on the latent genious of the rural masses. To correct the imbalance, remedial steps have been taken in the last few years to bring rural development to the forefront of national reconstruction. Accordingly, Government implementing a number of programmes for the sustainable development of rural areas. Watershed is one of them.

Watershed development refers to treatment of an area to get different direct and indirect livelihood benefits through studying, taming harvesting and utilizing water as it falls, flows or accumulates on a unit of land shaped by its influence. To tame the running water as well as to harvest it on site and reduce runoff and soil loss, soil and water conservation measures are applied. The effectiveness of these measures increases manifold when the water flow is treated from top to bottom across topo sequences on watershed basis tackling both cause and effect through preventive and remedial measures.

Watershed development has become a core strategy for poverty alleviation and rural development in India with its acceptance as a unit of planning for synergizing development by different ministries in ninth plan document. The main argument behind this approach is the higher incidence of poverty in drought prone, hilly or rain fed areas with an assumption that an area development may be able to mitigate the harsh living conditions in these regions. To ameliorate multiple dimensions of poverty, this essentially soil and water conservation tool with landscape focus and technology approach has become a holistic development tool to address livelihood issues (Carney (ed.) 1998). This development option is viewed as a panacea to dissipate spatial developmental inequality across the regions and landscapes by augmenting and diversifying employment and income while balancing production and conservation across temporal scales as well as ensuring enabling mechanism for appropriate livelihood entitlements. It exemplifies the potential of holistic, multidisciplinary and participatory approach in effecting envisaged transformation across social and natural layers (Rhodes, 2000)

Integrated watershed development is the cost effective method for socio-economic transformation of rural mass. It leads to sustainable production system and improvement in the quality of rural livelihood by means of effective management of natural resources and integrated initiative in a people centered and down to earth approach. Although it focuses on soil and water conservations for increase in economic activities and raising productivity of irrigated and rain fed agriculture.

The literally meaning of watershed is a "geo-hydrological unit draining at a common point by a system of streams" (Rajora, 1998). All land everywhere is part of some watershed. Essentially, a watershed is all the land and water area, which contributes runoff to a common point. It is a land area that captures rainfall and conveys the overland flow and runoff to an outlet in the main flow channel. It is a topographically delineated area draining into a single channel. This definition mostly postulated by hydrologists, depicts watershed as a hydrological unit. But it is beyond doubt that watershed is much more broader concept. In fact, watershed is a physical, economical, ecological and social system.

IMPORTANCE

Watershed development involves re-generation of the environment and management of the needs of human community in such a way that their demands match with the resources available likes land, water and vegetation within that particular watershed. The watershed project aims at treating degraded lands with the help of low cost and locally accessed technologies such as in-situ soil and moisture conservation measures, afforestation and their participatory approach seeks to secure close involvement of the user communities. Watershed development involves both the human resource development as well as livestock development besides improvement of environment in the identified area which will lead to increase resistance to drought and increase agricultural production augmenting food supply, fodder, fuel and timber. Thus rural poverty has been checked and present rural scenario has been changed with the increase in application of watershed development programme.

KORAPUT EXPERIENCE

In a district like Koraput, the simple ways through which society can progress are by increasing the productivity of economic activities raising the productivity of irrigated and rain fed agriculture combined with soil and water conservation techniques; keeping focus on environmentally benign and cost effective technologies essaying sustainability and by developing human resource through non formal education emphasizing on people centered and down to earth approach.

This has been fulfilled through watershed development and management at micro level, which focused on need based technological interventions.

By the intervention of watershed development programme, not only the social life of the people of the study area has changed but also the economic status of the poor people has gone up. Further productivity, cropping pattern and ecological stabilization has improved to a great extent that in turn has breathed a new life in natural resources of the projected area. People's response to the watershed development programme is significant and it seems from the study that watershed is a means, which pave the way in changing rural scenario in a positive direction.

OBJECTIVES OF THE STUDY

The objective of the study in nutshell is to ascertain the change in rural scenario after implementation of Watershed Project in the study area. To know the state at which the Watershed stands by now and what it was before intervention of Watershed. The other objectives include:

- To analyze the ecological/environmental impact
- Whether promotion of economic development of the village community has been given impotence
- To see improvement in agricultural productivity, crop diversification and other livelihood opportunities on a sustainable basis
- To see the women empowerment and gender bias if any in the identified areas
- To see the impact of the implementation of innovative/intervening technologies

METHODOLOGY

The study is mainly a case study of one watershed village i.e. Malkarbandha of Potangi block. Being one of the poorest blocks of Koraput district, the present study can be considered as a representative of the whole district. The findings of the study can be applicable to all irrespective of the changes in sample. The methodology adopted for the study is

Participatory Rural Appraisal and interview with the watershed functionaries, block officials, district officials, beneficiaries of villages etc. for collecting various information.

The PRA methodology is used basing on the following assumption:

- To learn directly in a face to face situation from the local people and to gain insight from their local physical, technical, social and psychological knowledge.
- Conscious exploration with the use of flexible methods and improvising, iterating and cross checking the methods with the process of time.
- PRA would provide the insight into people's perception, needs and aspirations that enable the stakeholders for the strategic development of training module, basing on the training needs of the women.
- Participatory assessment of progress would reveal whether the village had made any progress after the programme has been undertaken through the watershed development programme.

The data has collected from the households of watershed. The key informants and the traditional leaders are given due importance. Various tools are used to collect information from group and single individual. The demographic data of the village has collected from the concerned block office and are triangulated with the data collected through PRA. During data collection period care has taken to record data from village leaders, women and women SGH group, watershed members and as well as not part of the watershed living on the periphery of the village etc., thus covering all strata of the village.

RELEVANCE OF THE STUDY

In the district like Koraput, which is one of the most backward district in the state comes under TSP (Tribal Sub Plan) area with high density of schedule tribes population. 84% of the total households of the district still live below poverty line (1997). The rural people of the district heavily depend on agriculture. But the agriculture productivity of these small scale and marginal tribal farmers is very low. The uneconomic land holding, lack of technical knowledge and unavailability of proper watershed system further creates obstacles for sustainable livelihood opportunities of these people. All the plans and programmes implemented in the district have aimed at eradication of poverty and raising the economic standard of the poor. All-out efforts are made for increasing the productivity of economic activities, raising the productivity of both irrigated and rain fed farming with Soil Conservation techniques. Watershed development programme is one such effort to promote sustainability of human resources and ecology. This has lead to sustainable production system and qualitative improvement of rural livelihood by making them self reliant in managing and utilizing natural recourses in a systematic and scientific way. Present study taking into account *Malkarbhand Watershed village* of Potangi block of Koraput district in Orissa as a sample.

WATERSHED DEVELOPMENT IN ORISSA

Watershed based development initiative in Orissa began in Sundergarh district under Integrated watershed development programme (IWDP) in 1985. Thereafter, similar development activities were taken up in various districts under IWDP. Drought Prone Area Project (DPAP), Employment Assurance scheme (EAS) and Nation Integrated Development Programme for rain fed areas (NWDPRA).

Participatory watershed development programme in Orissa began after the introduction of the watershed Guidelines of 2001 developed by the Ministry of Rural Development, Government of India Janasahabhagita Guidelines of the ministry of Agriculture, Government of India. In order to facilitate Participatory watershed development programmes, the Government of Orissa (GoO) set up Orissa Watershed Development mission in August 2000. The OWDM is a registered body of the societies Registration Act. OWDM was created to plan, coordinate, supervise and monitor the watershed projects in Orissa. Since 2000, the OWDM is supervising watershed development scheme under

Table 1
Watershed Development in Orissa

Name of the Scheme	*No. of Water-shed*	*Total*	*Project Cost*	*Amount released by GOI & GoG as on March 2003*	*Amount spent by March, 2003*	*Area Treated*	*Balance Amount available as on 01.04.2003*	*Community Organization*		
Drought Prone Area programme (DPAP) 12527.15	684	354235	19099.99	4986.74	375109	85521	1234.65	4210	2950	
Integrated Watershed Drought Programme (I W DP)	417	2400491	12527.15	4736.01	3836.43	76910	899.58	4056	2362	79.25
Employment Assurance Scheme (EAS Watershed)	596	326598	12666.28	7210.46	6544.84	170860	665.62	8690	3958	55.39
National Watershed Development programme for Rain fed Areas (NWDPRA)	212	138186.26	6293.19	928.60	373.04	12390	555.56	1334	825	183.45
River Vallv Project (RVP)	29	26207	1195.51	175.28	115.80	3021	59.48			9.53
Additional Central Assistance (ACA)	314	170000	7650.00	1178.09	633.48	8476	544.61	1041	1011	23.11
Western Orissa Rural LivelihoodsProject (WORLP)	74	38170	3626.15	555.75	114.60	190	457.06		275	7.35
Total	3026	3453888	63058	19771	15370	357368	4417	19331	11381	358

Source: www. watershedmission.org

IWDP, DPAP, NWDPRA and EAS. At present more than 2000 watersheds are under the supervision of the OWDM throughout Orissa.

WATERSHED PROGRAMMES IN KBK (KALAHANDI, BOLANGIRI & KORAPUT)

The past development programmes in KBK region could not able to bring in the desired transformation as they were specific to sectors, locations or classes of society as per their design and scope, where as the regional problems are multi sectoral and interlinked socio-economically and ecologically. Moreover, hardly there was any programme where the end user's real need as well as the stake holders' aspiration have been tried to be tackled in a decentralized and bottom up framework in an integrated and equitable manner. Integrated and participatory watershed development programme, having promises to tackle head on the issues multi-stakeholder and multiple landscape through an equitable and sustainable fashion, has become the favorite development alternative at policy and donor level for this region.

The revised LTAP (1998-99 to 2006-07), thus focus on high priority schemes to deal with the basic problems of these districts. This project envisages an integrated approach for speeding up the socio-economic development of this region by synergizing effectively the various developmental activities and schemes under implementation both in Central as well as State sectors. The major objectives of the RLTAP are drought proofing, alleviation and development saturation as well as improved quality of life for local people.

WATERSHED DEVELOPMENT IN KORAPUT DISTRICT

DISTRICT PROFILE

Koraput is one of the poorest and underdeveloped districts in India despite an endowment of natural resources and beautiful climate. This district is situated between 17° 40′–20° 7′ North latitude and 81° 24′–84° 2′ East longitude with an altitudinal range of 600-1000 meters above the sea level. Its landscape is characterized by scattered, sharp, isolated hills with forest cover. The climate is warm and humid with high rainfall of 1521.8mm generally associated with incessant or high intensity storm events including runoff and soil loss. The soils are almost red with sandy loam to sandy clay loam texture. The cultivated land is around one third of the total area and with assured irrigation available only to one fifth of the cultivated area. While Jeypore sub-division lying on 2000′ plateau is relatively plain with more area under cultivation and irrigation, the Koraput subdivision on 3000′ plateau has an undulating topography and peculiar geo-hydrology restricting the expansion of the area under agriculture as well as under altitudinal advantage offer scope for horticulture development through seasonal and perennials. Paddy is the major crop followed by ragi and niger. Considering the terrain and about 15% land under stream–bed (Jhola) cultivation with perennial flow, there is scope of crop diversification. But the inequitable land ownership and incidences of higher poverty (84% BPL families) in general and among its two third of its population consisting mostly ST and SC in particular, calls for implementation of land and water development options with caution to avoid further marginalization of these vulnerable communities. As poverty alleviation is the main motive behind development action through watershed approach, probably, there is strong need to blend interventions to ameliorate the livelihoods of these weaker sections.

HISTORY OF WATERSHED ACTIVITIES IN KORAPUT REGION

Planned watershed (catchments) management has a history of half a century in Koraput. The soil conservation scheme in Machkund basin (750 sq km.) within the state falling in the district was taken up in 1956 with an objective to reduce silt flow into Jalaput reservoir and to persuade scheduled tribes to adopt permanent agriculture. It was basically a technical programme with an integrated five pronged strategy to take up contour bunding, plantation of economically important trees like cashew, bamboo and silver oak, agave plantation, coffee plantation and bench terracing. Three watershed management units of 10,000 acres each started in 1959, where contour bunding; tree planting and conservation farming were taken together. (DRDA, 2000–Status of implementation in Koraput District)

WATERSHED PROGRAMMES IN KORAPUT DISTRICT: THE PRESENT SCENARIO

In Koraput district watershed development has been taken as thrust area to ensure socio-economic upliftment of the poor tribal people. Watershed development programme has been taken up in the district since 8th plan period with the introduction of NWDPRA. Subsequently, watershed has been taken up under IWDP, RVP, EAS, ACA and OTELP. Besides, watershed development programme has also been taken up by the NGOs in the district with financial assistance from different funding sources like NABARD, CAPART and also from foreign Aid. Besides the above, five watershed development programme have also been taken up with financial assistance of Denmark Government through a project called IDCWDP.

The Koraput district comprises of four catchments namely Indravati, Machkund, Kolab, and Nagavali. The details number of sub-catchments, sub-watershed, mini watershed and approximate areas of the above four catchments is as given at Table-1.

Table 2
Present Scenario of Watershed in Koraput District

Name of the Catchments	*Number Sub-catchments*	*Number of Watershed*	*Number of Sub-Watershed*	*Number of Mini Watershed*	*Area in Ha.*
Indravati	03	08	73	132	177295
Machkund	1	2	16	32	46920
Kolab	4	12	109	279	329907
Nagavali	2	4	43	88	13610
Total	10	26	241	531	667732

Source: Status of Watershed in Koraput District – DRDA, 2000

WATERSHEDS IN KORAPUT DISTRICT: STATUS OF IMPLEMENTATION

The present status of implementation of Watersheds in Koraput district under Additional Central Assistance (ACA), Employment Assurance Schemes (EAS), Integrated Watershed Development Project (IWDP), National Watershed Development Programme for Rain-fed Agriculture (NWDPRA), Orissa Tribal Empowerment and livelihood Programme (OTELP) are given in the following table:

Table 3
Status of Implementation of Watersheds in Koraput District

Name of the Scheme	*No. of Watershed Under Implementation*	*Total Geographical Area in Ha.*	*Treatable Area*
ACA	84	52018	41401
EAS	72	40662	39383
IWDP-IV	24	12045	12045
IWDP-V	10	6035	5000
NWDPRA	12	7693.18	1500.00
OTELP	30	16720.7	14955.81

Source: Figure of DRDA, Koraput

CONVERGENCE OF WATERSHED PROGRAMME IN KORAPUT

In Koraput the watershed programmes under various schemes (EAS, ACA & IWDP) funded by ministries of Govt. of India have been in operation since 1998-99 in Mission mode through District Watershed Mission on the aegis of DRDA under chairpersonship of District collector. Watersheds are allotted as a sub-unit of development blocks and in most cases the BDOs are made the project implementing agency (PIA). PIA works through watershed development team (WDT) consisting of block level line department official and contractual professionals in NRM and Social Sciences. The mission approach as well as BDO- PIA has helped in convergence and delivery of services and actions to watersheds. The involvement of line department heads as members of district level Watershed Advisory Committee in monitoring and review of the programmes both in –situ and ex-situ has lead to the advantages of watershed projects through their professional advise, assistance and departmental resource mobilization. Constant monitoring and enthusiasm shown by mission leaders (District Collector) has also helped in instant decision-makings in dovetailing and ensuring intra-departmental collaborations. BDOs, being the coordinator for rural development programmes at the block level, have been able to channelize the required programmes through single-window to the watersheds as per the felt needs of the people.

In the convergence initiatives, the implementing stakeholders at PIA and district level have been able to dovetail facilities for basic livelihood amenities for human capital development like communication, education, rural housing and drinking water supply along with services that would augment livelihood viz. such as natural capital development through plantation, pisiculture and irrigation. It may be kept in mind that, the undulating terrains and scattered nature of settlements make most villages remain unconnected through road network and lack basic facilities like drinking water, housing and education and many watershed programmes in Koraput have done justice to these alienated communities not only through watershed Programme related interventions but also through this convergence approach with a human touch. In the convergence, more than 20 different schemes have been delivered to the watershed communities of the district as a whole with an average of 4.4 works per watershed. These include schemes of rural and tribal development, peripheral area development schemes of industries and agricultural intensification initiatives etc. It is also quite revealing that these schemes could be dovetailed primarily due to the coordination role of the block (as per initiatives if the PIA) through involvement of panchati raj institutions and ITDA (Integrated Tribal Development Agency). The potential of convergence could be realized from the fact that it could supplement the project with around half of the amount; project has spent on watershed development.

Table 4
Convergence Features in Koraput

Convergence	*Rs. in Millions*
Funds mobilized per Watershed	0.53
% of convergence amount to watershed fund spent	46.2
Number of Works converged per watershed	4.4
Amount spent per converged work	0.12
Range of amount spent per watershed	0.0 - 2.28
Sectors converged	Communication/ Drinking Water Supply, Education, Irrigation/Plantation, Pisci-culture, Rural Housing
Schemes Converged	ATMA/ C1C Grant, CRF, Cross bolder, DPEP, EAS, FDR, IAY, IHDP, ITDA, MLA LAD, Nalco Fund, OBB, PHD (RWSS), PMGSY, SGRY, SGSY, Tribal Coffee, United Fund, WFP, PMGAY,
Agencies Linked	Block, GP, ITDA, PS

Source: Choudhury P.R- Livelihood transformation through Watershed Development-Analysis of convergence perspective in Koraput District

WATERSHED DEVELOPMENT PROGRAMME IN POTTANGI BLOCK

BASIC INFORMATION

Pottangi Block started functioning from 1.4.1964 and now it is running its C.D Stage-II and T.D Stage. This Block is situated on the National High Way-43 (Waltair to Raipur) and 45 K.Ms from the District Headquarter Koraput. It is about 1015 meters above Main Sea level with a subtropical climatic condition.

This Block comprises of 100 Revenue villages and 345 Hamlets with an area of 320 Sq.K.Ms and most of the villages are situated either on top or gap of Hills. Its East and South touches Andhra Pradesh and North and West touches Semiliguda Block of this District. Pottangi Block has 14 G.Ps, 100 Revenue villages and 345 total numbers of Hamlets.

Table 5
Demographic Profile of Pottangi Block

Block	*Total Population*	*SC*	*%*	*ST*	*%*	*OC*	*%*	*Total works*	*Main worker*	*Marginal workers*
Pottangi 5352	52561	2737	5.2%	37527	71%	12497	23.8%	32418		27061

Source: Figures from Pottangi Block

Pottangi Block is one of the most backward blocks of the state with an area of 320 Sq.K.Ms square kilometers having 100 Revenue and 345 Hamlet villages in 14 G.Ps. The terrain is hilly and Vegetable cultivation is widely prevalent in the Block.

The demographic profile of the block is given below:

Table 6
Total Population of Pottangi Block

S.C Population	2737
ST Population	37527
O.C Population	12497
TOTAL	52761

Source: Figures from Pottangi Block

Pottangi Block is a tribal dominated Block, the ST population covers 71% of the Block. The total population of this block is 52,761 as per 1991 census as detailed below:

WATERSHEDS IN POTTANGI BLOCK: PRESENT STATUS

In Pottangi Block at present Twelve Watersheds in implementation under ACA, HAS and NWDPRA. The details are given in the following table.

Table 7
Present Status of Watersheds in Pottangi Block

Name of the Block	*Name of the Scheme*	*No. of Water-shed*	*Name of the Watershed*	*Total Geographical Area*	*Treatable Area*	*Area Treated So Far*
Pottangi	ACA	6	Deo- Pottangi, 04060104061 90202	640.00	500.00	205.00
			Badaliguda, 14-07030201	560.00	500.00	211.00
			Giriliguda, 1407030209	625.00	500.00	206.00
			Badapadu, 10-03020103	520.00	470.00	158.00
			Nuagaon, 10-04050201	580.00	500.00	230.00

Contd.

Name of the Block	Name of the Scheme	No. of Water-shed	Name of the Watershed	Total Geograp-hical Area	Treatable Area	Area Treated So Far
			Galigabadar-10-04050202	710.00	500.00	220.00
	EAS	5	Guntha-14-07020102	512.00	500.00	421.00
			Sepaiput, 14-07030202	504.00	466.00	422.00
			Malkarbandha, 14-07040102	512.30	500.00	410.00
			Bituguda, 14-07020201	523.00	500.00	0.00
			Setri,14-07020202	511.00	500.00	375.00
	NWDPRA	1	Sambai Nalla, ORK-6005	998.00	762.12	155.00

Source: Watershed Development Plan of Pottangi, 2000

MAJOR FINDINGS OF THE PRESENT STUDY

The paper *"People Centered Holistic Watershed Management for Sustainable livelihood of Rural Poor: A case study of Malkarbanndh Watershed of Koraput District in Orissa"* is an attempt to study the ecological, physical and social impact of Watershed Development Programme on the rural life of this region viz. Malkarbandha Village of Pottangi Block in Koraput District. This watershed comprises of two villages viz. Malkarbandha revenue village and part of Maliput revenue village. This watershed falls under Eastern Ghat high land Zone and characterized by vast stretch of undulating to moderately marginal lands with an elevation of 800 to 900 meters above mean sea level. After detail study it is observed that the watershed based development has emerged a major area to take care of problems related to resource management in agro-eco regions on the principles of watershed based resource identification, planning and implementation. Watershed is not just about soil and water conservation, but now it is proved that watershed development is also associated with individuals, villages, community and economic status of the area. It is Holistic Development Programme for the given area. The following are the major findings of the study:

- The Project under Study was started during the year 1999 under Employment Assurance Scheme.
- It was commenced with a treatable area of 466 Hectares and with a financial outlay of 17.25 Lakhs. The identified areas are mostly wasteland and there is a predominance of Podu cultivation in the area.
- The indicators are m *situ* soil and water conservations activities, plantation and demonstration of dry land horticulture, gully control, ravine treatment WHS, percolation tanks etc. Formation of groups, group dynamics, people's participation activities taken up for landless and "small and marginal land holders, user group formation, capacity building of WDT and other stake holders etc.
- One of the fact observed that the people's participation through formation of SHG is good. In order to ensure peoples participation uniformly, sufficient number of in-house and field level training have been provided to the watershed functionaries as well as to the villagers for the purpose.

The details of training conducted are as follows:

Table 8
Details of Training made in Malkarbandha Watershed Village

Focused Group	*Title of Training*	*Days*	*Organized*
Watershed Office Bearer	Rice Seminar Exposure Visit Trg. On Environmental pollution	4 days 3 days 4 days	RRTTSDRDA RRTTS
PRIs	Trg. On Floriculture Trg. On Horticulture	1 day 1 day	Pottangi Block
SHGs	Trg. On Mushroom & Honey Bee Trg. On different types of skill dev.Exposure Visit	1 day 1 day 1 day	Pottangi Block
UG	Maintain the project after compilation Mixed Fruit Plantation	1 day 1 day	Pottangi Block

- Community Participation has been given highest importance in the Watershed Project. The Watershed Development Team members has taken steps to celebrate all the important events like celebration of Water Month, Literacy Day, Health Day, Aids Day and all other important days, organize various training for formation of SHG, UG, Skill upgradation, Value Addition and for social mobilization.
- Watershed management has been proven to be capable of conserving rainwater and improving ground water recharge through simple contour cultivation, mechanical measures (e.g. bunds, bench terraces, nala, bunding, desilting of tanks) and construction of water harvesting structures (e.g. ponds, pits, percolation tanks). Recharge structures are constructed or existing structures are treated in regions where annual rainfall is inadequate or badly distributed over the season. Also a Field Channel has been constructed under WDP which is providing water to 45 Ha of land in the study area.
- After intervention of Watershed Development Programme, number of trees per acre has increased. As ascertained by the villagers during the year,1999 there was 152 number of fruit bearing trees and 3500 number of fuel wood trees available but now the number of fruit bearing trees has increased to 7800 and fuel and fodder trees increased to 15000. Farm fuel wood on individual land has increased enough so as to meet the household requirements for the whole year.
- Since implementing a watershed development programme involves farmers and landless people living in the Watershed area, it is necessary to upgrade their knowledge and to create potential awareness in the community on Watershed management. The district administration imparted training to VVC members (Chairman, President and Secretary) and some progressive farmers of watershed area on

different issues like watershed management, guidelines for watershed, accounting procedure, record keeping, agricultural interventions, training on coffee plantation, floriculture, dry land horticulture and other innovations in the Watershed.

- Spices Cultivation with a special reference to Ginger and Turmeric has been provided. This is done by conducting inter block exposure visit, inter district exposure visit and also inter state exposure visit. As a result of which the level of awareness has increased among the watershed functionaries as well among the villagers.
- Women empowerment has been given highest importance in Watershed Development Programme. Women have been taken as member in Watershed committee, which is the decision making body in the Watershed. Further, they have brought into the main stream of income generation through SHG groups. The SHG groups are earning income by engaging themselves in different activities like Duckery/ Fishery, vegetable cultivation, broom binding etc.
- A Composite Development Centre, namely "The Vikash Kendra" has been constructed in Malkarbandha Watershed under WDP which is the focal point for the Watershed where all the meetings of the Watershed Committee, SHG are conducted. The Vikash Kendra is also utilized for social functions of the villages. The researcher observed that by constructing a low cost permanent centre in each Watershed, the villagers could be united and a sense of belongingness for the assets created in the Watershed area. The details of work done, successful parameters of Watershed and other important points of Watershed are written in the Vikash Kendra for awareness and greater transparency.
- The monitoring mechanism developed under Watershed Development Programme in Koraput district is very good. Monitoring and review of the

progress of work of Watershed are conducted at three stages of implementation. In each Block, a WDT member has been assigned with one Watershed, who is supervising all the progress of that particular Watershed. Further to strengthen the technical team, a Graduate in Agriculture has been engaged in all the Watershed as Community Organizer who is coordinating all the works in the Watersheds of the Block. At the District level, a review meeting is held every month in a Watershed where besides the review the field visits of all the PIAs and WDT members are also organized.

- The project has changed the overall quality of life of the beneficiaries in the Watershed area. The employment generated during food scarcity period has provided food along with cash, which has positive impact on the inhabitants in the Watershed area. As such income generation activities like Mushroom, Goatery, Poultry, Duckery and Vegetable cultivation has provided additional benefit to the villagers besides ensuring them food security on a sustained basis.
- Under the works component various soil conservation measures and plantation work are being carried out in the various watershed areas. The higher ridge, middle ridge and lower ridge are treated according to the soil conservation measures. Among land development field bunding and contouring are done to reduce the run off losses. Under the drainage line treatments field channel, gully control and loose boulder check dams, bank stabilization and diversion weir are carried out for the treatment of middle ridge of the watershed. Among others creation of water bodies like percolation tank, village tank, farm pond, field channel are prepared which help in intensifying the agriculture production and productivity.
- Establishment of Nursery in the Watershed has been emphasized. One Nursery has been developed in

Malkarbandha village of Portangi block. In the Nursery along with fuel and fodder, saplings of fruit bearing vegetable, Neem and other species have been raised. An amount of Rs. 0.45 Lakh has been spent towards intensifying of Nursery.

- Plantation in the Community Wasteland has been taken up by the Watershed Committees in the study area.
- From discussion with the Villagers it is ascertained that after receipt of funds, people's participation as well as confidence of the people is regained. In the meantime the entire funds have already been utilized. The Committee did not observe any major flaws with the PIAs regarding the utilization of funds. Of course funds relating to the Works Component are directly released to the Watershed Committee and they are utilizing the same. The Committee has also been empowered in the meantime to utilize the funds in time. In other words at the Committee level also the members have become aware of the timely progress of works.
- 40% of the Villagers have been organized into three SHG and steps have been taken for formation of more SHG in the Study area.
- Watershed, a natural entity in itself, combines forest management, land use management and water management. If happens to be such a hydrologic or physiographic unit that it offers a very good unit for planning and implementing soil conservation, water harvesting, afforestation and environmental protection programmes. It is also considered a rational basis for optimum development of available resources. Watershed Programme has been effectively implemented in the Malkarbandha Village of Pottangi Block in Koraput District of Orissa State with the active involvement and cooperation of the beneficiaries.

RECOMMENDATIONS/SUGGESTIONS

Keeping in view the socio-economic, educational and occupational background of the people living inside the project area and the present status of land and green cover, the following recommendations are made. I hope this attempt will help for better and effective implementation of the programmes in this region besides helping the Planners and Scholars to explore more on Watershed Development Programme.

- Development of lands especially of the marginal and small holders to increase productivity is important to insulate them from vagaries of food in security.
- Agriculture intervention in the form of promoting locally relevant, drought resistant, crop mix are necessary to increase the land production and productivity, Input support through cheap credit is important in this connection.
- Introduction of remunerative cropping pattern, crop sequence and land and water management practices.
    - — Sustainable crop production techniques, Viz. Mixed farming, Mixed cropping, intercropping, companion Cropping, alley cropping for assured income.
    - — Land levelling, Land terracing/development in farmer's field.
    - — Contour bunding, vegetative bunding in hill slopes.
    - — Gully control, check dams, brushwood dam and water conservation measures in hills and dangers.
    - — Plantation of hardy trees like mango, guava, ber,cashew, tamarind, jackfruit, custard apple, medicinal plants etc. in danger and highlands not suitable for raising crops.
    - — Pasture and silvi-pasture development to address to the needs of livestock holders besides

conserving soil and moisture is to be taken up. The development of small ruminants in the Watershed may be encouraged.

— Alley cropping with nitrogen fixing trees and promotion of high value cash crops like potato, onion, yam, colocasia etc. are to be taken up to replace paddy, ragi, niger, mustard crops by improved variety of Arhar and high value beans in the degraded sloppy lands.

- Pisciculture program should be encouraged for the benefit of the marginal farmers and landless.
- Non-land based livelihood options for the poor need to be explored further, to enhance income of the landless and women.
- Wage employment measures for the landless are important to sustain Livelihoods of the landless. Wage opportunity on a sustained basis meeting during the lean agricultural season for a considerable period appears to be the key to enhance the resource base of the landless poor. All the wage employment programmes of Government have to be effectively implemented with wage payment in part and food grains in part.
- Families having forest based household production activities like Leaf Plate making and sale of Minor Forest Produces be identified and bottle necks like lack of market support, exploitation by middle man and the inability to process the products etc. are to be addressed properly for development of the identified families.
- Though there is a strong institutional arrangement prevalent in the implementation mechanism, for greater transparency and ensuring more democracy in the process, the local PRIs should be involved in the entire process of implementation of the programme.

- Community mobilization activities, celebration of National events/dates, inter block/Watershed competitions, Rallies, Awareness programme, observance of local festivals etc. should be continuous events and at no point there should be break in it. Awareness generation at Watershed Committee and PIA level on different topics is given priority on a continuous basis.
- Regular training at Watershed Committee, PIA/Block and District level should continue all along the year. Training on innovative activities, local skills, improved technology etc. should be given priority. In fact, a Training and Community Organization activities CALENDER be prepared and accordingly the programmes be organized.
- The position of organizing the population into SHG is not encouraging. As envisaged 80% of the population should be organized into SHG or UGs. The landless families should be organized into SHG.
- The On farm activities in the Watershed should be programmed in such a systematic manner that all land owning families be covered UGs.
- Nursery is a vital need in all the Watersheds. Provision of saplings of fuel and fodder plantation, fruit bearing trees, vegetable cultivation should be ensured at any cost either through individual Nursery at Watershed level or from a Central Nursery.
- Establishment of a Medicinal/ Herbal plantation garden is felt essential in the Watershed.
- Community based Grain Banks and Seed Banks should be established in the Watershed and Government support should be ensured at the beginning for food and seed security.
- Legal framework for migration and labour laws related to wage and movement of labour in the study area should be strengthened in order to benefit the poor sections.

- Women's involvement, socio economic upliftment of landless and disadvantaged sections of the community, equitable sharing of benefits and responsibilities were found important elements for long term sustainability of such interventions.
- Since the climate is conducive and there is high market value in our neighboring state, FLORICULTURE should be developed through the villagers for their economic upliftment.
- It is suggested that the User Groups be motivated properly and the benefit be accrued out of them should be explained to them exclusively so that they will contribute the more amount quite happily for post Project Management.
- The literacy status in the Watershed village is not up to the mark. Illiteracy needs to be addressed with utmost priority to bring development in the area.
- More emphasis should be given to Sanitation, safe drinking water, health and education, awareness and confidence building.
- More importance should be given to on off farm income generating avenues having linkages with local availability of input & Scope of marketing.
- Skill transfer for repairing & maintenance of assets should be ensured (Tube well/Biogas/Structures) & agri/horti/forestry practices should be ensured.
- For hills in the study area, mango, guava, cashew etc. are suitable fruit trees for taking up under WDP.
- Suitable forestry species for degraded hills in Pottangi are Acacia auriculiformis, Melia azaderach, and Gmelina arborea should be adopted.
- Pitcher irrigation for fruit plantations should be ensured.
- Emphasis should be given for trench-cum-bund planted with samuta, a local grass to protect the soil from erosion.

- Loose Boulder Check Dams should be constructed on community basis rather than by individual farmer.
- Agave, Sambuta and Bamboo can be used to protect small gully bed and drainage lines.
- Attempt should be made to overcome the shyness of the villagers, recognize their capabilities, understand their own needs, desires and limitations and develop a strong will to achieve their goals.
- If Watershed Management has to become peoples' movement, technologies would have to be simple, low cost and should be based on vegetative measures, which are self-regenerative. Claims are being made that watershed management would ensure supply of water to every field, remove hunger and poverty from poor areas, provide green cover over denuded areas, bring in more rains and improve environment, Watershed management is also described as a programme that holds the key to solve problems of employment, economy, ecology, export and equity.

CONCLUSION

Rural development is the overall development of rural areas with a view to improve the quality of life, which is a comprehensive and multi dimensional concept that encompasses the development of agriculture and allied activities, village and cottage industries, socio economic infrastructures, community services and facilities, above all the human resource development (Singh 1986).

Watershed Development is one such approach, which is eco friendly, and a hydrologically correct approach for efficient use of soil and water for more agriculture production. This refers to treatment of an area to get many direct and indirect livelihood benefits. The effectiveness of the measure would go manifold when bottom up approach of treatment is made. Watershed Development is a specific approach for sustainable development of people residing in the rain-fed or drought affected areas (Aggarwal, 2003)

The Watershed Development approach aims at augmentation and stabilization of production and productivity, maintaining ecological balance or to minimize ecological degradation, reduction in regional disparity and opening up of greater employment opportunities and means of sustainable livelihood to the rural poor (Gupta,1995)

Under Watershed Development Programme, along with the agricultural activities other activities like plantation of different species like mango, cashew etc. is undertaken, which yield greater economic benefits for the beneficiaries. Avenue plantation and mixed tree plantation are taken out in the project area to restore the ecological balance. Land development and measures to check soil erosion like construction of Mechanical filter strip; Gully Control structures etc. are carried out in the project area, which yield significant result.

Data reveal that people's participation in planning, implementation and community property resources has been increased, particularly of landless, small and marginal farmers. Participation of women in the decision making process has been increased manifold. Women organized in a strategic way forming Self Help Groups, which has synergetic affect in-the economic development of the households.

Increase in biomass through plantation and other relevant programmes have boosted animal husbandry' in the Watershed area. Rearing of high breed variety of birds and bovines increased the economic standard of beneficiaries.

As Watershed Development Programme is an integrated approach towards sustainable development, fishery and duckery are encouraged in the project. All these above mentioned programmes have increased the effective potential use of human resource and livestock in a systematic manner.

The main objective of the Watershed Development Programme, however, is to reduce poverty through efficient management of natural resources using cost –effective, socially acceptable environmentally sound technologies in participatory and bottom up approach. Ecological balance is restored by adopting programme measures, which are low cost, eco-friendly and sustainable in a long run. The disparity between irrigated and rain-fed areas is minimized in term of production, productivity and family income including gender equality. Employment opportunities are created which not only boost the income level, but also help to check migration in search of employment.

The current strategy for rain-fed farming is based on the concept of scientific conservation of rainwater for holistic and integrated development of the area and promotion of sustainable agriculture. Agriculture is directly linked to many aspects of sustainable development including alleviation of poverty, sustainable consumption and production, management of natural resources, capacity building as well. Agriculture Centers on integrated use of natural resources such as Soil, Water, Climate and biological diversity, which forms the basic part of Watershed Development Programme.

Modern methods and techniques have been used for better management of land and water in the Watershed area. Land use pattern has been changed dramatically with use of improved technology and High Yielding Variety Crops. Thus productivity has been increased. Proper treatment of land has been able to increase the soil and moisture level leading to better yield. Activities done under WDP like field bunding, Loose Boulder Check Dam, Gully Control Structure, Stone Wall Terracing, and Field Retention Wall have been able to check the soil erosion to a greater extent. Plantation of various species has increased the crown cover.

It is well noted that women have a substantial contribution towards rural economy, particularly among tribals. Due to Integrated Watershed Development Programme, the employment opportunities have increased manifold for them. Women are engaged in tending of livestock, crop production and other enterprises. Extension agencies working in the Watershed area promote participatory approach to enable people for initiating activities on their own and receive optimal advantage of other ongoing development programmes. The most important step for empowerment of the local community and assurance of their active participation in the programme is to entrust planning and execution of development works under the project to them. While the main development activities are carried out by the community itself, the overall facilitation, coordination and supervision of the whole programme is the responsibility of the extension personnel. The Watershed Approach aims at promoting equity of resource, which strengthens the socio economic status of rural people, especially the landless and women.

After intervention of Watershed in the study area, problems were addressed to generate various assets essential for enhancing sustainable livelihoods.

The initiatives taken through Watershed Development Programme has contributed to ecological stabilization of Malkarbandha Watershed area with increased ground water level which in turn has breathed a new life in natural resources of the project area. The programme should be upgraded so that whole community participates and the benefits are equally distributed. For strengthening this approach concerted efforts are urgently required to develop and adopt integrated approach through appropriate technological interventions in participatory mode to offset the looming crisis of natural resource degradation and increased demand of food for sustainable livelihoods. The need is to convert weaknesses into strengths and threats into opportunities by involving people in all management aspects related to conservation measures and repair of structures, diversified agriculture/ farming activities and benefit accrued should be shared or utilized. From the above discussion we came to conclusion that Watershed Development is the most effective approach in not only mitigating the environmental degradation but also increases the employment opportunities, ensures social security, equitable sharing of benefits and responsibilities, provide better sustainable livelihood opportunities etc. as a whole. *The Watershed Development Approach is the need of the hour to meet Social, Economical, Environmental and other community goals.*

REFERENCES

Aggrawal, S.K. (2003), Integrated Watershed Development Technology based Model for Rural Development, Kurukhetra, Vol.–51.

Carney, D. (ed.) (1998) , Sustainable Livelihoods; What Contribution We Can Make?, Paper presented at the DFID Natural resource Advisors Conference, London:DFID.

Choudhury, P. R. (2004), Convergence of Line Department, Lecture delivered to WDT Members of Koraput, March 2004 proceedings of the district level workshop for WDT members, Soil Conservation Division, Koraput.

Gupta, A. K. (1995), Rethinking Policy Options for Watershed Management by Local Communities: Combining Equity, Efficiency and Ecological Economics. Viabilityhttp://www.nird.org/_vti_bin/shtml.exe/papers/rethinkin.htm

Rajora, R. (1998), Integrated Watershed Management–Field Manual for Equitable Productive and Sustainable Development.

Rhoads, R. (2000), Participatory Watershed Research and Management: Where Shadow Falls, Gatekeeper Series (No.81), IIED, London.

Singh, K. (1996), Rural Development, Principles, Policies and Management, Sage Publication, New-Delhi.

CHAPTER–10

IMPROVING WOMEN'S SOCIAL CAPITAL–CAN WE SOLVE THE SHORTCOMINGS OF THE WATERSHED MANAGEMENT PROGRAMME IN INDIA?

Poulmi Banarjee

"Women play a central part in the provision, management and safeguarding of water."

–Dublin Principle 3, International Conference on Water and the Environment Development Issues for the Twenty-first Century, Dublin, 1992

INTRODUCTION

The Watershed Management Programme (WMP) in India has traversed a long journey from its earlier uncoordinated, sectoral approach to its current integrated bottom-up approach with a vision of providing employment, reducing poverty and securing livelihood for the millions of disadvantaged sections, specially women and dalits. Under this new endeavor, women's participation has been seen as the most important indicator of WMP success, as it attempts to incorporate women's concerns and experiences as an integral dimension of the design, implementation, monitoring and evaluation of policies and programmes in all political, economic and societal spheres. *(UNDP report: 2006)*. This has become particularly important over the last two decades with India being one of the signatories of the Millennium Development Goals. Since Agenda 21 of the MDG particularly promotes the involvement of women with water, there has arisen a plethora of conferences, discussion forums and workshops about the effectiveness of the gender sensitive participatory model. Although several successful case studies were highlighted, concerns were expressed time and again about the intent of such a noble mission and its actual implementation, with particular reference to the women's emancipation that it promises. The question that started bothering researchers is whether WMP has been able to make a difference in the lives of millions of vulnerable rural women, creating a platform for their voice and action, or if it has just remained another hollow initiative which promises a lot but fails to break the oppressive restraint of helpless marginalized women.

This problem is not unknown in India, where sociologists, eco-feminists and economists have talked a lot about loopholes in the policy imperatives, unrealistic programme packaging or lack of institutional backups deterring effective women's participation. Several case studies have been conducted that suggest that even the most "successful participatory programme", with considerable amount of women's involvement fails to sustain its vigor after seven to ten years with the withdrawal of the implementing agencies. However, very few attempts have been made in this direction to address the issue of exploring the causes behind such varying outcomes of the watershed programmes, even those implemented by a single agency. The following paper therefore attempts to look into the dynamics of social capital as an answer to solve the dilemmas of gender relations in WMP in India. The paper tries to look into the intricate balance of power existing between social perception, trust, values, and norms, that secludes or includes women in the loop of mainstream development programme like WMP and to see how far it is responsible for the long term success or failure of these initiatives in India *(Pantoja: 2000; Aggarwal: 2000)*

HOW GENDER AND POVERTY AFFECT ACCESSIBILITY TO SOCIAL CAPITAL

Social capital may be defined as a) the quantity and/or quality of resources that an actor (be it an individual group or community) can access in a social network and b) an actor's location in the social network. *(Christiaan and Thierry, 2001, Lin 2000)* It is obvious that not all individuals or social groups uniformly acquire social capital or receive expected returns from the social capital. In the words of Granovetter, "social capital penetrates irregularly and in differing degrees in different sectors of social life." *(Pantoja 2000)* There are two factors responsible for such differential accessibility of social capital by different actors in the societal process. Firstly, the historical and institutional factors, which point out that each society structurally provides unequal opportunities to members of different groups defined over several dynamics, like race, caste, religion and gender. Secondly, *Homophily*, which is the general tendency for an individual to interact and associate with those of similar groups or socio-economic characteristics. Inequality of social capital is increased when disadvantaged individuals cluster around others in the same situation, thus embedding themselves in networks poor in resources and social capital. This acts as a vicious cycle, pushing the poorly equipped section further down in the power spectrum. This is most visible among the vulnerable rural women who have good horizontal connections with peers but little vertical networking with people outside of their gender or socio-economic class. Apart from some notable exceptions, natural resource management initiatives, like WPM, have failed to alter this gloomy reality. These WPM should be designed with a more truthful background, and not treated as a cooperative performance of a homogeneous populace, since this is not the case. Rather, research into these programs should work on understanding the inequalities caused by gender relations within the context of social capital and the dynamics of equity and sustainability in the collective action.

HOW COMMUNITY AND HOUSEHOLD DYNAMICS AFFECT ACCESSIBILITY TO SOCIAL CAPITAL

In every society, women have been entrusted with very distinctive roles. For instance, in traditional agricultural tribal societies, like the Apatanis of Arunachal Pradesh and Garhwalis of the Western Himalayas, Mizos, Naga and hill tribes of Western Ghats of India, men and women share equal work load and responsibilities. This form of networking has helped them to conserve resources for generations in an informal but more effective way. Men and women equally share the knowledge of selection of species, (particularly medicinal plants), conservation of resources, breeding and managing livestock, and other necessary survival tasks. This knowledge is passed through generation within and across households and, in turn strengthens their networks, helping to develop reciprocity and trust among themselves. On the other hand in some agriculturally developed areas where market forces had penetrated deeply, women are largely secluded from the mainstream agricultural scenario and instead, occupy a peripheral position, restricted within the household. These differences in societal structure lead to differences in women's access to social capital. In the mentioned traditional societies women develop strong networks, involved with core organizational activities (both formal and informal). However, in the other heterogeneous societies, women's access to these valuable forms of social capital and other resources becomes highly restricted. *(Pantoja: 2000)*.

Differing laws and standards of women's rights also affect accessibility to social capital.. For instance women in the North East tribal provinces of India (e.g Khasi, Jaintia tribe), or Nair women of Kerala, have higher economic status in the form of rights to property, and thereby accessibility to most of the family assets. This economic freedom has given them greater autonomy to access a greater social network and build power relations. Thus they are in better position to bargain over the use, reuse, or revitalization of social norms, values and attitudes present in the society. However, for North West India, particularly where Hindu succession law-Dayabhaga prevails, women do not own family property naturally (particularly land rights) and have less accessibility to land or any other form of wealth and thus have less bargaining power as compared to men. As a result of such differing social networks and correspondingly different levels of access to information, women from different areas experience different hierarchical and economic positions in their societies.

Different communities also place different importance in women's work. In some agricultural societies, women's work is not recognized even when it makes up 50% of the work done. Instead, it is merely seen as part of her husband's work. Sometimes, she is not paid for her work except as a portion of her husband's wage. This further lowers the position of women and decreases their access to social capital.

Social position, religious and ethnic dynamics also determine the degree of accessibility of social capital by women. Often women of the lower caste and dalits enjoyed more mobility in the society as compared to the upper caste women. Among scheduled castes and tribes, women are appreciated as an *economic asset*. In fact, literature substantiate that "...the poorer the family, the greater its dependence on women's economic productivity" (World Bank report 2001). Extreme poverty and social seclusion often forced the women to search for means of survival and thus many times they were able to move out and form horizontal networks with larger civic organisations. Women in upper castes, without this freedom to work outside the family, may not have this access to social capital.

In addition to community and social expectations, another factor affecting accessibility is the power dynamics that operate between men and women at the household levels. Gender relations are at cutting edge competition, to win over the scarce resources. In this power game who will gain depends on several interconnected variables like economic, political and social position of the actors (especially women), linkage to outside world, perception and rights enjoyed by them and specific institutional arrangements that structured everyday life. For instance, even with the higher respect given to a tribal woman, there has remained a subtle difference in the power and position that she enjoys as compared to her male counterparts. These women are not often equal to men, who represent the family in the main social organizations and tend to have control over the household resources. Tribal women, regardless of the dominant place that they occupy in agriculture and in domestic labor, are not perceived as producers, but a subordinate labourers where all the monetary transactions to the outside world is mediated by men (Janet, Batra and Sarin, 2000). Even though poor low caste women can move out of their house in search of livelihood (which upper caste rich women can't do), they still often have to give away their earning to their husbands, even if he then spends it on alcohol or other unproductive pursuits. Thus, even when a woman escapes "the inside," and is allowed by society to access other forms of social capital, they can still be prevented from fully developing social capital because of hous-hold politics.

HOW WOMEN'S LOW ACCESSIBILITY TO SOCIAL CAPITAL AFFECT THE WMP

Technically, "watershed" is a geographic area that drains to a common point, which makes it an attractive unit for technical efforts to conserve soil and maximize the utilization of surface and subsurface water for crop production (Kerr, Pangare 1999). In terms of development, however, "watershed" indicates a holistic approach to improvement in land, water and vegetation with active involvement of the common people.

Although it dates back to the colonial age, the Watershed Management Programme began in 1994 to focus on a bottom up, integrated, participatory model rather than solely technological models. For the first time, emphasis was placed on the management, restoration and revitalization of Common Property Resources (CPR) with a vision of promoting equity in sharing benefits to the hitherto deprived landless and women. CPR serves as an important means of livelihood for the vulnerable landless and marginal farmers in the fragile ecosystems. It particularly affects women because they are responsible for collecting fuel, fodder and drinking water from it. Thus, any change in its spatial coverage and qualitative upgradation will therefore tremendously impact the economic, and socio political life of the women. For instance, decline in the extent of CPR forces the women to spend more time and travel longer distances in procuring water, fuel and fodder. This not only increases the cooking time from substituting with inferior fuels, decreases livestock population resulting in income reduction, affects women's health, education and overall livelihood security, but it also has much deeper social consequences. For instance, access to the village commons is usually linked to membership in the village community, and therefore, with CPR, women are not excluded in the way they may be in a system of individualized private land rights. This acquires additional importance in regions with strong norms of female seclusion, where women's access to cash economy and to markets is strictly controlled by male relatives (Aggarwal, 1995)

Therefore, these new WMP agendas appeared to offer a way out of stagnation and degradation for all those areas that development seemingly bypassed. *(Joy, Shah, Parenjape, Badiger, Lele: 2006)* However, evaluative studies and reviews point out that in many instances WMP could not kept pace with expectation. Instead, it essentially benefited the big land holders, bypassing the women, landless and dalits for whom all the promises were made. The arena of CPR, has been grossly mistreated in WMP, mostly to avoid the problem of accountability and overlapping conflicts across interest groups that generally plagued the open access land in rural India. When CPR is ignored, this alters the power balance and value system of the community, eventually eroding away the trust, bonds and reciprocity, or in other words various facets of cognitive social capital across gender.

WMP has also failed the cause of women in other ways. Even though gender analysis has been taken as one of the integral component in WMP, it only talks about women's participation in terms of attending meetings and forming Self Help Groups and revolving funds. It has failed to take the larger social dynamics where gender relations ultimately determine the success of the programme. Because of this, WMP many times accentuates, rather than improves, the gender gap and power politics among men and women. Since is essentially a land based activity, women get less share of the benefits because of the lack of rights enjoyed by them with regard to land property. WMP initiatives often focus on changing cropping patterns from food to cash crops increasing intra-village inequality and making poor women and the landless more prone to casualisation of labour. The increase in cash income is more often reflected in the purchase of family resources and assets, which primarily benefit men (bicycles, mopeds, etc), rather than those that lower women's work burden and drudgery (say hand pumps, improved cooking stoves etc) (Krishna, 2001).

The sporadic success stories where gender participation shows a higher trend are ones where implementing agencies speculated the dynamics of gender and social capital and tried to formulated their polices accordingly in order to strengthen the social network for the women in much more harmonious manner. Several case studies can be cited to show the importance of taking gender analysis into account when implementing watershed programmes. For example, a study conducted by TERI in T.Begur watershed of rural Bangalore district in Karnataka exhibits the differences caused by differences in the social capital available to women. T.Begur watershed consists of four villages-Hosur, Marohalli, H.G. Palya and T.Begur-located in the Kumadvati River system. Despite being within the same agro climatic zone, T.Begur (the down stream village) is remarkably different from the upstream villages of Hosur, Marohalli or H.G. Palya, not in physical dynamics, but in micro social perspective. Trust, reciprocity and bond among the villagers, attitudes, value system and norms with regard to power and functions of women in natural resource management is much more open and broad in upstream villages as compared to the heterogeneous downstream village of T.Begur. As a result Hosur, Marohalli and H.G. Palya were able to sustain their traditional agriculture amidst of chronic ground water shortage and rapidly approaching urbanisation, which T.Begur could not. Land convertibility, factianism, power politics, aggression among villagers and extreme women seclusion from the mainstream economic activity is much higher here. Several agricultural interventions under the preview of watershed programme like construction of farm ponds, developing micro finance group in T.Begur, were not able to make any instrumental change in this stagnating social structure. This is noticed with the presence of nine dysfunctional women's micro finance groups in the village, which although have one crore of funds, had not been involved in any kind of developmental activities for years. On the other hand, in Hosur or any of the other upstream villages, although no proper government initiatives have taken place for last 10 years, villagers, even women, were quite enthusiastic and able to bring about a change in their stagnated situation. These clear differences shows the need for on the part of the implementing agencies to actually understand the dynamics of gender and social capital before initiating any watershed interventions.

A successful implementation example can be seen in the Gauriya village of Sagar district of Madhya Pradesh, where an all women committee in watershed programme has been able to overcome extreme poverty and subjugation in the village and break out from patriarchal dominance. In this case, sufficient time and energy was invested by the implementing agency (a government–NGO partnership) to understand gender dynamics, women constraints in developing informal networks, attitudes, values and norms of the society towards women's contribution in agriculture etc. In this way, they were able to strengthen the trust network among women across vertical and horizontal levels, with sufficient cooperation and support from the men members of the society.

With the 73rd amendment, women's position and responsibilities were guaranteed at a constitutional level. In tune to this, most of the developmental initiatives like WMP, started recongnising the role of women by according them reservations at the institutional levels. Even with reservations, however, the participation of women is very unequal to men. The following tables show this small women's representation at all levels of projects :

Table 1
Participation at the National Level

Implementing agencies	*Project Directors*		*Monitoring Development Team (MDT)*		*Watershed Development Team (WDT)*		*Watershed Committee (WC)*	
	M	*F*	*M*	*F*	*M*	*F*	*M*	*F*
Government	84%	16%	99%	<1%	95%	<5%	75%	25%
NGOs	75%	25%	60%	40%	60%	<40%	60%	40%
Bilateral/Multilateral and goverment	50%	<40%	70%	40%	70%	30%	70%	20%
Government and NGOs	60%	40%	50%	50%	65%	<40%	70%	<20%

Source: Compiled from the literature review.

Table 2
Participation at the Grass Root Level

	SHGs		*UGs*	
PIA	*M*	*F*	*M*	*F*
Government	0	100%	98%	<2%
NGOs	0	100%	80%	20%
Bilateral/Multilateral	0	100%	80%	20%
Government and NGO	0	100%	75%	<20%

Source: Compiled from literature

Even those levels with higher than normal levels of women do not necessarily mean a success. Unfortunately, mandatory requirements of 3/4th participation of women in government-run projects encourages tokenism and does not demonstrate a committed effort to involve women in the decision making. In many situations, women's involvement is only accounted in terms of their attendance even when their voices at these meetings are not considered seriously. In some NGO implemented watershed programme women are appointed at the post of chairman, but without assigning her the real power. In most of the cases, women either don't come for the meeting or sit at the back without uttering a single word. Thus, in actual practice, all the decision-making is still generally taken up by her husband or the other male members of the committee. Simply putting women in positions using the reservations system does not necessarily increase her social capital or do anything to increase the role of women in WMP.

This tokenism can especially be seen in institutions like the Watershed Development Team (WDT) and Monitoring Development Team (MDT). These provide technical support to the community and generally are comprised of four to five experts with skills in civil engineering, forestry, veterinary medicine, soil and water conservation, and community development. The Common Approach for Watershed Development (GoI, 2000) states that *"one of the WDT members should be a woman"*. But in both the Government implemented projects or a NGO implemented one, WDT and MDT are dominated by men, because of the dearth of women experts. Even if a woman member is an expert, she will often be treated as less important than the men on the team. The role of women is maximum in self-help groups (SHGs), but here also, it is restricted to generation of revolving funds. On a larger scale, they are still kept outside the planning of natural resource development. Since there is no organic linkages to these wider scale projects, the strength of the group ends once the revolving fund is distributed and any social capital that might have developed just remains on paper.

CONCLUSION

It is not mere collective action or on-paper gender mainstreaming that provides an answer to this complex issue of equity and sustainability of WMP. It has to be viewed through the lens of social capital, so as to have a proper understanding about the intricate social relationships operating across gender in heterogeneous social structures. In India, informal social networks forms the backbone of life for millions of vulnerable rural women. Intricate power politics between genders often determines the rights and social economic position of women. All these factors in turn hinder vertical and horizontal linkages and thus, women's accessibility to social capital. These social, and specifically gender, dynamics can affect the efficacy of development initiatives. Deeper understanding of both formal and informal networks, norms, values, and trust systems across gender lines is very crucial before implementing any programme meant to accomplish anything for women. These gender analyses likely hold the key to resolving the problem of equity and sustainability in WMP. A community may not ready to accept any developmental change for women and so needs to be sensitized very carefully, so that the informal value chains do not break up and proper vertical and horizontal integration is possible. The solution to WMP inability to sustain improvements for women is to create a more congenial environment where women emancipation is not viewed by the male as threat to the society but a benevolent helping hand ready to share the responsibilities of eradicating poverty and attaining sustainable livelihood. WMP can only succeed in its stated goals by taking into account women's accessibility to social capital.

REFERENCES

Agarwal Bina (2003), *"Gender Inequality, Cooperation and Environmental Sustainability"*: Sage Publication.

Agarwal, Bina (2000), *"Conceptualizing Environmental Collective Action: Why Gender Matters"*: Cambridge Journal of Economics, 283_310

Agarwal Bina (1997), *"Bargaining and Gender Relations: Within and Beyond the Household"*,; Feminist Economist 3(1), 1-51.

Christiaan Grootaert (2001), Thierry Van Bastelaer, *"Understanding and Measuring Social Capital, A Synthesis of Findings and Recommendations from the Social Capital Initiatives"*, World Bank Report April.

Dick Ruth Meinzen(2006), Pandolfelli Lausen, Dohrn Stephen and Athens Jessica,; *"Gender and Collective Action: A Conceptual Framework for Analysis"*.11th Biennial Conference of the International Association for the Study of Common Property (IASCP) 19-23 June, Bali.

D'Silva, Pai Sudha (2003), *"Social Capital and Collective Action"*, Vol.38, No14, April 05-April 11.

Joy. K.J, Shah Amita (2006), Paranjape Subhas, Badiger Shrinivas, Lele Sharachchandra, *"Issues in Restructuring"*, Economic and Political Weekly, Vol.41.No 27 and 28, July8-July21.

Kerr John, Pagare Ganesh (1999), *"Participatory Watershed Development; Challenges for the Twenty Forst Century"*, Vedams Books, Delhi.

Krishna Anirudth (2003), *"Understanding, Measuring and Utilizing Social Capital: Clarifying Concepts and Presenting Field Application from India"*, CAPRi, Working paper no.28, January.

Krishna Sumi (2001), *"Towards A Genderscape of Community Rights in NaturaL Resource Management"*, Indian Journal Of Development Studies, Vol.8, No 2, 151-174.

Lin Nan (2000), *"Inequality in Social Capital"*, Contemporary Sociology, Vol 29, No.6(November, pp785-795

——(2006), *"Mainstreaming Gender in Water Management"*, UNDP Report, November.

Pantoja Enrique, *"Exploring the Concept of Community based Development: The Case of Coal Minning Areas in Orissa, India"*; Social Capital Initiatives, World Bank, Working Paper No. 18.

Seeley Janet, Batra Meenakshi and Sarin Madhu, *"Women's Participation in Watershed Development in India"*, Gatekeeper Series No 92, iied.

CHAPTER–11

SUSTAINABLE MANAGEMENT OF FARM LAND: A CASE STUDY FROM BIHAR

Vijay Laxmi

INTRODUCTION

Watershed development refers to the conservation, regeneration and judicious use of all the resources–natural and human-within a particular watershed. The management of watershed can bring a balance in the environment that can be sustained. Therefore, mechanism of watershed develop-ment requires an integrated approach of soil and land development, crop management, water management, livestock management, rural energy management, human resource development etc. Land being a very important resource plays a very crucial role in this endeavor.

Land resources in India are under heavy pressure due to growing human and livestock population, conversion of public forests and revenue lands, unwise use of chemical fertilizers and pesticides, thoughtless and careless disposal of industrial wastes, and some economic policies. Approximately 57% of total geographical area is degraded to varying degree (Table 1). Although there is a wide variation in the estimates of wastelands due to different approaches adopted by different agencies, physical degradation ranges from 53.3 mha (NRSA 1985) to 187.7 mha. (Sehgal and Abrol, 1994). The cultivable wastelands account for about 16 % of TGA (Chadha et al, 2004). Among the different categories of land, the land under cultivation faces the highest problem followed by grazing and pastureland, and forests. Therefore, there is a need to take urgent care of land degradation in crop cultivation. This need becomes even more pronounced in the wake of current situation of reducing/stagnant growth in agriculture, no possibility of increase in land for agriculture purposes in near future, and population growth. Therefore, there is a need to increase the food production with fewer resources. The significant part of increased food production has to come from rice wheat farming systems (RWS) (Srivastava & Mukhopadhya, 1997). Approximately three-fourth of the total rice area and half of the wheat area in India are under RWS and contributes about one third to total cereal production. However, studies have shown that growth in productivity of this m Vijay Laxmi, IGIDR, Mumbai cropping system is either stagnated or is declining mainly due to over exploitation of natural resources (Ladha *et al*, 2003; Kumar *et al.* 2002).

Therefore, there is an urgent need to address the issue of food and nutrition security through sustainable agriculture. A sustainable agriculture is such a system, which meets biophysical, environmental, economic and social objectives. For such a system, proper policy options and adoption of appropriate and improved agricultural technologies, becomes imperative for increasing productivity and conserving natural resources. This process will also help in addressing some of the issues of achieving the Millennium development Goals (MDG) specially those of MDG 1 (reducing poverty and hunger) and MDG 7 (sustaining environmental quality).

With this background, the objective of the present paper is to look into the issues of reducing land degradation and increasing the productivity of farm land with the use of some appropriate resource conservation technologies (RCTs) in Bihar state. For the effective adoption of any technology, it is important to understand peoples' perception. Therefore, peoples' perception and the factors, which affect the adoption of one such technology, are also discussed in this paper. Bihar is one of the poverty stricken states (41 per cent population below poverty line) with the proportion of agricultural labourers in the total workers being about 51% (NIRD, 2003). Rice wheat farming system (RWS) is the major farming system and approximately 36% of total geographical area (TGA) is under land degradation. The agriculture in this state is less capital intensive and the yield is much below the potential yield. Therefore, to improve the income and livelihoods of the people in Bihar, there is a need to increase the land productivity through new agronomic and improved crop management technologies, which also takes care of the natural resources. Section II deals with the land and soil resources of Bihar, while section III deals with principal crops. Issues related to RWS are discussed in the next section IV. Section V gives a brief description of the resource conservation technologies that can be used to increase the system productivity. In the sixth section, farmers' perception on one of the most adopted RCT, i.e., Zero Tillage in Bihar is reported followed by the factors responsible for adoption of ZT in section VII.

Table 1
Estimates of Degraded Land in India

(In Thousand Hectare)

States	*Total Geographical Area (TGA)*	*Net Sown Area*	*Degraded Land Area*	*Degraded Land As a % of TGA*
Andhra Pradesh	27505	10736	15662	57
Assam	7844	2762	2807	36
Bihar	17388	7329	6291	36
Gujarat	19602	9605	10336	53
Haryana	4421	3601	1384	31
Himachal Pradesh	5567	563	3008	54
Jammu & Kashmir	22224	734	2225	10
Karnataka	19197	10515	7681	40
Kerala	3886	2267	2608	67
Madhya Pradesh	44345	19773	26209	59
Maharashtra	30771	17894	13328	43
Orissa	15571	6089	6121	39

Contd.

States	Total Geographical Area (TGA)	Net Sown Area	Degraded Land Area	Degraded Land As a % of TGA
Punjab	5036	4139	896	18
Rajasthan	34244	16683	13586	40
Tamil Nadu	13006	5414	5273	41
Uttar Pradesh	29441	17437	15253	52
West Bengal	8875	5463	2752	31
Total	328726	142820	187700	57

Source: National Bureau of Soil Survey (NBSS) and Land Use Planning (LUP) (2000)

LAND AND SOIL RESOURCES OF BIHAR

Bihar is part of Indo Gangetic Plains and falls in the middle Gangetic plain region. The agro-climatic zones (ACZs) are South Bihar Alluvial Plain Zone-C3, North-West Alluvial Plain Zone-C4, and North East Alluvial Plain Zone- C5. ACZ C3 lies to the south of the Ganga river with the Sone river as the major tributary. It is comparatively free from recurring floods. The soils are well drained and water availability is very high. ACZ C4 lies on the east of river Gandak and north of Ganga river and is most frequently flooded. ACZ C5 is the second most severely affected flood prone area of the state after C4 (Narang & Virmani, 2001).

Bihar is the playing field of eight major rivers. The soil is mainly young loam, rejuvenated every year by constant deposition of silt, clay, and sand brought by different streams. The soil is generally deficient in phosphoric acid, nitrogen and humus. But potash and lime are usually in sufficient quantity. The state can be broadly divided into two parts, north Bihar and south Bihar. North Bihar is mainly flood affected and has problem of sodicity. Rainfed rice is grown in 60% of the area and farmers diversify crops due to varying topography. South Bihar has generally loam to silty clay loam soils and has canal irrigation system.

As per the National Bureau of Soil Survey and Land Use Planning, (Indian Council of Agricultural Research), extent of various kind of land degradation in Bihar (Bihar + Jharkhad) is given in Table 2. It shows that problem of water erosion and water logging is very high in the state. Out of the 93.6 lakh hectare of total geographical area in Bihar approximately 10% (9.41 lakh hectare) land is water logged (http://wrd.bih.nic.in/activities.html). The land utilization pattern of Bihar shows (Table 3) that area under current fallows is about 11.3% of net sown area, this area does not include the culturable wastelands. Thus a large portion of land is unutilized/under utilized for cultivation purposes in a given year. This under utilization is generally in low lying areas (chaur, diara, tal, and barind lands). Therefore, there is an urgent need to adopt appropriate crop establishment and agronomic practices to utilize these under utilized lands for enhancing the livelihood opportunities of the people.

Table 2
Extent of Various Kinds of Land Degradation in Bihar (Bihar+ Jharkhand) (Area in Thousand Hectare)

Geographical Area	17387
Degraded Area	6283
Water Erosion	3024
Wind Erosion	0
Water Logging	2001
Salinity/ Alkalinity	229
Soil Acidity	1029

Source: www.indiastat.com

Table 3
Land Utilization Pattern in Bihar (1997-98). Area in Thousand Hectare

Total geographical area	9350
Area under non-agricultural uses	1616
Forest area	616
Barren & unculturable wasteland	436
Permanent pastures & other grazing land	19
Land under misc. tree crops & groves	233
Culturable wasteland	51
Fallow land other than current fallow	152
Current fallow	632
Net sown area	5603
Area sown more than once	2343

Source: www.indiastat.com

PRINCIPAL CROPS OF BIHAR

Rice is the major crop grown in Bihar followed by wheat and maize (Table 4). The high yielding variety of paddy and wheat were grown in 1697 thousand and 1611 thousand hectare area respectively in 2001-02 (Table 4). The HYV are generally grown in irrigated areas. Rice wheat farming system (RWS) is being followed in approximately 1830 thousand hectare (Pal et al, 2003).

Table 4
Area (In Thousand Hectare) Under Principal Crops in Bihar

Crops	*1990-91*	*1991-92*	*1992-93*	*1993-94*
Rice	5390	5099	4510	4718
Wheat	1965	1985	1974	2070
Barley	55	51	41	38
Maize	665	689	697	722
Pulses				
Gram	168	150	127	132
Masoor	188	182	169	180
Arhar	66	65	66	76
Khesari	304	271	208	208
Peas	37	32	31	20
Commercial Crops				
Sugarcane	149	145	133	120
Tobacoo	15	15	16	14
Potatoes	160	168	159	183
Jute	137	155	107	121
Chillies	5	6	11	7

Source: http://www.indiastat.com

Table 4
Area (In Thousand Hectare) Under Cereals in Bihar (2001-2002)

Crops	*H.Y.V*	*L/V*	*Total*
Paddy	1697	1855	3552
Wheat	1611	515	2126
Maize	205	389	594
Barley	–	22	22
Ragi	–	20	20
Other millets	–	12	12
Total cereals	3513	2813	6326
Irrigated Area of Cereals Crops			

Contd.

Crops	*H.Y.V*	*L/V*	*Total*
Paddy	1329	601	1930
Wheat	1503	411	1914
Maize	122	223	345
Barley	–	–	–
Ragi	–	–	–
Other Millets	–	–	–
Total cereals	2954	1235	4189

Source: http://www.indiastat.com

Rice and wheat are the main crops, but the farmers diversify RWS with oilseeds, pulses, sugarcane, maize etc., mainly as a risk management strategy. Some farmers even take three crops of rice in a year, viz., aus, aman and boro rice. The major farming systems practiced by the farmers are as follows (Chandan, Parvesh, 2007).

Rice – potato - wheat

Rice - jute/rice

Rice - wheat/boro rice

Rice – potato - winter maize

Rice – potato - rice (boro)

Pigeonpea + green gram - wheat

Rice – potato + maize/boro rice

Rice +sesame + maize + mungbean – boro rice

ISSUES RELATED TO RWS IN BIHAR

As rice wheat farming systems (RWS) is the major farming system in Bihar. Therefore, there is a need to look into the issues involved with its cultivation. Some of the important issues are as follows

- Late planting of wheat
- Rice fallow
- Excessive moisture
- Water logged areas
- Salt affected soils
- Lack of infrastructure

LATE PLANTING OF WHEAT

Late planting of wheat is one of the major problems. It is estimated that if wheat is planted by third week of November, it will have the best yield. After that a yield decline at the rate of 1-1.5% per day is reported (Oritiz-Monasterio et al,1994; Randhawa et al 1981). Late planting also reduces the input use efficiency. On an average 15-33% loss in yield is estimated due to late planting of wheat. This is primarily due to the fact that wheat is a temperature sensitive crop and if planting is done after November in Bihar it gets short window available for growth and reproduction. It is being reported that approximately 26% (475 thousand Hectares) of total wheat planted in Bihar is under late planting. The potential yield of RWS in Bihar at optimal conditions are 16.4 t/ha (Aggrawal, 2000) whereas, current productivity of this system is only 4.5t/ha. Therefore, there is a wide yield gap, which needs to be tapped for sustaining not only the food security but also the livelihood of the people. Although realizing the potential yields in all the farmsers' field may not be economically viable and environmentally feasible, it definitely points towards the possibility of improving the productivity in the state.

The delay in planting of wheat crop is mainly due to the late harvest of the previous crop and/or a long turn-around time (Malik et al, 2002; Malik et al, 2004). The late harvest of the previous rice crop can be linked to both the late rice establishment and the duration of the rice crop. For instance, some farmers grow fine quality rice, which takes longer time to mature. The long turnaround time often reflects intensive tillage operations, soil moisture problems (too wet or too dry), unavailability of draught and mechanical power for plowing, and the urgency to store the rice crop before preparing land for wheat cultivation (Vijay Laxmi et al, 2007). In addition to this, there is a common practice of drying rice in the field itself for several days before threshing. This process further delays faster drying of soils in the wet soils. In the flood prone low-lying areas (ACZ C4 & C5), water recedes slowly. Thus takes a long time for land preparation through conventional intensive tillage. Need for intensive tillage for wheat is perceived by the farmers due to the difference in soil management practices for rice and wheat–the former being grown under anaerobic conditions and the latter under aerobic conditions. It has been reported that in Bihar, farmers go for on an average 6-7 tillage operations before wheat sowing (Vijay Laxmi et al, 2003).

RICE FALLOW

A large area in Bihar remains fallow after the kharif season rice crop. It has been reported by ICRISAT that approximately 37% of rice area remains fallow in Bihar. The main reasons for such fallows are unavailability of irrigation water for preparatory tillage in uplands and midlands and late receding of flood water, excessive soil moisture etc. in low lying areas. It is possible to improve the productivity of cropping system, by timely planting of rice and timely planting of wheat or other winter crops in the uplands or midlands. To realize this, there is a need to conserve some ground water for raising paddy nurseries so that transplantation is possible with the onset of the monsoon rains.

EXCESSIVE MOISTURE AND WATER LOGGING PROBLEM

As stated earlier, approximately 10% of crop land in Bihar is faced with water logging problem. Improved technologies can be adopted to increase the overall productivity of the cropping system by utilization of these lands.

SALT AFFECTED SOILS

In Bihar, around 1,53 thousand hectares land is salt affected (CSSRI, Karnal). Most of the salt affected soils are alkaline in nature (approximately, 1,06 thousand ha) having pH > 8.4 and ESP (exchangeable sodium percentage) > 15. These soils need special treatment for crop cultivation.

OTHERS

Lack of infrastructure viz., road, quality input supply system, electricity, proper irrigation facility at the appropriate time are also reasons for lower productivity of the RWS. Further, fragmented holdings and poor on-farm development also add to this under utilization. Therefore, there is need to enhance cost competitiveness in RWS. Farmers will have to produce more with fewer resources and with even less environmental degradation. This is possible by addressing these issues, through adoption of appropriate and improved agricultural technologies that are more productive and conserve resources.

RESOURCE CONSERVATION TECHNOLOGIES TO ADDRESS ISSUES RELATED TO RWS

Resource conservation technologies (RCTs) are the practices, which result in higher production at less cost with more efficient use of resources (both natural and man made), to produce a crop (Hobbs & Gupta, 2003). Some of the RCTs that can be practiced in the field by the farmers for addressing the problems listed in the earlier section are briefly described in this section.

FURROW IRRIGATED RAISED BEDS

In this system, crops are planted on top of raised beds that are usually superficially reshaped for sowing the next crop. Irrigation is applied through the furrows between the beds. There is water conservation (approximately 50% in rice crop) and good drainage conditions can be maintained (Hobbs & Gupta, 2003). The benefit from bed planting for crops and especially for wheat production is enhanced field access, which facilitates controlling of weeds and other pests, handling nutrients, reducing tillage, and managing crop residues. Studies have shown that raised bed gives farmers more yields with increased water use efficiency. Diversification of crop is possible with it and is very helpful in the long run. This method can be used in the upland and midland areas where water availability during wheat crop is a problem. To tackle the problem of salt affected soils and use them for cultivation, soils can be reclaimed by chemical treatment and treated soils can be used for bed preparation. The bed will give sufficient depth for rooting. Even in the areas where water recedes late from the field, timely establishment of the crop on the bed is possible.

LEAF COLOUR CHART (LCC)

The LCC is a good eco-friendly cheap tool in the hands of small farmers to approximately optimize N use, irrespective of the source of N applied-organic, bio-, or chemical fertilizers for rice crop. It was observed during a study that 74 per cent of the farmers obtained equal or higher yields in LCC N-managed trails and saved N on an average 25 kg/ ha (Balasubramanian et al., 2003). This chart will be very helpful for the resource poor farmers in Bihar.

LASER LEVELING

Leveling of field is required for uniform seeding and good water control that results in relatively higher yields. Land leveling becomes faster, easier and more precise with the use of laser technology. The laser-leveling system consists of a laser transmitter, a laser receiver and mast (a control box for tilt control) and a hydraulic interface. There are two types of laser leveling, dry and wet laser leveling. Studies have shown that with the adoption of laser leveling farmers were able to reap significant savings in irrigation water, efficient use of inputs and higher yields (Balasubramanian et al., 2003).

ZERO TILLAGE AND REDUCED TILLAGE

Zero tillage (ZT) technology is one of the most widely adopted RCTs in the IGP for RWS. ZT implies planting crops in previously unprepared soil by opening a hole, narrow slot, or trench, to obtain proper coverage of the seed. "Though the name refers to only one practice, zero till actually is a farm management system that involves many agricultural practices, including planting, residue management, weed and pest control, harvesting, and rotation" (Ekboir, 2002).

The existing ZT technology in the rice-wheat systems uses a tractor drawn zero-till-seed drill to establish wheat in the rice stubble. Field experiments for ZT dry seeded rice after ZT wheat are also showing good results in Bihar. But till date ZT wheat is the only RCT which is being widely adopted on the farmers' field. Zero-till-seed-cum-fertilizer drill is often made up of a conventional seed drill fitted with sharp edged modified furrow openers, a calibrated engraved disc, and a cup mechanism for placing fertilizer. The machine opens a number (6-11) of narrow slits for placement of seed and fertilizer at the depth of 7.5–10 cm into the soil (Mehla et al., 2000). Many farmers go for reduced tillage where they go for one or two tillage operations before using ZT drill machine. In this process also total number of tillage operations reduce from conventional tillage practices.

Thus ZT greatly reduces the turnaround time allowing wheat establishment in a single pass almost immediately after rice harvest (Malik et al, 2002; Vijay Laxmi et al, 2003). Studies have shown that ZT technology by reducing soil movement serves as an effective control measure of important weed of wheat, *P. minor* (Malik et al., 2002). ZT potentially reduces irrigation water use and thereby reduces pressure on aquifers and soils.

There are manifold advantages of ZT technology. It generates higher yields at lower production costs. It is an environmental friendly practice and saves irrigation water requirement, and reduces soil and air pollution (Vijay Laxmi, et al, 2003; Hobbs et al., 1997). A study by Vijay Laxmi, et al, 2007a, has shown that investment towards ZT technology R&D produces high welfare gains. A conservative ex-ante assessment by this study shows that it has a benefit cost ratio of 39, and net present value of US$ 94 million.

This technology can be adopted for addressing the issue of late planting of wheat and any other crop. If rice crop leaves the farm late or excess moisture preclude from seed establishment, ZT provides an opportunity to catch up with the time. Thus helps in reducing the rice fallow. Saving in time can also be used for the diversification of RWS by adopting short duration leguminous crop in between wheat and rice crop.

SURFACE SEEDING

One of the major problems in Bihar is excess soil moisture. This excessive soil moisture prevents field operations using machines. In such a situation, farmers can go for surface seeding for timely sowing of the crop. This method is best suited for fine textured and poorly drained soils. In RWS, wheat seeds can be directly broadcasted on the moist soil. No machines are required and it saves labour and tillage and hence it is very cost effective. Care is needed to ascertain the optimum amount of wetness. As excessive moisture will cause seed to rot and too little will affect germination adversely. It is being reported that in Patna, Bihar surface seeded wheat yield was much higher (33.3 qtl/ha) than the conventional farmer's practices (28.1 qtl/ha) (Chandna et al, 2004). Care needs to be taken for weed management. This method can be used to address the late planting of crop and rice fallow problem.

DRY SEEDED RICE ON NONPUDDLED SOILS

In this method, dry seeds of rice are grown on well prepared dry or moist soil without puddling it. Seed-cum-fertilizer drill can be used to sow the seeds. The rice can be grown as aerobic rice without standing water in the bunded field. Crop can be supplemented with irrigation if necessary. This method allows for early establishment of the crop but will increase the crop maturity time by 15 days (Balasubramanian et al., 2003). However, this increase in time is being compensated to some extent by the savings made in puddling and transplanting operations. Further, management of weeds becomes a major problem. If weeds can be controlled, this method is very cost effective and resource saving.

The problem, of no utilization (culturable waste land, fallow land), under-utilization of farmland and increasing the productivity of the system, can be addressed though adoption of appropriate mix of complementary resource conservation technology. Such problem cannot be addressed at broad watershed level, but requires area and site specific planning. Therefore, involvement at gross root level, in this case farmer, is must. Thus getting feed back from them about their perception and suggestions for improvement of technology application becomes imperative. In the next section farmers' perception about one such technology is presented.

ROLE OF RESOURCE CONSERVATION TECHNOLOGIES-FARMERS' PERCEPTION

After discussing these technologies, there is a need to analyze benefits accruing to the farmers and to understand their perceptions. For this purpose, the results of a study conducted for one such widely adopted technology i.e., ZT is reported. For this study the primary data was collected from Begusarai district of north Bihar. Equal number of both adopters and non-adopter were selected from this district. Thus a total of 200 households were selected for analyzing the economic benefits and farmers' perception. This survey was apart of the survey conducted for "Roles of Agriculture" project funded by FAO (http://www.fao.org/es/ESA/Roa/ROA-e/case_studies-e.htm#India).

The data were collected in collaboration with Rice Wheat Consortium (RWC) for the Indo Gangetic Plains. The questionnaire was tested and modified after the pilot survey in the field. Data were collected during the period May 2003-June 2003. The information recorded from the farmers included different input use in the field, different farming operations performed and yield. Perceptions about ZT were recorded from both adopters and non-adopters for different set of questions.

SAMPLE DESCRIPTION

The sample description is given in Table 5. The average size of family for ZT adopters is 7 whereas for non-adopters it is 6.

Table 5
Description of Sample

Variables	*ZT Adopters*	*Conventional Tillage (CT)*
Sample size	96	100
Family Size	7	6
Age	42	47
Area (ha)	1.11	1.37
% of non-farm income in total income	38.6	50.5

Operational holding of adopters is 1.11 hectare as against 1.37 hectare for non-adopters.

FARM OPERATION IN WHEAT CROP IN BIHAR

The survey results presented in Table 6 show that in the selected village of Begusarai district the conventional tillage requires about five passes of tractor before sowing of seeds, whereas for ZT/RT it is one. Thus total savings in land preparation is of four tillage operations. The labour hours involved per tillage operation is approximately 22 hours and amount of diesel required per tillage is 18.5 liters per hectare (See Table 6). The ZT saves on these because of only one tillage operation performed. Sowing charges for ZT and CT are Rs 319 and 283 respectively. Sowing charges for ZT is relatively high because rental charges of seed drill cum zero tiller is also included in it. CT requires more labour hours for sowing as compare to ZT. The analysis has shown a significant increase in the wheat yield due to adoption of ZT with a net saving of Rs 2185 per hectare.

Table 6
Farm Operation in Wheat

Variables	*ZT*	*CT*
No. of tillage	1	5*
Labour hour involved in land preparation (hrs/ha)	5.9	21.7
Amt of diesel (lts/ha)	3.44	18.5*
Sowing charge (Rs/ha/lab)	318.6	283
No. of irrigation	2	2
Time taken for first irrigation (hrs/Ha)	17.0	17.6
Yield (quintals/hectare)	27	25*

Note: * Significant at 5% level of significance
Source: Adopted from Vijay Laxmi et al. 2003

FARMERS' PERCEPTION

The perceptions were recorded from both adopters and non-adopters of ZT technology for wheat. Except for common questions to get general perceptions: there were different set of questions for both. Table 7 shows that about 64 per cent of adopters and 63 per cent of non-adopters view availability of labor as 'not easy'. Both adopters and non-adopters viewed possibility of increase in yield due to zero tillage. Early sowing and early germination of seed due to ZT was perceived higher by the non-adopters than by the adopters.

Table 7
Perception of All Farmers-Bihar

	ZT		CT	
Query	*Frequency*	*Percentage*	*Frequency*	*Percentage*
Availability of labor for cultivation				
Easy	1	1.04	14	14
Ok	34	35.4	21	21
Not easy	61	63.6	63	63
Increase in yield				
Yes	84	87.5	82	82
No	9	9.4	11	11
No response	11	11.5	7	7
Possibility of early sowing				
Yes	93	96.9	91	91
No	1	1.0	6	6
No response	2	2.1	3	3
Early seed germination				
Yes	82	85.4	90	90
No	2	2.1	4	4
No response	12	12.5	2	2

Source: Adopted from Vijay Laxmi et al 2003

PERCEPTION OF ADOPTERS

The survey data show that it is friends, relatives and other farmers who were the services providers and also the source of information as per Table 8. The role of agricultural university, extension worker is not perceived as significant. Reduction in fertilizer use was reported by 49 per cent of adopters whereas 45 per cent were of the view that there is no change. Additional saving due to adoption of ZT was perceived highest (25%) in the range of Rs 401 to Rs 600 per hectare. Decrease in weed infestation was reported by 85 per cent of the adopters. About the increase in the disease infestation, 74 per cent of the adopters were of the view that it has not increased whereas 11 per cent were of the view that disease infestation has gone up after adoption of the technology. (see Table 8).

Table 8
Perceptions of Adopters of ZT: Source of Information, Input Use and Savings

Questions	*Responses Percentage*
Source of information	
Department of agriculture/Extension worker	13.5
Agricultural University	2.1
Friends/Relatives/other farmers	83.3
Other sources	0.00
No response	1.0
Reduction in fertilizer use	
Yes	49
No	44.8
No response	6.3
Additional savings (Rs)	
200-400	12.5
401-600	24
601-800	20.8
801-1000	16.7
1001-2000	8.3
2001-4000	5.2
>4000	3.1
No response	8.3
Increase in yield	
A great extent	17.7
Some extent	69.8
Did not increase	9.4
Decreased	1.0
No response	2.1
Change in weed infestation	
Increased	1.0
Decreased	85.4
Can not say	12.5
No response	1.0
Increase in disease infestation	
Yes	11.5
No	74
No response	14.6

Source: Adopted from Vijay Laxmi et al. 2003

Improvement in the soil quality to a large extent was reported by only 10 per cent of the farmers, whereas 38 per cent reported the improvement moderately. Use of irrigation water efficiency was reported by the 84 per cent of the adopters where as 2 per cent of the adopters were of the view that irrigation water requirement has gone up. About 47 per cent of adopters were of the view that about 20-30 per cent of water is being saved due to ZT (Table 9).

Table 9
Perceptions of Adopters of ZT: Natural Resources

Questions	*Responses Percentage*
Improvement in soil quality	
To large extent	10.4
Moderately	38.5
Very less improvement	4.2
No improvement	14.6
Decreased	3.1
No response	29.2
Quantity of water	
Increased use	2.1
Decreased use	84.4
No change	12.5
No response	1.0
Reduction in water requirement	
upto 20 %	24
20%-30%	46.9
30%-40%	12.5
40%-50%	14.6
No response	2.1

Source: Adopted from Vijay Laxmi et al. 2003

Table 10
Perceptions of Adopters of ZT: Suggestions to Improve Application

Question	*Response Percentage*
Make available the spare parts	40.6
Initial training of machine operation	1.0
Regular monitoring of running machine is required	0.0
Timely availability of machine	10.4
1,2 & 4	1.0
2, 3 & 4	8.3
2, 3 & 5	1.0
No response	37.5

Source: Adopted from Vijay Laxmi et al 2003

Suggestions to improve the ZT application, by the adopters were: make available the spare parts (41 per cent), followed by timely availability of the machine (10 %). Approximately 37 percent of the adopters have not responded to this query (Table 10).

PERCEPTION OF NON-ADOPTERS

Most of the non-adopters (97%) were aware of the ZT going on in the nearby area. Those who were aware, 92 per cent of them were willing to adopt ZT. But the constraint in adoption was the query recorded as 'others' for 65 per cent of respondent. Under this category, farmers reported the discrimination in availability due to caste and social status. Non-availability was reported by only the 26 per cent of the respondent. Those who were not interested in adopting ZT perceived no benefit in it and are the ones who are not aware of this technology (Table 11).

Table 11
Perception of Non Adopters

Query	*Response Percentage*
Awareness of ZT going on in near by area	
Yes	97
No	3
If yes, interested in adopting the technology	
Yes	91.8
No	8.3
If interested, what are the constraints	
Availability of technology	25.8
Cash constraint	2.1
Others	65
No response	7.2
Reasons for not interested in adopting ZT	
Very expensive	
Time consuming	
I don't see any benefit out of it	3 (people not aware

Source: Adopted from Vijay Laxmi et al 2003

From the perception of both adopters and non-adopters given above it is seen that farmers perceive very high benefits from adoption of ZT. It will be interesting to look into the factors that are responsible for adoption of ZT. The next section deals with the same.

FACTORS RESPONSIBLE FOR ADOPTION

The factors responsible for adoption of ZT have been reported by Vijay Laxmi and Vinod Mishra (2007). They have used the same data set that was collected for recording the perception in the Begusarai district of Bihar. The results of the study indicate, that the probability of adoption is higher for the experienced but relatively young farmers. There is a need to have resource allocation to improve the human capital mainly through mass media exposure for adoption of the technology. Though extension programmes, village community meetings, farmer fairs etc. are deemed to improve adoption but in this case, role of these factors have shown insignificant effect. There is need to focus on this issue, as in Table 8a also it is identified that source of information is mainly friends, relatives and friends, not the formal government sources. Further, availability of credit both formal and informal is being identified as important factor. Therefore, for promoting new technology, availability and accessibility of credit should be ensured.

CONCLUSIONS

Land is one of the most important components of watershed development. Ownership of and access to productive land is very important resource for promoting economic well being and socio-cultural identity. Land resources in India are under heavy pressure due to increase in human and livestock population, poverty and economic policies. Approximately, 57% of total geographical area is degraded to varying degree. Among the different categories of land, the land under cultivation faces the highest problem. Therefore, there is a need to take urgent care of land degradation in crop cultivation.

It is being recognized that to meet the demand of the growing population the Indian farmers will have to produce more with fewer resources. The significant part of this increase has to come from RWS. However, studies show that productivity of this cropping system is either stagnated or decreasing due to over exploitation of natural resources. Therefore, there is a need to focus on sustainable agriculture which will address some of the issues of achieving the Millennium Development Goals (MDG 1 and MDG 7). RCTs such as bed planting, ZT, LCC, etc. can help in such an endeavor. The mix area/site specific appropriate complementary technologies need to be adopted for improving system productivity and conservation of natural resources. Therefore, it becomes imperative to understand farmers' perception on these technologies. To address this issue farmers' perception on widely adopted technology, i.e., ZT is reported.

The records of farmers' perception show that farmers are willing to adopt ZT in Bihar. Farmers perceived very high economic benefits from adoption. The main constraint in adoption for technology as perceived by the farmers was timely availability of the ZT machine. This calls for better public-private partnership. The study shows that government extension officers and agricultural college need to play a more active role in disseminating the awareness about new technologies. Further, there is a need to have resource allocation to improve the human capital and availability of credit for enhancing the efficiency of adoption.

Therefore, there is need to implement the complementary resource conservation technologies suitable to the particular area. Policy reforms are needed to create enabling environment for sustainable agriculture. Further, RWS needs to be diversified with introduction of short duration paddy crop and leguminous crops. This is possible by adopting suitable resource conservation technologies.

REFERENCES

Aggarwal., P.K., Talukdar, K.K., and Mall, R.K. (2000), Potential Yields of Rice-Wheat System in Indo-Gangetic Plains of India. Rice Wheat Consortium paper Series 10. 16 p.

Balasubramanian, V, Ladha J.K., Gupta R.K., Naresh R. K.,. Mehla R.S, Singh B. and Singh Y. (2003), Technology Options for Rice in Rice -Wheat System in South Asia. In: Ladha, J.K.et al (Eds.), Improving the Productivity and Sustainability of Rice-wheat

Systems: Issues and Impacts. ASA Special Publication Number 65. ASA-CSSA-SSSA, Madison, Wisconsin, USA, pp. 115-148.

Chadha, G.K., Sen, S., Sharma, H.R. (2004), *State of the Indian Farmer*, Academic Foundation, New Delhi.

Chandna, P., D.P. Hodson, U.P. Singh, A.N. Singh, A.K. Gosain, R.N. Sahoo, and R.K. Gupta (2004), Increasing the Productivity of Underutilized Lands by Targeting Resource Conserving Technologies-A GIS/Remote Sensing Approach: A Case Study of Ballia District, Uttar Pradesh, in the Eastern Gangetic Plains. Mexico D.F.: CIMMYT.

Ekboir, J. (2002), Developing No-Till Packages for Small-Scale Farmers. In: Ekboir, J. (Ed.), CIMMYT 2000-2001 World Wheat Overview and Outlook. CIMMYT, Mexico,DF, pp. 1-38.

Hobbs, P.R., Giri, G.S., Grace, P. (1997), Reduced and Zero Tillage Options for the Establishment of Wheat after Rice in South Asia. Rice-Wheat Consortium Paper Series 2. RWC, New Delhi, India.

Hobbs, P.R., Gupta, R.K. (2003), Resource-Conserving Technologies for Wheat in the Rice-Wheat System. In: Ladha, J.K.et al (Eds.), Improving the Productivity and Sustainability of Rice-wheat Systems: Issues and Impacts. ASA Special Publication Number 65. ASA-CSSA-SSSA, Madison, Wisconsin, USA, pp. 149-172.

Kumar, P., Jha, D., Kumar, A., Chaudhary, M.K., Grover, R.K., Singh, R.K., Mitra, A., Joshi, P.K., Singh, A., Badal, P.S., Mittal, S., Ali, J. (2002), Economic Analysis of Total Factor Productivity of Crop Sector in Indo-Gangetic Plain of India by District and Region. Agricultural Economics Research Report 2. Indian Agricultural Research Institute, New Delhi, India.

Malik, R.K., Balyan, R.S., Yadav, A., Pahwa, S.K., (Eds.) (2002), Herbicide Resistance Management and Zero Tillage in Rice-wheat Cropping System. Proceedings of International Workshop, 4-6 March, 2002. Chaudhary Charan Singh Haryana Agricultural University (CCSHAU), Hisar, India.

Mehla, R.S., Verma, J.K., Gupta, R.K., Hobbs, P.R. (2000), Stagnation in the Productivity of Wheat in the Indo-Gangetic Plains : Zero-till-seed-cum-fertilizer Drill as an Integrated Solution. Rice-Wheat Consortium Paper Series 8. RWC, New Delhi, India.

Narang, R.S. and Virmani S.M. (2001), Rice-Wheat Cropping Systems of the Indo-gangetic Plain of India. Rice Wheat Consortium Paper Series 11, 36 p.

——(2003), NIRD, Rural Development Statistics 2002-2003. p 55.

Sehgal J. and Abrol, I.P. (1994), Soil Degradation in India: Status and Impact, Oxford and IBH Publishing Co.

Srivastava, J.P. and M. Mukhopadhya (1997), Sustainable Intensification of Rice-Wheat Cropping Systems in India. Prepared for the Seminar on "Sustainable Intensification of Agricultural Production Systems", Learning and Leadership Center. The World Bank.

Ortiz-Monasterio, J.I., Dhillon, S.S., Fischer, R.A. (1994), Date of Sowing Effects on Grain Yield and Yield Components of Irrigated Spring Wheat Cultivars and Relationships with Radiation and Temperature in Ludhiana, India. Field Crops Research, 37 (3) 169-184.

Pal, S., Jha, A.K., Goel, R., Gulia, P.K. (2003), Ploughing Against Traditional Wisdom: Impact of Resource Conservation Technologies for the Rice-wheat System. National Centre for Agricultural Economics and Policy Research, New Delhi, India.

Randhaw, A.S., Dhillon, S.S., Singh, D. (1981), Productivity of Wheat Varieties, as influenced by the time of sowing. Journal of Research. Punjab Agricultural University, Ludhiana.

——(2004), RWC, Highlights 2003-2004. Rice-Wheat Consortium for the Indo Gangetic Plains, New Delhi, India.

Vijay Laxmi, Gupta, R.K., Swarnalatha, A., Perwaz, S. (2003), Environmental Impact of Improved Technology-Farm Level Survey and Farmers' Perception on Zero Tillage (Case Study). Paper presented at Roles of Agriculture Workshop 20-22 October, 2003, Rome, Italy. (http://www.fao.org/es/ESA/Roa/ROA-e/case_studies-e.htm#India).

Vijay Laxmi, Erenstein O., Gupta R. K. (2007a), "The Case of Zero Tillage Technology in India" in *The Impact of Natural Resource Management.*

Research: Studies from the CGIAR, edited by Hermann Waibel and David Zilberman. CABI. pp 68-91.

Vijay Laxmi, and Mishra V. (2007), "Factors Affecting Adoption of Resource Conservation Technology: Case of Zero Tillage Technology in Rice Wheat Farming Systems", *Indian Journal of Agricultural Economic*, vol. 62 (1), pp. 126-138.

CHAPTER–12

REDEFINING WATER REGIMES FOR GROWTH: AN IMPACT ASSESSMENT OF WATERSHED APPROACH

S.C. Srivastava

:"Once upon a time this universe was made of darkness, without anything that could be discerned, without any distinguishing marks, impossible to know through reasoning or understanding, it seemed to be entirely asleep. Then the lord who is self existent, himself unmanifest, caused this universe to become manifest; putting his energy into great elements of everything else, became visible and dispelled the darkness——first he emitted water—. "

(Manusmriti)

INTRODUCTION

Water In Government Policy: Since independence till recently, that is before the emergence of the concept of community based watershed projects, water has been treated in the government policy mainly from two perspectives- irrigation and drinking water. And the majority of schemes under these two were government owned. Water regimes, for the first time assumed greater significance during the late sixties and more intensively since around the beginning of the seventies, thanks to New Agricultural Technology (NAT)-so heavily dependent on water-both within the region and among the individuals. The

NAT basically altered the entire water usage pattern within regions and within villages and also affected the traditional institutions and traditional systems.

With the advent of Green Revolution in country, the efforts were focused on bringing more area under cultivation and increasing the crop productivity per unit hectare. This resulted in over exploitation of groundwater resources. However, the 'betting on strong' along with government initiatives to develop irrigation water led to disparities among different categories of the farmers and changed the traditional arrangements of crop sharing practices. The net result was an acute growth in the landless and agricultural labourers. The focus of the government policy therefore, was shifted for the first time in Fourth Five Year Plan on small and marginal farmers and agricultural labourers. Moreover, the geographical barriers to development were also recognized during the same plan and proper emphasis was put on Drought Prone and Desert areas. Thus during the Fourth Five Year Plan some specific polices were initiated to help the poor most of whom belong to the category of marginal farmers and even small farmers in geographically chastised areas. No need to mention, land and water were the prime criteria to categorize farmers and areas, respectively. The policy initiative indirectly accepted the fact that institutional arrangements under the government mainly benefited the rich and the various incentives to develop own irrigation sources also went in their favour as they had the capacity to invest. This had implication for ground water use in the country. As practically the ground water is a matter of private ownership and use under the Easement Act, the net results was that in a few states this potential had been overexploited to meet the demands of green revolution and is a major point of concern now.

The Costs of Distortions: While the use and exploitation was done by the rich, the burnt were felt mainly by the poor. For the poor, the government started thinking since Fourth Five Year Plan. Almost all the programmes initiated since then, mainly in the name of development, talked about development of minor irrigation for the benefit of the poor (small and Marginal farmers, landless and agricultural labourers). Since then the shape of these programmes has changed drastically but the central theme remains to be there- water as the major natural resource and instrument for the uplifting of the poor. However, despite all theses initiatives, more than 60 percent of cultivated land in the country remains to be dependent on monsoon.

REDEFINING WATER REGIMES THROUGH WATER-SHEDS

There is long history of water management regimes n the country with the traditional institutional arrangements now operational only in a few places. These institutional arrangements in general have been relegated to the background in the past few decades, especially since the advent of New Agricultural technology. Most of these institutional arrangements unfortunately belonged to the common property regimes. The tank irrigation showed decline in terms of net irrigated area and siltation is common in many tanks. In this condition, creation of watersheds covering wider area seemed promising for rainwater harvesting potential and conservation and developing bio-mass and fuel wood. It is an area based approach which would cover the ridge, middle and valley portion of the watercourse. The approach of the guidelines of watershed encompassed lands of all sections of the population and assumed to involve the whole community in the development and maintenance of watersheds. Instead of going into the details of watershed guidelines, all that we can say here is that these guidelines seek gainful and transparent utilization of public funds for watershed development, with a view to promoting the overall economic development and improving the socio-economic condition of the resource poor and the disadvantaged sections of the people inhabiting the project areas.

The objectives of Watershed Development Projects are as follows:–

(i) Developing wastelands/degraded lands, drought-prone and desert areas on watershed basis, keeping in view the capability of land, site-conditions and local needs.

(ii) Promoting the overall economic development and improving the socio-economic condition of the resource poor and disadvantaged sections inhabiting the programme areas.

(iii) Mitigating the adverse effects of extreme climatic conditions such as drought and desertification on crops, human and livestock population for their overall improvement.

(iv) Restoring ecological balance by harnessing, conserving and developing natural resources i.e. land, water, vegetative cover.

(v) Encouraging village community for

(a) Sustained community action for the operation and maintenance of assets created and further development of the potential of the natural resources in the watershed.

(b) Simple, easy and affordable technological solutions and institutional arrangements that make use of, and build upon local technical knowledge and available materials.

PRESENT STUDY

NEED

The issue of water regimes, in recent times, have attracted good amount of attention mainly on part of activists, human rights' associations, development economists and development practitioners. One prime reason for this increased attention has been the recent methodologies adopted on part of the Governments in developing countries and Civil Society Organizations, especially through the informal structures at the grass roots level. The right to use water for development purposes as bestowed in the state itself is now challenged. The prolonged protests over multi purpose dams like Sardar Sarovar is living example where the right of livelihoods of the common people and the development interventions of the state are at conflicting ends. At the micro level, the philosophy of promotion of the watershed management committees, water users associations, irrigation society's etc have put a new thrust on the natural resource management through participatory efforts.

MAJOR OBJECTIVES OF THE STUDY

In view of the above present study was undertaken with following objectives-

- To analyze the changing pattern of access and management of water resources from a demand and supply perspective.
- To study the role of emerging formal and informal organizations in changing the access to water resources in the common pool.
- To explore impact of the watershed project on socio-institutional and socio-economic dimension of the village economy.

STUDY AREA AND COVERAGE AND SCOPE

The study area covers one of the drought prone districts in the country–Rajkot district in Gujarat The study confines to emerging patterns of the water management institutions, use and accessibility patterns of water and implications of these new patterns on the traditional rights of the poor.

RESEARCH METHODOLOGY AND ANALYTICAL FRAME-WORK

The study is conducted with the help of primary and secondary data obtainable from various sources. Data is also be collected from the households especially poor, women and other sections of the society. Different local institutions available in the area like Panchayats, Village Councils, Programme Implementing Agency for Watershed implementation, Water users Associations, Irrigation Committees, etc., were contacted for the purpose of gathering information adopting the Participatory techniques.

AMARAPAR WATERSHED PROJECT: BROAD FEATURES

The present study explores the impact of one watershed project in Amarapar Village of Rajkot district of Gujarat The Amarapar watershed project was initiated in 1998 under National Watershed Programme and is one among 437 watershed projects in Rajkot district of Gujarat state under NWDP. The district is one of the seven districts in the Saurastra region of the state. This region is essentially dry region and classified as Draught Prone Area as per the agro climatic zoning of the country. Also this is the region which got worst affected during 2000 earthquakes rocking almost two third of the state.

THE ENTRY POINT VILLAGE

Amarapar village is located about sixty km. in the Northern side of the Rajkot district headquarters and falls under the Tankara Block. Till recently the village formed a part of Maurbi block, a well known name now courtesy the 2000 earthquakes. The village has a population of 1160 persons (590 males and 570 females) in 250 households. Of these 250 households, almost 160 had lost their houses during the great earthquake. All these houses are now rebuilt by people's courage and government assistance. Based on the damages caused by the earthquake in 2000 the village was put in G5 category. 82 households received earthquake grants to the tune of Rs. 95000/ each for reconstruction. At the time of the visits to the village, the adverse impact of the earthquake was totally invisible as people had already recovered from it with government assistance, their hard work and their brave attitude. The village has a history of cohesive and harmonious relationship.

Compared to male literacy rate of sixty percent the female literacy rate is just half bringing down the average literacy rate in the village to 45 percent which is much below the district average of sixty percent.

Out of 1160 persons 575 are working people in the village which means the work participation rate is very high at nearly fifty percent. Majority (71 percent) is engaged in self cultivation followed by sixty persons (10.46 percent) working as farm labourers (Table 3)

Table 1
Caste wise Distribution of Households

Details	*Farmer*	*Other*	*Total*
S C	10	m	11
ST	–	–	–
OBC	9	3	12
Others	224	3	227
Total	243	7	250
BPL Households	–	–	40

Table 2
Literacy Status

Details	*Male*	*Female*	*Total*
Literate	354 *(60)*	*171* *(30)*	525 *(45.26)*
Illiterate	236 (40)	399 (70)	635 (54.74)
Total	590 (100)	570 (100)	1160 (100)

Table 3
Employment Activity

Details	*Number*			
	Male	*Female*	*Total*	*Approximate Annual Working Days*
Self farming	210	200	410	170
Farm labour	35	25	60	200
Involved in sahkari mandali-	–	–	–	
Employment other than farming	25	5	30	265
Maldhari	15	55	70	300
Other	15	–	15	180

LAND USE AND AGRARIAN STRUCTURE

The village has a total area of 748 hectares of which more than 68 percent is put to cultivation. Apparently 200 hectares of the 513 hectares under cultivation, is under irrigation but the intensity of irrigation is just once a year. Another nine percent of the total village area is under wasteland. Nearly nine percent of the village land is under the Panchayat control (Table 4).

Table 4
Village Land Use and WDP Coverage

Area	*Total Area*	*Area Covered Under Watershed Project*
Total geographic area covered under the Watershed Programme	648 (86.63)	648
Private land		
irrigated	200	200
unirrigated	313	313
Total under cultivation	513 (68.58)	
Forest Area	–	–
Waste land	70 (9.36)	70
Panchayat land-Govt. Waste land	66 (8.82)	66
Other area	100 (13.37)	
Total	748	648

Source: DRDA, Rajkot

The village has a mixed topographic structure. Out of 648 hectares under the watershed treatment, 500 hectares or seventy seven percent is flat land and 100 hectares (15.43 percent) is under small hills (Table 5). The soil by and large is black cotton type with low permeability of water Table 6).

The average rainfall in the study area is just 400 mm per annum distributed over four months with a total of 24 rainy days in the year (Table 7).

Table 5
Topographic Features

Area	*Total Area*	*Area Covered Under Watershed*
Flat land	500	500
Undulating land	–	–
Ravine area	–	–
Hilly area	100	100
Other	48	48
Total	648	648

Table 6
Soil Type

Area	*Total Area*	*Area Covered Under Watershed*
Sandy soil land	–	–
Black cotton soil	500	500
Latretic soil	–	–
Stony thin soil	100	100
Others	48	48
Land slope	–	–
Total	648	648

Table 7
Rainfall and Month wise Distribution of Rainfall

Months	*Number of Rainy days*
June	5 days
July	9 days
August	7 days
September	3 days
Total	24 days

CROPPING PATTERN

Cotton is the main crop of the village. Cotton alone accounts for more than fifty eight percent of total cropped area. Only thirty three percent of the cropped area under cotton is under irrigation. Wheat (13.64 percent) and groundnut (11..70 percent) are other two important crops in terms of area under cultivation. Besides, some other crops which are essential feature of any dry land cropping like Bajar and Jowar are also being grown in the village.

Distribution of Land and Irrigation Resources: The village scene is dominated by some inequalities in terms of land holdings. We have seen earlier that in the present scheme of things under the watershed programme landholding is one of the major determinants of benefits of the project. Out of 243 farmer households 110 or more than forty five percent are small farmers. The forty five percent of small farmers, however, own only twenty three percent of the land. On the other hand four percent of the big landowners own more than seventeen percent of the land. Similarly, forty one percent of the medium farmers acquire nearly fifty six percent of land. The benefit of any scheme aiming at improvement of irrigation facilities are likely to be favorable to the big and medium farmers. Well is the major source of irrigation. Out of 195 wells, 125 are owned by big and medium farmers. The small farmers mainly depend on pond (only one in the village) and a nearby canal, which is more often than not in dried state.

Table 8
Distribution of Area Under Crops

	Crop Land (Ha in 2000)			*Approximate Production (Kg per Ha)*	
Name of Crop	*Irrigated**	*Unirrigated**	*Total***	*Irrigated*	*Unirrigated*
Bajra	5 (33.33)	10 (66.67)	15 (2.92)	1200	240
Wheat	70 (100)	–	70 (13.64)	3000	–
Cotton	100 (33.37)	200 ((66.67)	300 (58.48)	6000	1500
Gram	–	5 (100)	5 (0.97)	–	240
Groundnut	10 (16.67)	50 (83.33)	60 (11.70)	800	400
Jowar	–	50 (100)	50 (9.75)	–	–
Maize	–	5 (100)	5 (0.97)	–	–
Jeera	8 (100)	–	8 (1.56)	400	–
Total	193 (37.62)	320 (62.38)	513 (100)		

* Figures in parenthesis show percent of total area under the respective crop.
**Figures in parenthesis show the area under crop as percent to total cultivated area

Table 9
Land Distribution

Details	*No. of Farmer*	*Total Acquired Land (Ha)*
Marginal farmer Irrigated: 0.75 Ha; Unirrigated : 3.50 Ha	23 (9.47)	20 (3.26)
Small farmer : Irrigated : 1.50Ha; Unirrigated : 7.50 Ha	110 (45.27)	140 (22.84)

Contd.

Details	*No. of Farmer*	*Total Acquired Land (Ha)*
3 to 10 Ha	100	343
	(41.15)	(55.95)
10 to 15 Ha	10	110
	(4.12)	(17.94)
15 to 20 Ha	–	–
More than 20 Ha	–	–
Total	243	613
	(100)	(100)

VILLAGE INFRASTRUCTURE

Except for one Sahakari Mandali, there is no other financial institution in the village. The nearest health faculty is located at a distance of six Kilometers in Tanakara Village. Table 11 shows the status of the village with regard to some of the other infrastructure facilities.

Table 10
Irrigation Sources

Details	*No.*	*Previous Years Irrigated Area (Ha)*
River-Nala plug	=	–
Pond (dam)		–
Well	195	75
Irrigation canal		–
Others	–	–

Watershed Project Under ORPAT Charitable Trust: The Watershed Project covering an area of 640 hectares (Table 2.4) involving an estimated cost of Rs.60/00 lacs under the National Watershed Programme was launched in the village in 1998 with Orpat Charitable Trust as the Programme Implementation Agency. As per the programme guidelines, the cost estimation is only for a project covering 500 hectares of land. However, due to cost reduction by people's planning, the PIA was able to cover 640 hectares. The project was completed before the due date. As we have earlier seen the watershed guidelines in chapter one, we shall not go into the details of the implementation process. Instead it would be much more worthwhile to account the benefits and changes that the project has brought to the life of people in the village and then go to explore some of the issues which have emerged during the discussions with the villagers.

Table 11
Other Facilities in Village

Details	*Facility Available in Village*	*If Not in Village, Nearer Place (Km)*
Approach road	NO	Tankara 6 Km
Kachchha road	YES	-
Pakka road	NO	Tankara 6 Km
Metal road	YES	-
Railway station	NO	Vankaner 20 Km
Electricity	YES	-
Kinder garden	YES	-
Primary school	YES	-
Secondary Higher Secondary school	NO	Tankara 6 Km
Drinking water facility (well, bore, danki)	YES	-
Gram Panchayat office	YES	-
Other	Bus stand	-

PROJECT IMPLEMENTATION- THE ADMINISTRATIVE STRUCTURE

All the members of the gram sabha are the members of the Watershed Association and pay an annual membership fee of Rs.11/00. Members of the Association elected the 13 member Watershed Committee which at the end of the project phase is now converted into Village Development Committee. The composition of the Committee is as follows–

SC/ St	3 members
Women	3 members
Pachayat member	1 member
Cooperative Bodies	1 member
User Groups	5 members

The tenure of the Committee is three years and their membership is subject to final approval of the Gram Sabha. The Gram Sabha has the right to change the membership even before the completion of the term if somebody is found wanting in duties.

WATER HARVESTING AND CONSERVATION- THE SUPPLY SIDE OF THE PROJECT

The basic philosophy behind the watershed approach is not only to develop on area basis but also create a balance between demand and supply of water. The system, thus has two components- water source on the supply side and alternative uses of water on the demand side. While the works undertaken under the watershed project affect the supply side by harnessing the surface and flow water from the environment, the effects are also felt on the ground water level. Most the works undertaken as mentioned above, have resulted in level the ground water resources in the village as clear from the recharging of the wells. In fact one well, about ten meter deep was overflowing when the study team visited the project site Following observations were made during the study visit about the works done during the project period affecting the supply side of watershed project-

(i) As against targeted 46 check dams total number of sixty eight check dams (including six earthen check dams) were constructed.

(ii) The sight of the dams and project design was done by the villagers themselves. This helped them in cost reduction and getting works done in time and above the target numbers.

(iii) With such an extensive networking of the check dams, the dry village has now taken the shape of an Iceland surrounded by water and greenery from every side.

(iv) Besides the formation of new structure, one old pond constructed originally under relief works during 1988-89 has also been renovated. This had added to the strength of irrigation potential and ground water recharge capabilities.

Land Works Affecting Supply Side: While above works were done with the project money, most of the land works were done mainly at private cost but on highly cooperative basis. As mentioned earlier, more than 500 hectares of area in the village was of black cotton soil. Hence the permeability of the water was very low. To overcome this problem, the villagers used tractors to remove the top soil of the earth. In some of the field almost two feet of the top soil was removed.

The removal of the top soil has two implications–

(a) It allows greater permeability,

(b) It enables cultivation of other crops also, besides the normal crop of cotton. Consequently the cropping pattern in the village has already undergone some change during last two years period.

WATER USERS' GROUPS AND WATER USE: THE DEMAND SIDE

From the demand side water may be looked upon according to different uses to which it is put to. The demand side, of course is to be seen from the angel of particular setting. Some of the major aspects of the demand for water are- use for drinking water, irrigation, household and public utility water needs, requirements for natural vegetation and requirements for marinating the ecological balance.

DRINKING WATER

Amarapar ahs no problem of drinking water as Government supplies drinking water through piped water supply system which is sufficient to take care of household and public utility water needs. There are no industries in the village to demand water. Hence irrigation remains to be the basic source of demand for water in the village. Demand for irrigation water, in turn is directly related to the size and ownership of land holding. Hence it is obvious that the demand will vary from individual to individual.

IRRIGATION

As per the guidelines of the watershed projects, therefore, all the water users have to form a water users' group. The basic objective behind the formation of the group is two fold- determine the pattern of water use on a cooperative and participatory basis (management of demand), and management of the water structures (maintenance of water supply). The formation of the water users' group in Amarapar is, however, on slightly different principles. It is formed on the basis of farmers covered under a particular check dam, that is, all the farmers using water from the particular reservoir form a group. Thus overall 46 water users' groups covering 243 farming households are formed in the village.

The water users' groups have not evolved any principle of water usage so far. Evolving a principle for water sharing is essentially a phenomenon of shortages. Since at the very micro level, check dam level, no such shortage is felt so far since last two years, such evolution has not taken place. As per the assessment, if the normal rainfall takes place, all the farmers will get two to three rains depending on the requirement and nature of the crop grown. This throws light on another determinant of water use- the cropping pattern. As mentioned earlier, due to removal of top soil and now with the availability of water, the cropping pattern itself is likely to undergo changes (villagers have reported that such changes have already started). Sooner or later, therefore, principles of water use have to be evolved.

MAINTENANCE

Their prime responsibility so far is of maintenance. The project has evolved principles for maintenance of the water harvesting structures. As per the project design, all the users' have to contribute twenty percent of the cost of the project of which ten percent has to be in cash. So far a pool of Rs. 2.87 lacs is contributed by the water users. This amount is put in fixed deposit in bank. The initial period of deposit is 37 months and is subject to renewal. In the event of need for maintenance expenditure, fifty percent of the expenditure cost will be met from the interest of the deposit and remaining fifty percent will be contributed by the users. The extent of the contribution by each user will depend on the quantum of land holding he has. Thus the user charges for maintenance will vary according to the land size.

EMERGING BENEFITS

The watershed project in Amarapar has brought about socio-economic changes in the village life. An increase in productivity of two of the main crops, cotton and groundnut is reported. And the increase has been phenomenal. The productivity of cotton has gone up from 1.5 quintals on unirrigated land and six quintals on irrigated land earlier to around 12-12 quintals after the availability of sufficient water.

Table 12
Emerging Benefits of Watershed Project: Few Aspects

Indicators	*Pre Project*	*Post Project*
Cotton yield per hectare	1.5 to 6 quintals	10-12 quintals
Groundnut	Upto 2 quintals subject to rainfall	10-12 quintals
No. of tractors	12	31
No of wells	195	300
New Crops Initiated after the project	–	Vegetables, Fruit bearing plantation, improved variety of gram and introduction of other pulses
New Occupations		Bakery
Milk Production per day	200 ltrs.	1000 ltrs.
No of Buffalos	215	490
Literate Males	354	418
Literate females	171	399
Motorbikes	26	146
Refrigerators	Nil	190

Thus the income from one crop alone has gone up substantially. Similar result is reported in case of groundnut, another major crop of the village. Vegetable growing and marketing has emerged as new and profit making avocation in the village. The growth in number of well (for irrigation) and tractors also reflect the growing agricultural economy of the village. The impact of agricultural growth is also witnessed in livestock growth. The buffalo population in the village has grown by more than one hundred percent in last two years, giving a boost to dairy and bakery industry. One basic feature of dairy sector in Amarapar is that it is totally in the hands of the women.

The very fact that milk production has increased from 200 ltrs. Per day to 1000 ltrs. Per day itself reflects the change in the economic status and contribution of the women towards that. Some of the social variable used as indicators for increased socio economic conditions reflect remarkable impact of the project. At the beginning of the project there was no refrigerator in the village. Today 190 households are already having refrigerators Similarly the number of motor cycles in the village has gone up from 26 to 146. The literacy rate is nearly 100 percent (Table 12).

IMPACT ON MIGRATION

The most significant impact of the project has been on migration. Earlier about 120 persons use to migrate fort doing labour works in Rajkot and Ahmadabad. With the access to water for irrigation, all these people are now settled in cultivation. Besides about thirty five persons are now coming from outside to do farm woks in the village on wage basis.

EMERGING ISSUES

The project has been instrumental in bringing about socio economic changes in the village society. Through its impact on migration and through formation of seven Self Help Groups (five women groups, one Shepard group and one landless group) involving exclusively the people below poverty line, it has affected the status of the poor also. Most of these groups are involved into livestock activities. Yet the prime question remains- in view of any formal or informal understanding on the right to use the water, what should be next step so that right of the poor are protected. As we have seen, prima facies no inequality is noticed in the water use pattern as such. Whatever, inequalities are noticed are because of the inequalities in land holdings. In this context, three primary issues emerge which may have to be addressed in future, if not right now-

(1) How to incorporate the issue of land reforms (from redistribution point of view), with the practical orientation of watershed projects so that land and

water both the resources get distrusted equitably, rather than the poor merely contributing their labour for the growth of the land owners?

(2) Presently, the right to use water is free for everybody. Rajkot is also known for manufacturing of water pumps. Hence almost every farmer is having pumps to lift water from the reservoir as per his needs and capacity. Since the distribution of the water users is as per the reservoir, so far no conflict has taken place in this context. However, as mentioned earlier, the cropping pattern is slowly changing and as this is an area where the major emphasis is on cash crops, sooner or later conflicts in water usage rights are bound to arise. The villagers so far have not evolved any guideline in judicious and just use of water. How to evolve that?

(3) The third issue is of macro in nature. As per the topographical requirements, all the water harvesting structures try to arrest the surface water flowing from the ridge to valley, apart from harvesting the rain water. There are discussion already taking place in the urban areas of Rajkot that due to such interruptions in free flow of water, the river base as the major source of drinking water in the urban areas is dwindling. The city is now trying for br.inging water from Narmada river, about 100 km. away through laying down pipelines. Thus how to restore the balance between the harvesting local water and at the same time allowing water to flow to the terminal rivers is another issue of significance which needs to be addressed at this stage.

CHAPTER–13

WATERSHED APPROACH-A FEASIBLE PROPOSITION FOR RESOURCE MANAGEMENT AND CROP PRODUCTIVITY GROWTH IN RAIN FED AREAS

C. Sekar

According to the UN estimates, the total amount of water on earth is about 1400 million cubic kilometer. However, the fresh water constitutes a very small proportion of this enormous quantity. About 2.7 per cent of the total water available on the earth is fresh water of which 75.2 per cent lies frozen in Polar Regions and another 22.6 per cent is present as ground water. The rest is about 2.2 percent available in lakes, rivers, atmosphere, moisture, soil and vegetation (www.wrmin.nic.in). But water available for consumption and other uses is a small proportion of the quantity available in rivers, lakes and ground water. The crisis about water resources development and management thus arises because most of the water is not available for use and secondly it is characterized by its highly uneven spatial distribution. Accordingly, the importance of water has been recognized and greater emphasis is being laid on its economic use and better management.

WATER HARVESTING AND THE NEED FOR CONSERVING WATER

Water harvesting in short is a small-scale concentration, collection, storage, and use of rainwater runoff for both domestic and agricultural use. The ratio of catchment to command is inversely related to the amount and intensity of rainfall, the impermeability of soil and the slope of the land on which it falls. Rainfall intensity is particularly important, since intense storms generate the most runoff. The term water conservation is generally associated with the management of water resources under scarcity.

Indian villages for the most part have traditionally relied on local rainfall for meeting the water requirements of agriculture and domestic activities. A rich and varied array of techniques, adapted to local conditions, have been evolved over centuries for harvesting rainwater and conserve it in small surface storages and underground. These are still in active use but have been overshadowed by large reservoirs and energized pumping of ground water, which are made possible by technological advances in civil engineering and water lining devices. In India, the quantum of water harnessed by these means has expanded phenomenally and now far exceeds the quantity obtained by traditional devices. However, it is becoming apparent that (i) the demand for water for all uses has grown largely and continues to grow at an unprecedented rate, (ii) while supplies have increased, all parts of the country have not benefited uniformly from it, (iii) nearly two thirds of the country's cultivated land still depends entirely on rainfall, (iv) a large proportion of the population does not have adequate quantity of water, (v) the scope for augmenting supplies from surface sources is limited and diminishing even as there are clear signs that ground water resources are being already over exploited and subjugated and (vi) competition between different uses and among users for the limited supplies of water has been greater than before in many areas. In this context, conservation and prudent use of water from surface sources are imperative and warranted.

IMPORTANCE OF WATER RESOURCE IN RAIN FED FARMING

The importance of rain fed crop production is partly due to the dominance of rain fed agriculture. More than 80 percent of cereal area in developed countries is rain fed, much of which is highly productive maize and wheat land such as that in the Mid-western US and parts of Europe. Rain fed yields in developing countries are projected to increase from 1.5 metric tonnes per hectare to 2.1 metric tonnes per hectare by 2021-25, and rain fed area in developing countries will account for 43 percent of total cereal area, and rain fed areas will account for 40 percent of growth in cereal production. Rain fed wheat production contributes 33 percent of the total yield in developing countries, 81 percent in developed countries, and 52 percent worldwide. Maize is grown under rain fed conditions more often than rice and wheat. Of the total 138 million hectares of maize in the world, 82 percent is rain fed, while only 18 percent is irrigated. Developing countries occupy over 60 percent of the total maize area worldwide. The average rain fed maize yield in developed countries is 3.4 tonnes per hectare, while that of developing countries lags behind at 1.8 tonnes per hectare. Rain fed maize production contributes 66 percent of the total yield in developing countries, 81 percent in developed countries, and 74 percent globally. It is a matter of fact that just about 62 million hectares of soybeans are harvested worldwide, of which 53 million hectares are rain fed. Developed countries plant 91 percent of the total soybean area using rain fed agriculture, while 80 percent of the area in developing countries is rain fed. In developing countries, the irrigated yield is only marginally higher than the rain fed yield, with both at approximately 1.8 tonnes per hectare (IFPRI Report, Feb 2002). The foregoing discussions clearly explicate the importance of rain fed areas in the food production front and its contribution in the global food basket.

WATER RESOURCES AND FOOD PRODUCTION INDIAN SCENARIO

India has 2.45 percent of world's land, 4.9 percent of fresh water resources and 17 percent of population. From the reported area of 306 million hectares, the present cultivated area is 142.5 m.ha (47%).Out of the cultivated area, 40 percent area is irrigated which produces 55 percent of food and the remaining 60 percent area is rain fed which produces 45 percent of food. Amongst the net irrigated area, 17.7 m.ha (31%) are benefited from canal water, 33 m.ha (58%) from ground water and the balance 6 m.ha (11%) from tanks and other sources (CWC, 2003).

The water resources potential of the country, which occurs as a natural run off in the rivers is about 1869 Billion Cubic Meters (BCM). It constitutes a little over 4% of the total river flows of the world. However, due to various constraints in topography and uneven distribution over space and time, only about 1122 BCM of the total annual water potential can be put to beneficial use. This can be achieved through 690 BCM as utilizable surface water and 432 BCM through ground water. In majority of river basins, present utilization is significantly high and is in the range of 50% to 95% of utilizable surface resources. While water for drinking purpose has been accorded topmost priority in water use, irrigation is the major consumer of water. Ultimate irrigation potential which can be created making use of the utilizable surface water resources through major, medium and minor projects would be about 75.9 m.ha. Irrigation potential making use of ground water has now been assessed as 64 m.ha. Thus the total irrigation potential from surface and ground water sources would be about 139.9 m.ha. Besides this, the additional irrigation potential of about 35 m.ha can be created by taking up long distance inter basin transfer of water from surplus to deficit basins. Water Resources potential in the major river basins is given in Annexure 1. In order to appropriately address the present and future water and food grain requirements of the society within the available financial resources, Ministry of water resources has identified the following key areas for water resources related issues.

(i) Water harvesting and water conservation methods
(ii) Improving water utilization efficiency
(iii) Command area development and participatory irrigation management
(iv) Flood management and erosion control
(v) Protection of costal erosion
(vi) Dam safety and rehabilitation
(vii) Revival and restoration of existing water bodies
(viii) Appropriate regulation and management of groundwater
(ix) Ground water recharge
(x) Inter-linking of rivers
(xi) Rural drinking water supply and sanitation.

As the variability of rainfall over the country is well known, the development of water resources for irrigated agriculture received high priority in the different plan periods. Expansion of irrigation facilities, along with consolidation of the existing systems, has been the main strategy for increasing production of food grains. Irrigation support is provided through major, medium and minor irrigation projects and command area development. With sustained and systematic irrigation development, the irrigation potential has increased from 22.6 m.ha in 1951, during the first five year plan began in India, to about 93.98 m.ha at the end of IX five year Plan (CWC, Annual Report 2004-05).

IRRIGATION POTENTIAL IN TAMIL NADU

It is understood that the full irrigation potential of the state has already been realized and the per capita availability of water is lowest in Tamilnadu. As per the World Bank reports, the per capita availability of water resources in the state is 900 cubic meters (40.9%) in a year as against 2200 cubic meters in India. Well irrigation is dominant in Tamilnadu. Of the 1.8 million wells, approximately 10 per cent are defunct. The depth of bore wells in hard rock is between 600 to 1000 feet. This situation implies that water harvesting is the priority area both for the farmers and the implementing authority. Gross area irrigated to gross cropped area was in the order of 55 per cent in 2001-02, 50 percent in 2002-03 and 47 percent in 2003-04. It indicates the fact that the fortune of agriculture still significantly relies on quantum and spread of precipitation. Of the irrigated area, the share of wells is 60.5 percent, canals 20.5 percent, tanks 17.9 percent and others 0.7 percent during 2003-04. Irrigation by canals has been influenced by factors such as the flow of Cauvery River to a great extent. So the dependence on ground water has been increasing and it will indirectly accelerate rapid depletion of available ground water. The problem of salinity and alkalinity of the soil is posing additional problems. In this scenario, micro irrigation techniques viz., drip and sprinkler irrigation and precision farming are becoming increasingly relevant and hence the government is stepping up investment in these areas. The irrigation profile of Tamilnadu is presented in the Table 1.

Table 1
Irrigation Profile of Tamilnadu

Particulars	*2003-04*
Total rainfall (mm)	1034.6
Net irrigated area (lakh ha)	21.5
Canals (lakh ha)	4.5
Tanks (lakh ha)	3.8
Wells (tube and ordinary wells)	13.0
Others	0.2
Gross area irrigated (lakh ha)	24.8
Net area sown (lakh ha)	46.9
Irrigation intensity (%)	115.3
Cropping intensity (%)	113.4
Net area irrigated as percentage to net area sown	45.8
Total food grain production (lakh tonnes)	43.12

Source: TN- An Economic Appraisal, 2004-05.

IMPACT OF RAIN WATER HARVESTING–A FIELD LEVEL EXPERIENCE

A micro level investigation was undertaken by the second author of this research paper in association with the first author in 2004 to analyze the impact of rainwater harvesting on the socio-economic characteristics of the user groups. The study was carried out in Pongalur block of Tiruppur taluk in Coimbatore district of Tamilnadu, where the watershed activities are carried out by the development departments in association with the farmers and user groups of the village commons. The Integrated Watershed Development Programme (IWDP) has been implemented in the study area on a large scale. The various water harvesting activities undertaken in study area are percolation pond, minor check dam, major check dam, land leveling, farm ponds, contour bunding, summer ploughing, agro-forestry etc. The current investigation primarily assessed the cost economics of different water harvesting structures and also examined the comparative performance of agricultural and other socio economic parameters between WTA (Watershed Treated Area) and NTA (Non Treated Area) through indicators like cropping pattern, cropping intensity, water quality, crop productivity etc.

GENERAL CHARACTERISTICS OF THE STUDY AREA

The study was conducted purposively in Pongalur block of Coimbatore district in Tamilnadu because of the following two reasons. i) This block was the site of implementation of water harvesting structures under the Integrated Watershed Development programme (IWDP) and ii) the study area was also the location of many watershed treatment activities. For the study 120 sample respondents were contacted. Among the six panchayats in the block, Kattur panchayat was randomly selected for the study. From the above panchayat, two villages for WTA and two villages for NTA were selected randomly. From the sample villages, two broad categories of 60 beneficiaries from WTA and 60 non- beneficiaries from NTA were selected randomly for the study.

ECONOMIC EFFICIENCY ANALYSIS

An economic efficiency analysis is a systematic way to compare the streams of benefits and costs. In the present study, the benefits and costs of the different water harvesting structures were studied to determine whether the technology had been economically efficient or not. Three principal undiscounted measures used in economic efficiency analysis were 1) Net Present Worth (NPW) 2) Benefit-Cost Ratio (BCR) and 3) Internal Rate of Return (IRR). The costs and benefits of the watershed components were studied for a period of five years since the project was implemented only five years ago. The data on costs were collected through primary survey from the sample farmers and also through secondary data from the development department. The data on the benefits of the water harvesting structures were calculated based on the increase in gross cropped area and also the change in yield for the individual crop in the sample farms due to the positive externalities of the water harvesting structures. Every care was taken to isolate and quantify both the costs and benefits of the water harvesting structures from the other means practiced by the sample farmers so as to get as precise information as possible.

HEDONIC PRICING ANALYSIS

Hedonic price function relates to an individual's willingness to pay for environmental attributes, specified between the market prices and all the relevant attributes of the commodity. For the estimation of the hedonic price, the marginal implicit price of the environmental attribute needs to be considered. Thus it includes a price paid for a better environmental attribute, in the absence of which the value of land is equal to the cost of the land without appropriate mark ups for environmental benefits. In the present study, the hedonic price function was employed to estimate the marginal price of the different attributes of the WTA. The preliminary analysis inferred from the primary data revealed that the prices of the agricultural land had shown variations with respect to the extent of watershed activity in the area. Hence, the hedonic pricing function was employed to study the impact of land quality, water quality, proximity of farm household to the water harvesting structures, depth of water table in the open wells, the proportion of cropland to the total land area and the value of the farm products in the farm on the price of the agricultural land.

The hedonic price function employed in this study was of the following form.

$$PRICE = f\,(LQI,\ WQI,\ PROX,\ PCLA,\ WTDEP,\ VAP)$$

Where,

PRICE	=	Value of agricultural land in rupees per hectare
LQI	=	Land quality index (1- Poor, 2- Average, 3- Good)
WQI	=	Water quality (1-Poor, 2- Average, 3- Good)
PROX	=	Proximity of sample farm to the watershed (metre)
PCLA	=	Proportion of cropland area to total farmland area (%)
WTDEP	=	Depth of water table in open-wells in the farm (metre)
VAP	=	Value of farm products (rupees per hectare)

Key Findings of the Field Level Observations

The details of the soil and water conservation structures adopted by the sample respondents and the unit cost of the conservation structures are presented in Table 2.

Table 2
Unit Cost of the Water Harvesting Structures

Soil and Water Conservation Structures	*Number of Structures Adopted*	*Unit Cost of the Structure (Rs.)*
Major check dam	4	70000
Minor check dam	6	8000
Percolation pond	7	75000
Contour bunding	10	998 (Rs/ha)
Land levelling	10	3200 (Rs/ha)

SOIL AND WATER HARVESTING STRUCTURES- COST ECONOMICS

The cost economics of the water harvesting structures in the study area were analyzed to assess the returns on investment on water harvesting structures. Hence, discounted financial measures such as Net Present Value (NPV), Benefit Cost Ratio (BCR) and Internal Rate of Return (IRR) were calculated. The results of the analysis are reported crop wise for different water harvesting structures in the Table 3.

Table 3

Cost Economics of Water Harvesting Structures

Discount rate – 10 percent.

Crops	*Maize*	*Chillies*	*Onion*	*Coconut*
Major Check Dam				
BCR	1.29	1.42	1.20	1.58
NPV (Rs.)	9445	11426	8256	13677
IRR (%)	23	29	19	35
Minor Check Dam				
BCR	1.50	1.57	1.27	1.71
NPV (Rs.)	10256	11048	7482	12633
IRR (%)	32	35	22	40
Percolation Pond				
BCR	1.54	1.52	1.08	1.63
NPV (Rs.)	3382	13134	6794	3679
IRR (%)	32.24	32.12	14.3	37
Contour Bunding				
BCR	1.38	1.44	1.28	1.18
NPV (Rs.)	915	994	796	678
IRR (%)	27	29	22	18.23
Land Levelling				
BCR	1.19	1.35	1.43	-
NPV (Rs.)	976	1768	2164	-
IRR (%)	19	16	23	-

From the Table 3, it could be elaborated that the BCR ranged from 1.08 for Percolation Pond to 1.71 for minor check dams. The BCR for percolation ponds varied from 1.08 for onion to 1.63 for Coconut. The range of BCR for contour bunding for the above crops varied from 1.18 for coconut to 1.44 for Chillies. The BCR for major check dams though above unity were low ranging from 1.20 to 1.58 for onion and Coconut. The reason for this could be attributed to the higher investment in the major check dams and the longer benefit realization period of the structure.

The NPV of crops for the different water harvesting structures reflect the impact of implementation of different harvesting structures. It is noticed from the Table 3 that among the water harvesting structures, major check dams had the highest NPV of Rs.13677 followed by percolation pond with the NPV of Rs.13134 for chillies. The major check dams had an NPV ranging from Rs.8256 for onion to Rs.13677 for coconut. Contour bunding and land levelling showed an NPV ranging from Rs.678 for coconut to Rs.2164 for onion.

The minor check dam had the highest IRR (40.12 percent for coconut). It was then followed by percolation pond with an IRR value of 37 percent for coconut.

The major check dam gave an IRR value of 35 percent for coconut. However, contour bunding and land levelling had the IRR values ranging from 16 to 29 percent. The BCR, NPV and IRR values for conservation structures like major check dam and minor check dams for coconut were found to be high. The reason for this could be attributed to increased realization of benefits by the coconut crop under these structures. The overall results on feasibility analysis for the various water harvesting structures, which include contour bunding, land levelling, minor check dams, major check dams and percolation ponds across the selected crops are encouraging and reiterated the advantages of the water harvesting structures in the watershed areas.

COST AND RETURNS AND PRODUCTIVITY OF CROPS

It was understood that the cropping intensity of the sample farms in WTA was higher (114.31 percent) than the sample farms in NTA (102.90 percent). Enhanced cropping intensity in WTA could be attributed by the meticulous adoption of water harvesting structures. The comparative costs and returns of sample farms between WTA and NTA were analyzed by calculating the cost and returns of some of the dominant crops discretely and presented in Table 4. The percentage difference in costs and returns was also computed individually to understand the efficacy of the water harvesting structures. It could also be known from the table

Table 4

Comparative Study of Cost and Returns of Major Crops in WTA and NTA

(in rupees)

Particulars	*Coconut*		*Maize*		*Chillies*		*Sorghum*		*Onion*	
	WTA	*NTA*	*WTA*	*NTA*	*WTA*	*NTA*	*WTA*	*NTA*	*WTA*	*NTA*
Preparatory cultivation	j	j	536.66	512.63	472.22	422.56	550.00	500.00	554.54	500.00
Labour	2854.23	2120.25	2694.66	2428.41	2844.40	2520.28	800.00	730.00	3110.00	2565.00
Seed	j	j	693.00	450.00	211.11	195.84	530.00	470.00	1359.09	1124.61
Manures	2065.38	1874.63	1200.00	900.00	1005.60	982.54	j	j	381.81	250.41
Fertilizers	1489.23	1290.26	922.00	678.58	1025.60	910.75	j	j	1059.09	785.64
Plant Protection	1471.92	854.31	250.00	200.00	344.44	254.21	j	j	404.54	352.19
Total Cost	8290.76	6139.45	6046.33	5169.62	6245.00	5286.18	1980.00	1700.00	6869.07	5577.85
Total Return	61211.50	47692.10	20966.70	16500.00	21456.00	17500.00	5010.00	4380.00	22772.70	17996.50
Net Return	52920.80	41552.70	14920.30	11330.40	15211.00	12213.80	3030.00	2680.00	15903.70	12418.70
Percentage difference (Net return)	27.35		31.68		24.54		13.06		28.06	

4, that coconut, maize, sorghum, chillies and onion had shown a positive additional net return of 27.35, 31.68, 13.06, 24.54 and 28.06 percent, respectively. Thus it is clear that the net returns of major crops in the study area had been found high in the sample farms of WTA than the sample farms in NTA.

PRODUCTIVITY AND YIELD DIFFERENCE

The productivity of major crops and their yield difference were analyzed to study the differences in yield among the sample farms in the WTA and NTA. The results are reported in Table 5.

Table 5
Productivity of Major Crops and their Yield Difference

(Kg/ha)

Crops	*WTA*	*NTA*	*Percentage of Yield Difference*
Coconut (in numbers)	14170	12280	15.39
Maize	4869	4194	16.08
Green Chillies	10640	9350	13.00
Onion	31710	28801	9.20
Sorghum	747	694	7.64

It could be observed from the Table 5, that the yield of maize showed the highest increase in productivity (16.08 percent) followed by coconut (15.39 percent). It is also clear that the crops like chillies, onion and sorghum also indicated increase in productivity to an extent of 13.00 percent, 9.20 percent and 7.64 percent, respectively. Thus it could be concluded that water-harvesting structures had a significant impact on the productivity of the crops.

WATER QUALITY

The water quality of the sample farms in the WTA was assessed through collection of opinions from the sample respondents. The respondent's opinion for different quality attributes of water are tabulated for easy interpretation. From the Table 6, it could be interpreted that about 37 percent of farmers in WTA perceived that the water quality had been good, while only 21.67 percent of farmers in NTA observed that the quality of water was good, which shows the indirect benefit received by the adopters of water harvesting structures in WTA. About 47 percent of the farmers in WTA perceived that the water quality was medium while only 43.33 percent of the farmers in NTA reported that the water quality was medium. Thus it could be concluded that the overall quality of water in WTA had been superior to NTA.

Table 6
Opinion of the Sample Farmers about Water Quality

	WTA		*NTA*	
Water Quality	*Number*	*Percentage*	*Number*	*Percentage*
Good	22	36.67	13	21.67
Medium	28	46.66	26	43.33
Poor	10	16.67	21	35.00
Total	60	100	60	100

HEDONIC PRICING ANALYSIS

In hedonic pricing analysis, the implicit prices for the various qualitative and environmental characteristics were estimated by looking at the real markets in which that distinctiveness are effectively traded. Differences in these qualitative features of the land were thought to affect the flow of benefit from the property implicitly. Hence, to appraise the qualitative attributes of enhanced land use for agriculture and also to evaluate the improved values of the cropland, the data collected were subjected to hedonic pricing analysis. The results of the hedonic pricing estimates are represented in the Table 7.

From the Table 7, it could be noted that the coefficient of WQI was positive and significant at ten percent probability level. It could be inferred that an increase in water quality resulted in significant positive change in the land value in the WTA. The distance of the sample farmer from the water harvesting structures showed a negative influence on land value but it was not significant. It could also be observed that proportion of cropland to the total land area had exerted a positive influence and was significant at one percent level of probability. It could be discussed that for every one-hectare increase in the proportion of cropland to total land holding, the land value would increase by Rs. 57432 by keeping the other variables constant. This variable had the expected sign. Similarly, the depth of water table showed a negative influence on the land value. However, this variable was not significant. As expected, the product value of the sample farm showed a positive relationship with land value and was significant at one percent level of probability. Hence it could be implied that for every unit increase in product value, the land value would increase by Re. 0.17 by keeping the other variable constant. Thus, from the above analysis, it could be concluded that the water quality, proportion of cropland to the total land parcel and product value showed a significant influence on the land value. Though, the distance and water table depth exerted a positive influence on the land value, the estimates of them were not significantly different at five percent level.

Table 7
Hedonic Pricing Estimates for WTA and NTA

Variables	*Coefficients for WTA*	*Coefficients for NTA*
Intercept	483740	265396.6*
	(17.7451)	(11.3885)
WQI	5086.89***	23065.18*
	(1.6364)	(4.7328)
PROX	-45.10	-24.05289*
	(-1.5603)	(-4.5151)
PCLA	57432.12*	14260.58
	(2.7300)	(0.8160)
WTDEPTH	-716.67	-1136.276*
	(-1.4886)	(-3.2458)
VAP	0.178146*	0.002028
	(4.2228)	(0.0561)

Figures in parenthesis indicate the 't'value.
* Significant at one percent level.
** Significant at five percent level
*** Significant at ten percent level.

The Table 7 also explains the hedonic pricing estimates for farms in NTA.

Since the sample farms of NTA were located outside the geo-hydrological boundaries of the watershed, the sample farms did not experience any of the effects of the watershed. From the Table 7, it could be observed that the coefficient for water quality was positive and significant at one percent probability level. It could also be implied that an increase in water quality resulted in increase in land value by Rs.23065 by keeping the other variables constant in the NTA. The distance of the sample farmers from the water harvesting structures showed a negative influence on land value and was significant at one percent level of probability. The reason for this could be attributed to the higher implicit value that the sample farmers in the NTA assign to the proximity to watershed components. Thus it could be inferred that for every one meter increase in distance from the water harvesting structures (major and minor check dams, percolation ponds) the land value decreased by Rs. 24.05 by keeping the other variables constant. The proportion of cropland to the total land holding though positive was not significant. It could be explained that for every one hectare increase in the proportion of cropland to total land holding, the land value increased by 14261 rupees by keeping the other variables constant. The depth of water table showed a negative influence on the land value and was significant to one percent level of probability. It could be implied that for every one meter increase in depth of water table, the land value decreased by 1136 rupees by keeping the other variables constant. The product value of the sample farms reveals the positive relationship with land value. Thus from the above analysis, it could be concluded that the water quality, proportion of cropland to the total land holding and product value showed a significant influence on the land value.

GARRETT'S RANKING

Garrett's ranking technique was applied to rank a set of benefits obtained from the impact of watershed development activities. The order of merit assigned by the sample respondents in the WTA was transmuted into scores using the formula given by Garret and Woodworth (1977). The results of the Garrett scores obtained for different activities are tabulated in the Table 9 for easy understanding.

Table 9
Garrett's Score Value for the Benefits Obtained from Different Watershed Activities

Benefits	*Mean Garrett Score*
Improvement in soil and water conservation	78
Enhanced soil fertility	66
Change in cropping pattern	57
Increased cropping intensity	50
Yield enhancement	43
Ground water recharge	34
Resource conservation	22

It could be inferred from the above table that among the benefits listed, the highest score was recorded for soil and water conservation (78). This in turn had indicated that the construction of different water conservation measures such as percolation ponds and check dams have greater impacts on the conservation of water and controlling of soil erosion. This benefit was then followed by the improvement in soil fertility with a score of 66. The results of the table also ranked the other benefits like cropping pattern, cropping intensity, yield increase, ground water recharge and resource conservation with Garrett scores of 57, 50, 43, 34, and 22, respectively.

CONCLUSION

The basic problem of rain fed areas is degradation of natural resource base like soil and water through poor management leading to low productivity, low income and low surplus. This in turn leads to over exploitation of the existing natural resource base like groundwater. Among the natural resources water is the most crucial resource for the existence of living beings. Therefore, in order to obtain sustainable agriculture production as well as to improve soil productivity and ecosystem of vast rain fed agriculture, the efforts to conserve as much rainwater and to prevent soil erosion are considered vital. This can be implemented effectively and economically by adopting various water harvesting structures of cost effective integrated approach. In order to conserve the precious natural resources *viz.*, soil, water etc. and also to sustain the existing resource endowments for future entitlement, the Government of India has formulated water-harvesting structures.

The field level experiences also indicated that the cropping intensity of the sample farms in watershed treated area (WTA) was higher. The financial measures of water harvesting structures also indicated a favourable trend with IRRs ranging from 14.3 to 35. The water conservation works extend the beneficial effects on recharge of ground water, control soil erosion, and alters the cropping pattern and cropping intensity with positive effects on productivity of the crops. Hence the water harvesting structures may be scaled up and implemented in dry lands on large scale to reap the real benefits of the rainwater harvesting, sustainability of natural resource base and strengthening of economic prosperity of our country.

REFERENCES

Alagumani, T. (1991), "An Economic Evaluation of Soil Conservation in Avinasi Taluk, Coimbatore District. Tamil Nadu", *Indian Journal of Agricultural Economics,* 46(3): 300–301.

——(2004-05), Central Water Commission, Annual Report.

——(2003), Central Water Commission: Pocket Book on Water Data, CWC, MoWR, India.

Chaurasia, S.P.R. and L.R. Singh (1991), "Optimal Cropping Pattern for Minimizing Soil Loss in Nauraar Watershed of Almora District in Uttar Pradesh. Parameters", *Indian Journal of Agricultural Economics,* 46(3): 320.

Lal, B. (2001), "Impact of National Watershed Development Project on Rain fed Agriculture in Alwar District of Rajasthan", *Agricultural Science Digest,* 21(3):157-160.

Lata.S.L, R.C. Koushal and S.S. Grewal (1994), "Economic Viability of Watershed Management Project Selected to Rehabilitate

Degraded Aravali Foothills of Haryana", *Indian Journal of Agricultural Economics*, 49(4): 591-600.

Mahandule, D.K., R. Pawar, D.L.Sale and S.A.Kadam. (1991), "Effects of Watershed Development Programme on Resource Use Structure and Returns of Farms in the Drought Prone Area of Western Maharastra", *Indian Journal of Agricultural Economics*, 46(3): 287.

Manhot, S.C., P.K. Singh and V. Sharma (1992), "Socio Economic Evaluation of Watershed Management Project–A Case Study", *Journal of Rural Development*, 11(2): 219-227.

——Ministry of Water Resource Management, India. (*www. wrmin. nic.in*)

——Ministry of Agriculture and Co-operation, GOI, (www.agri coop.nic.in)

Padmavathi, M. and M.S. Reddy (2002), "Personal and Socio-Economic Characteristics of Mitra Kisans in National Watershed Development Project for Rain fed Areas", *Journal of Research ANGARU*, 30(1): 71-75.

Pereira Luis S., Cordery Ian and Iacovids (2002), Coping with Water Scarcity, International Hydrological Programme, IHP-VI, Technical documents in Hydrology,No.5, UNESCO, Paris.

Sekar, C. (2001), "Externality Effects of Common Property Resource Degradation", *Indian Journal of Agricultural Economics*, 56(3): 346-357.

Senthil Nathan, S. and Sekar, C. (2004), "Soil and Water Conservation Activities in Watershed– Technology, Production and Economics, Research Report, 2004, Department of Agricultural Economics,Tamil Nadu Agricultural University, Coimbatore.

LIST OF ABBREVIATIONS USED IN THE STUDY

BCM	—	Billion Cubic Metre
BCR	—	Benefit Cost Ratio
CWC	—	Central Water Commission
ERM	—	(Extension/Renovation/ Modernization)
GOI	—	Government of India
IRR	—	Internal Rate of Return

M.ha	—	Million Hectares
MoWR	—	Ministry of Water Resources
NPW	—	Net Present Worth
NTA	—	Non-Treated Area
WTA	—	Watershed Treated Area

Annexure 1
Water Resources Potential in the Major River Basins of India Unit: BCM

Name of the River Basin	*Average Annual Potential in the River*	*Estimated Utilizable Flow (Excluding Ground Water)*
Indus (up to Border)	73.31	46.00
Ganga	525.02	250.00
Brahmaputra, Barak and others	585.60	24.00
Godavari	110.54	76.30
Krishna	78.12	58.00
Cauvery	21.36	19.00
Pennar	6.32	6.86
East flowing Rivers betweenMahanadi & Pennar	22.52	13.11
East Flowing Rivers betweenPennar and Kanayakumari	16.46	16.73
Mahanadi	66.88	49.99
Brahmani & Baitarni	28.48	18.30
Subarnarekha	13.37	6.81
Sabarmati	3.81	1.93
Mahi	11.02	3.10
West Flowing Rivers of Kutch,Saurashtra including Luni	15.10	14.98
Narmada	45.64	34.50
Tapi	14.88	14.50
West Flowing Rivers from Tapi to Tadri	87.41	11.94
West Flowing Rivers from Tadri to kanyakumari	113.53	24.57
Minor River Basins drainage toBangladesh & Myanmar	31.00	–
Total	1869.35	690.32

Source: CWC Publication – Handbook on Water and Related Information, Jan 2005

CHAPTER–14

WATERSHED DEVELOPMENT: A SOURCE OF SUSTAINABLE LIVELIHOODS FOR THE RURAL POOR

Dalip Kumar

INTRODUCTION

A watershed is a community based programs that is organized in a specifically earmarked area with a defined time frame and focuses on a wide range of issues and activities for integrated development of the village. The main focus is laid on water, food and fodder security and employment generation. It eliminates unscientific land use, inappropriate cropping patterns and soil erosion, thereby improving and sustaining productivity of resources leading to higher income and living standards for the inhabitants in the watershed area. It, therefore, involves restoration of the ecosystem, protecting and utilizing the locally available resources within a watershed to achieve sustainable livelihood for rural poor.

This paper assesses the impact of policy interventions through watershed development on the livelihoods of rural poor in India.. Land, water and forests are vital resources for the rural economy. A host of livelihood options of these resources are offered to the rural poor. The remote rural areas especially tribal pockets are facing the [problem of degradation of natural resources, low productivity, obstructed access to natural resources and the markets as well. The ongoing strategic development of the poverty-ridden pockets is boosting the confidence of the poor people. Strategically designed activities aiming at generating livelihood options are building a congenial atmosphere in which the poor could have sustained productivity from agriculture and forests with improved volume of water.

The original concept of watershed management or rehabilitation focused on the management of these resources in medium or large river valleys, in a way that would prevent rapid runoff of water, and so would slow down the rate of salutation of reservoirs and limit the incidence of potentially damaging flash flooding in river courses. (Paul 1997). The watershed cannot bring direct irrigation benefits on a large scale. Watershed development is a necessary but not a sufficient condition for sustaining rural livelihoods. While the focus of watershed development is primarily on strengthening the ecological base such as water bodies (including traditional tanks), grazing lands and wastelands, it should be complemented with other programmes that focus on landless poor households in order to make it pro-poor. In the context of low rainfall regions where improvement in irrigation facilities is slow, agriculture alone cannot support the communities. Policies and programmes should aim at creating an environment for diverse livelihood activities, which are the choices of the household rather than distress activities.

Watershed Development (WSD) is the development of a physiographic unit and can be used productively for integrated development of small natural unit areas. It is a holistic approach and can be viewed as an efficient and effective way of not only restoring the environment but also addressing the issue of poverty and unemployment in rural areas. The watershed development approaches aimed at treating degraded lands with the help of low cost and locally developed technologies like in–situ soil and moisture conservation measure, afforestration, horticulture, pasture development, upgradation of community land resources, employment generation and integrated development in a specific unit areas.

These plans take into consideration the land capability, local needs of the people and constraints to development.

A number of researchers have evaluated the ecological and socio-economic impact of these water shede development programmes. A vast majority of studies not only confirmed the economic viability of the programme but also indicated the fact that watershed programme is the only alternative to develop the rainfed agriculture in India (Raju, 2004). While the focus of watershed development in India has modified over the last 20 years from soil conservation to water conservation, now include a more participatory planning approach, evaluation studies estimating the distribution or magnitude of social impact from watershed development are often unclear or disputed (Kerr et al., 2002; World Bank, 2004). Improved knowledge will help determine how watershed projects affect intended beneficiaries in order to evaluate the performance of current watershed projects and to aid the appropriate design to future projects(Farrington et al.,1999).

The watershed development approach is based on totally on agricultural production in the areas where it is inadequate to meet the need of the rural poor and where the problem of food insecurity looms large. The increasing unemployment in the rural sector is likely to have serious ramifications on India's socio-economic and political balance. The WSD approach seeks the participation of the local people. For this purpose, several programmes have been launched by the central and state governments envisaging some promising results at different points of time.

In India, micro-watersheds are generally defined as falling in the range 500-1000 hectares. A mini-watershed comprises a number of micro-watersheds and covers around 5000 hectares. A macro-watershed is equivalent to a river basin and may encompass many thousands of hectares. The micro-watershed concept aims to 'establish an enabling environment for the integrated use, regulation and treatment of water and land resources of a watershed based ecosystem to accomplish resource conservation and bio-mass production objectives' (Jensen et al. 1996).

AVAILABILITY OF WATER

The relevance and urgency of watershed development programmes can be understood by recalling some facts and figures related to water which is viewed not only as a social but also economic good. The three forth of the earth's surface is covered with water but only a small portion of it is fresh water. The fresh water is obtained from surface run-off and ground water which is continuously being recharged and renewed through the hydrological cycle ensuring that water is a renewable resources. 96.5 per cent of total volume of water on the earth is estimated to exist in oceans. The fresh water is only 2.5 per cent. Out of this 70 per cent occurs as ice sheets and glaciers and about 30 per cent are estimated as ground water in the world's aquifers. India receives about 4 per cent of global precipitation. The total renewable water of India is estimated at 1897 Sq. k m per annum. It is feared that by 2025 India will become one of the water-scarce countries. (UN World Water Development Report–2003). At present we have utilised only 61% of our total irrigation potential in the major, medium & minor irrigation sectors. In fact on conventional calculations India's storage capacity compared to annual availability is very low - 207m^3 against 1820m^3 per-capita availability. Storage as a percentage of per-capita availability is only 11.4 per cent in India as compared to Australia (18.4%), China (49.1%), Turkey (50.5%), Spain (50%), Mexico (27%), USA (18.1%). The low ratio in India is all the more telling when we consider that the per-capita availability in Australia and USA is much higher than in India: 25,708m^3 and 10,837m^3 respectively compared with India's 1,820 m^3.

Further, the availability of water resources is uneven. It varies over time and space due to wide variations in seasonal and regional annual preipitation. The problem of water scarcity is worsening day by day due to over exploitation, excessive use and unequal access to water among different social groups.

Realizing the importance of water, from time immemoral, people in India gave religious sanctity to water by worshiping rivers like the Ganga, the Yamuna, the Kaveri, and the

Narmada and by associating several rituals with other water bodies like lakes, wells and ponds. Many such rites and rituals are being performed in and around water bodies. These social and philanthropic activities add to their social status and dignity in Indian society. It reflects the place of water- storage, and conservation and cleanliness in the mindset of Indian people including the elite's and common man all through the ages. There are numerous evidences to recall the tradition and practices of water conservation by rulers and elites in India.

HISTORICAL BACKGROUND

In the first century B.C. there was very sophisticated water-harvesting system channeling the floodwater of the river Ganga at Sringaverapura near Allahabad. Dams, lakes and irrigation systems were extensively built during the rule of Mauryan kings. The famous Sudarshana Lake was built during the rule of Ashoka, the great and Gupta rulers repaired the lake. Sophisticated irrigation system was developed in Kalinga (Orissa), Nagarjuna Konda (Andhra Pradesh), Bennur (Karnataka), Kolhapur (Maharashtra) and at many other places. In the 11th Century, the artificial Bhopal Lake was built. The Delhi Sultan Iltutmish had built tank in Hauz Khas to supply water to Sirifort area (Agrawal and Nrayan-1997).

The long tradition of constructing sophisticated hydraulic structures like dams, reservoirs, Lake Embankments and canals for irrigation continued in modern India. More stress was given on multi-purpose river valley projects, which were called by Jawaharlal Nehru as new temples of modern India because of their significant contributions to the integrated development of agriculture and rural economy with rapid industrialization and faster growth of Indian economy.

With the changing needs and problems, there has been shift in the international goals from merely increasing food production and poverty reduction to environmental sustainability. Greater emphasis should be given on checking the exploitation of natural resource base, soil-erosion, and land degradation coupled with the declining per capita availability of soil and fresh water. Hence, there is dire need of efficient and effective management of natural resources for increased productivity of soil and sustainability of environment.

Several governmental and non-governmental agencies have launched watershed development projects to tackle some of the generic problems with the objectives of soil conservation, improving the land-productivity, and promoting appropriate technologies for efficient and sustainable use of natural resources. But the success of watershed projects depends on people's participation from the stages of designing of projects, and project implementation levels.

STRATEGIES AFTER INDEPENDENCE

In India, watershed development programme was launched in 1970's to prevent land-degradation and to increase the soil productivity. It had no special significance for the development of the community. By the end of 1980's the policy changed radically. It was thought that technical and physical works alone would not lead to the desired objectives of watershed development and it must also concentrate on social financial and institutional aspects of rural development. Watershed development projects have been launched over diverse range of rainfed agro-climatic regions. These are grouped into five agro-climatic zones-

(a) Trans-Gangestic plain zone
(b) Western Himalayan zone
(c) Western plateau and Hill zone
(d) Gujarat plain and Hill zone
(e) Southern zone.

In 1944, Ministry of Rural Development issued a set of guidelines for implementation of watershed programme. This progressive policy was people-centric. It incorporated the good practices from NGOs and governmental policy like awareness creation, bottom-up planning, and partnership with NGOs and community partnership.

THE CONVENTIONAL APPROACH

The conventional approach was "top-down" approach in which local people were not consulted in project designing. (Rhoades. and Elliot, 2000)

Due to several weaknesses, this approach resulted into the failure of projects in achieving the desired goals. Any watershed project becomes more effective and efficient when users are given role in managing their own watershed resources (Johnson et al –2001).

The conventional approach was based on the assumption of technology-transfer rather than the development of technology on people's land and their surroundings. In this approach training was imparted by Agricultural Research Institute and Agriculture Universities which are capable in technological aspect of watershed project but weak in social science aspects of institution building as well as forging links with non-farm sector to generate value-added products from watershed (SRISTI-2005). The conventional approach does not stress the local knowledge on local soil types and conditions for sustainability of technology, which is soil specific. The top-down approach was not conducive for indulging the stakeholders participation in designing the programme, which are targeted to their improvement. There was a mismatch between the needs of the stakeholders and the activities for implementation of watershed development. Responding to these shortcomings in the conventional approach there has been a paradigm shift over the years..

PARTICIPATORY APPROACH

The new approach to watershed development is the participatory approach. It is directed towards more decentralized and greater participation of the people for whom projects are made. This approach enables the Natural resource management to face the new challenges by strengthening the capacity of local people. This approach is based on the concept of watershed development projects "of the people, for the people and by the people". It emphasises on inter-disciplinary, inter-sectoral and multi-institutional mechanism (Rhodes and Elliot 2000).

The participatory watershed management is defined as a process, which aims at creating a self-supporting system, which is essential for sustainability. (Wani, et al, 2005). It provides opportunities for stakeholders to jointly negotiate their interest, set priorities, evaluate, opportunities, implement and monitor the outcomes. Gradually the concept involved people's institutions like zila parishad, SHGs and watershed implementing committees in the project management system.

The seeds of the participatory management were sowed in a small village Ralegan-Siddhi in Maharashtra where in a social activist Anna Hazare had initiated movement for social change. He played a pioneering role in soil and water conservation, family planning, ban on alcohol, protection of non-arable lands against open grazing, felling of trees and voluntary labour for community welfare and several other measures which could help in restoring natural resources base in the village. (Kerr, et al, 2002)

In last three decades the management of watershed development has significantly developed. In 1970s and 1980 focus was on bio-physical criterion. In late 1980s, there were significant changes looking beyond soil and water conservation to include improvement in the productivity of natural resources. In 1994-95, the govt. of India issued strict guidelines to achieve multiple objectives like productive social, ecological/environmental and equity issues, optimum utilization of natural resources of the watershed, employment generation and development of other eco-resources in the village as well as easy and affordable solution to the problems faced by village people. The government guidelines outline the various stages of implementation of watershed development projects, the operational procedures and provision for sufficient operational flexibility at state, district and project levels so that the project can respond to differing situations and aspirations of the local rural community. The guidelines encourage the involvement of user groups (Ugs) and SHGs.

CHANGING OBJECTIVES

There have been significant changes in the focus on watershed development to achieve the objectives of overall enhancement of sustainable rural livelihood for reducing the incidence of rural poverty. Watershed Development Projects are planned and operationalised with a set of objectives like rising farm income, increasing agricultural productivity, soil and water conservation, employment generation in rural areas, risk-reduction by diversifying crops in rain-fed areas. Needless to say that all these objectives are to be achieved by greater participation of the people at the grass-root level which is the real spirit of democracy.

WATERSHED DEVELOPMENT AND FOOD SECURITY FOR RURAL POOR

The Indian Constitution does not explicitly mention the right to food as a fundamental right, it is implicitly enshrined in Article 21 of the Constitution as the fundamental right to life of every Indian citizen. Article 47 of the Constitution (in the Directive Principles of State Policy) is unambiguous: "The State shall regard the raising of the level of nutrition and the standard of living of its people and the improvement of public health as among its primary duties..."

Watershed development can be the only feasible solution to increase the foodgrain production, improve irrigation facilities and create employment opportunities for the rural poor in the short run. WSD should be the good tools for accelerating agricultural growth. It can offer unique opportunities to improve their economic situation and enhance their status in society. It has a notable impact on employment and income opportunities, food security, fodder, fuel and water availability and access to credit (D'Souza, 1997). Public Distribution System (PDS) and Anthyodaya Anna Yojana (AAY) are the two important strategies and intended to serve as safety net for food security to rural poor. As around 30 crore people in our country are nutritionally at risk, the PDS reforms have focussed more on the people living below the poverty line. The PDS has always been supplemental in nature and partly met the full requirements of the majority of the population. However, the benefits of the subsidy have thinly spread among about 6.5 crore BPL families in the country. The overall foodgrain production has increased from 50 million tonnes in 1950-51 to 209 million tonnes in 2005-06. Adequate food availability is necessary both for stabilizing prices and ensuring the operations of an effective PDS beamed at rural pool households. Foodgrains from the governments stocks are being made available through the PDS to HHs through a countrywide network of about 4.6 lakh fair-price shops. Despite PDS reforms and several new initiatives the food security scenario of the country is not satisfactory. The country is witnessing on the one side huge stock of food and on the other side the food security of the poorest of the poor at the household level is yet a far cry. Besides, NSS survey points out that the 5% of the total population of the country sleeps without two square meals a day. The Anthyodaya Anna Yojana has targeted hungry and the poorest of the poor households of the country. There is hardly any study based on the results of implementation of Anthyodaya Anna Yojana Scheme. Therefore it is necessary to ascertain the benefits of the scheme accrued to the rural poor.

But the present PDS is inherently costly as it is based on surpluses of two superior cereals-rice and wheat- generated by some green revolution pockets like as Punjab, Haryana and Western UP. This system is practically absent in some of the hard-core poverty areas like Orissa, Bihar and North-East region. PDS covers a large section of the population but its benefits do not always reach the targeted groups. Lastly we cannot be sure that PDS is really going to secure food to the rural poor. There are large number of literature on this theme explains the inadequacies of the present food security system.(Details see Mahendra Dev 1996, Swaminathan, 1998, Mahendra Dev and Suryanarayanana, 1993, Jharwal, 1998 etc.). The hard reality is that we need to produce foodgrains on a much larger scale to meet fully domestic consumption requirement, for instance, food production needs to be raised to 250 million tonnes by year 2025 (Majumdar-2007). the

Planning Commission did an evaluation of the PDS and found that 57 per cent of the poor had been actually excluded from the BPL system. Earlier, the Abhijit Sen Committee had also come up with similar findings, pointing to the utter failure of the targeted system, and suggested a return to the universal PDS.

Now there is a question, whether the country will continue to be self-sufficient in the food production? There is a big demand for foodgrains and cereals in coming period. The projection indicate that our population will be 1.5 billion by year 2025. Rising population and per capita income are pushing up the demand, which needs to be met through enhanced productivity per unit area, input and time, the annual increase in demand in India is estimated to be 2.6 million tonnes in rice, 2.2 millon tonnes in wheat, 1.6 million tonnes in pulses, 4.2 million tonnes in fruits, 2.5 million tonnes in vegetables, 7.8 million tonnes in milk and 0.6 million tonnes in fish. As against the Tenth Five Year Plan target of 4 per cent growth rate in agriculture, the growth of agriculture GDP, including forestry and fishing, was only 1 per cent per annum in the last three years of above plan. (Rai, 2006). But the past trends of supply had been showing the slow down in the production of foodgrains and per capita availability of cereals. The overall availability of cereals has decreased from 469 gram per capita per day in 1991 to 391 gram per capita per day in 2005-06. Net availability of foodgrains has also gone down from 510 gram per capita per day in year 1991 to 422 gram per capita per day in year 2005.

The wheat production rose from 6.45 million tonnes in 1950-51 to 76.37 million tonnes in 1999-2000 and now decreased to 73.70 million tonnes during 2006-07. Rice production also increased up from 21 million tonnes in year 1950-50, to 93.34 in 2001-02 and now fell down to 91.79 million tonnes in 2006-07. Trends of production of rice and wheat are going down during last five years. There is an increasing gap between demand and supply of food grain. Food security issues differ across the states. Punjab is a food surplus state while Kerala is a food deficit state. North-eastern states have also same problem. To meet the national food demand, we need to raise investment in agricultural research and education irrigation along with watershed development. Watershed development as sustainable sources for food security in the backward states, provide more income generating opportu-nities among the rural poor households.

Self sufficiency in foodgrains has driven the development of irrigation facility in India. About 60 per cent of the crop output now originated from under irrigated areas., which account for about 42.2 per cent of total cropped areas. The productivity of rice and wheat in Punjab was more than double their productivity in Bihar. The reason for such differences in productivity became clearer when we look at the level of irrigation in Punjab and Bihar. Around 95 per cent of gross cropped area in Punjab was irrigated compared to 48 per cent in Bihar. Thus Punjab is almost fully irrigated and productivity of irrigated land for rice and wheat is much higher than non-irrigated land. (Kumar Pramod, 2006) .According to the Deputy Chairman Planning Commission, at the present rate of incremental addition to irrigated area, it will take 30 years to complete all the ongoing large and medium irrigation projects (Ahluwalia, 2006). Raising the ground water level to promote irrigation facilities s the primary objective of most watershed development programmes. Indian agriculture has been sustained by natural and traditional man-made water bodies such as *Ahar, pokhar*, tanks, lakes, ponds etc. , but many of them are in bad shape. Now it needs to be restored urgently. For the irrigation facility maintaining the canal system is important. Poor maintenance of canal system, results into the loss of much water in non-productive manner. A watershed is an area from which runoff resulting from precipitation flows past a single point into a large stream, river, lake or pond. Each watershed is an independent hydrological unit. It has become an acceptable unit of planning for optimum use and conservation of soil and water resources. The concept of integrated watershed development refers to the development and management of the resources in the watershed of achieves higher sustainable production without deterioration of the resource base and any ecological imbalances.

Now Prime Minister Manmohan Singh called for a second Green Revolution:-" I believe we do need a second Green Revolution in agriculture .... based on the application of new technologies and modern business practices. New technology will enable farmers to make more informed choices and undertake product planning in a demand driven rather than supply- driven mode"(Singh, Manmohan ,2005). Mr. Jeffrey Sachs, who has emerged as a modern development *guru*, has endorsed the Prime Minister's statement. " Agriculture has not done well. The Prime Minister is right when he says that the second Green Revolution, is needed but in poorer states."(Sach,2006). Prime Minister has been calling for a second green revolution. It will be appropriate to restrict the use of this term to enhancing the productivity, profitability, and sustainability of dryland farming, that is, raising crops solely based on rainwater. If the first green revolution benefited farmers in irrigated areas, the second should help farm families in rainfed, and semi-arid areas also . In both cases, the pathway used for yield enhancement should be the evergreen revolution approach. The Prime Minister said that an important dimension of the new deal is aimed at ensuring food and nutritional security of the people, while at the same time augmenting farm incomes and employment through launching of the second green revolution

WSD AND EMPLOYMENT GENERATION

WSD aims to increase employment through labour- intensive soil and water conservation. The implementation of the WSD programme can affect migration though and increase in short-term employment as well as long–term productivity gains. It will create a sustained employment opportunities for the rural community including the landless rural poor .WSD should be the good tools for accelerating wage employment. It has a notable impact on employment and income opportunities. The historical evidence suggests that the watershed programmes successfully met the initial three principal objectives of raising income, generating employment and conserving soil and water resources. Employment is continuing to decline in the traditional natural resource extraction and agricultural industries that once supported rural economies. To survive and prosper, rural communities must attract new people and investments that can establish businesses and create jobs.

The National Commission for Enterprises in unorganised Sector, Government of India has also views convergence of watershed development activities with other programmes as an issue of high importance. A number of activities undertaken in the Watershed Development Programme (WDP) pertains to wage employment. These activities can be covered with NREGP and SGRY. Shelves of projects related to water conservation, plantation and afforestation, renovation of the existing Watershed Development Work Plans at Block level. The Watershed Development Teams should work for convergence of WDPs with NREG activities. Panchayats should be trained to ensure convergence in implementation. The Eleventh Plan has recommended preparation of district plans with activity planning for different levels of the PRIs. Integration of land and water improvement programmes should be ensured in activity mapping and in the district plans.

EVALUATION OF WATERSHED PROGRAMME AND ITS IMPACTS

Analyzing the comparative performance of watersheds in the scarcity zone and the transition zone, Deshpande (1997) maintains that

- Incremental income generated per unit of investment is higher in the scarcity zone than in the transition zone.
- Sources of income generated per household differ substantially in the two zones.
- Income generated from agricultural sector per hectare is inversely related to the size of the holding.
- A higher level of farm asset creation takes place in the scarcity zone as compared to the transition zone.
- The magnitude of reduction in runoff/soil loss is also found to be higher in the scarcity zone.

Singh et. al (1991) studied the Kandi watershed, in one of the economically backward tracts of the Punjab state. The different components of this project were forestry, animal husbandry, soil conservation, horticulture, and irrigation and the rates of return on them were 12 per cent, 9 per cent, 10 per cent, 22 per cent and 2 per cent respectively. The overall project ERR of 8 per cent represents a substantial shortfall from the earlier expectations of 12 to 20% according to the feasibility studies. However, the internal rates of return and benefit cost ratios are 38% and 2.30 for kinnow, 26 per cent and 2.48 for mango, and 44 per cent and 2.30 for guava respectively. Increase in cultivated area was from 80.34 to 99.33 while irrigated area increased from 11.36 per cent to 48.93 per cent.

In a more recent study, Shah (1997) has examined watershed programmes in Western Gujarat. A yield gain of 20 to 30 per cent is expected with an average investment of about Rs.6000 per hectare. In terms of the acceptability of different components of watershed technology, she reports that in a dynamic rainfed region, returns from capital intensive measures such as land leveling, water harvesting and commercial plantation are likely to be higher and are also likely to evoke more interest and participation. In situ conservation measures by themselves (including vegetative barriers) may not succeed unless accompanied by measures that are perceived to be income enhancing. She also maintains that farmers need appropriate technology, even if it is not a low cost one.

It is true that many rural development programmes launched by the government have resulted in utter failures but it is a matter of great satisfaction that the watershed development. Programme designed with people centric approach has succeeded in having their positive impacts to a large extent on the life of the rural community. Some of the impacts can be counted as under.

The watershed development projects have increased the area under irrigation, which helped in increasing crop productivity (Shah-2001)

Increase in productivity can be seen more in case of rain-fed crops like legumes and soyabeans, which witnessed rise by about 280 per cent. (Renfro-2005)

As a result there has been increase in the farm income and better livelihoods of the poor in fragile and high-risk areas.

These programmes have helped in improving the moisture content in the soil creating new opportunities for crop diversification. It also helped in the increase in the crop-intensity by 13-25 per cent.

Several studies reveal that watershed development projects have their positive impacts on controlling the soil erosion. This impact was more significant in case of rain-fed areas.

Watershed development projects are very much helpful in augmenting water storage capacity and improving local water resources by reducing the water run-off and increasing the recharge of ground water.

Watershed development has more potential to generate employment opportunities for rural poor. This is due to the increased availability of water resources, diversified cropping pattern including cultivation of labour intensive vegetable and other horticultural crops. The additional employment generation from watershed programme varry across regions depending on the crop-intensity. The employment generation potential has got impetus from National Rural Employment Guarantee Act in those areas where the act is being implemented.

Once the villagers realised that they could work together, they decided to take matters into their own hands and build a well to tap water from a small stream that flowed beside the village. The water could be used to irrigate their fields. The increasing employment opportunities reduced the burden of surplus labour engaged in agriculture. It has not only increased the income of the rural poor but also minimized the forced migration of labour from rural to urban areas in search of livelihoods.

PROBLEMS

A lack of project sustainability and equity was another problem in India's watershed management programme. Many projects failed to develop strategies to maintain assets once project support ended. Feedback from several projects indicates that many farmers benefited from watershed projects only through obtaining short-term paid labouring work. Because communities see few long-term benefits emanating from these projects, they have little interest in operating and maintaining project assets. Moreover, some property regimes in rural India contradict the requirements of watershed management guidelines. Land is inequitably distributed and rights over groundwater are bundled with landownership. Most watershed development projects have a clear hierarchy of benefits and beneficiaries. Farm households benefit most, with improved irrigation; they are followed by those farmers who receive on-farm treatments such as field bunds. The landless and those who do not own livestock benefit the least. These issues have been treated as inevitable, and have not been made the object of a participatory process. There is a need to Efficient programmes of natural resources management is possible only if they prove to be catalysts for initiating sustainable development process. This is true in particular in developing countries initiate negotiations among different beneficiaries and stakeholders.

CONCLUSIONS & RECOMMENDATIONS

- Increased productivity of land and water have the potential to create the path of economic growth even without further investment. Focussing on this fact those programmes should be made which may argument the natural resources development. These programmes are superior to traditional investment in employment or assets creating schemes.
- The unit of operation of the watershed development programmes must capture a large part of externalities, which are the essence of natural resources management.
- Watershed Management done in smaller privately owned units have failed in its attempts at soil and water conservation. It affects downstream areas. So emphasis should be given on watershed development in

comparatively bigger areas to make the programme more cost effective.

- Any water shade Development programme should be area specific, such programme should be made considering the problems and prospects in specific agro-climatic zones.
- Any people–centered programme can succeed if it has the whole hearted support of the people at large. Most watersheds contain a mix of government, private, common property and open access to land. Decisions regarding the use of resources are taken by the respective owners within the framework of social and administrative structures. Sometimes, these decisions are taken in the interest of respective owners but not in the interest of sustainable use of resources like water and soil. The dichotomy between decision on the basis of ecological imperatives and property rights creates the problem for the success of WSM programme. The watershed programme should be made on the basis of agreement among a large number of stakeholders with regards to the sharing of costs and benefits.
- Success of any programme depends not only on its aims and structure but also on the implementation machinery. That requires efficient implementation machinery and strict monitoring. Any programmes becomes the victim of corruption, irregularity, mismanagement of funds, lethargic tendency and all these lead to its failure.
- A process of social mobalisation is required to involve and encourage communities and households to under take water management to meet their water needs.
- Awareness component of watershed development is also very important.
- WSD programme should more socially less technically.

There should be focus on creating more and more awareness among the masses about the need and various aspects of watershed development programme from the stage of conceptualization to planning, implementation and routine appraisals. It helps the programme and that ensures greater success. Improved evaluation of watershed projects is necessary to provide information on what work (Good design), for whom(beneficiary impact) and how(resource efficiency). (Hope, 2007). WSD programme can ensure food security, reduce poverty and generate employment opportunities and will be a source of sustainable livelihoods for the rural poor.

REFERENCES

Agrawal, Anil & Sunita Narain (1997), *Dying Wisdom: Rise, Fall and Potential of India's Traditional Water Harvesting Systems.* (State of India's Environment–A Citizens' Report, No. 4), Centre for Science & Environment (CSE), New Delhi.

Ahluwalia, S. Montek (2006), "Reducing Poverty and Hunger in India: The Role of Agriculture" *Annual Report 2004-05*, International Food Policy Research Institute, Washington, D.C.

Ahluwalia, S. Montek (2006), "Agriculture Situation: Policies for Achieving Production Increase in Indian Agriculture" *Economic Development in India* , Vol.93, Academic Foundation, New Delhi, p–57.

Deshpande, R.S. and N. Rajsekharan (1997), "Impact of Watershed Development Programme: Experiences and Issues", *Arthvignana,* Vol. 39(3), pp. 374-390.

D'Souza, Marcella (1998) 'Gender and Watershed Development', *Agricultural Research and Extention Network Newsletter* 36, July 1997, Overseas Development Institute, London

Farrington, J.,Turton, C.& James, A.J. (1999), *Participatory Watershed Development: Challenges for the 21st Century*, New Delhi, Oxford University.

GOI (2007), *"Report on Conditions of Work and Promotion of Livelihoods in the Unorganisd Sector,"* National Commission for Enterprises in the Unorganised Sector, Government of India, Academic Foundation, pp. 188

Hope, R.A.(2007), Evaluating Social Impacts of Watershed Development in India, *World Development*, Vol. 35, No8, Pp 1436-1449, Oxford University Centre for the Environment (OUCE), UK.

Jensen, J., Seth, S.,Sawney, T and Kumar, P. (1996), 'Watershed Development: Proceedings of Danida's Internal Workshop on Watershed Development. Watershed Development Coordina-tion Unit, Danida, New Delhi.

Jharwal, S. M. (1998), *Public Distribution System in India Reassessed,* Manak Publications, New Delhi

Johnson, N, Ravnborg, H. M, Westerman, O. and Probst, K. (2001), "User Participation in Watershed Management and Research"., Working Paper No–19, APRI, IFPRI, Washington D.C.

Kumar Pramod (2006), Economic Reforms and Agricultural Economy A Comparative Analysis of Punjab and Bihar, *Agriculture Summit 2006*, Ministry of Agriculture, Government of India. pp. 21-32

Kerr, J., Pangare, G., & Pangare V. L. (2002), *Watershed Development Project in India- An Evaluation.* Research Report No. 127, IFPRI, Washington DC.

Mahendra Dev, S. (1996), "Food Security: PDS Vs. GS: A Tale of Two States" *Economic and Political Weekly*, Volo.31, No,27

Mahendra Dev, S and Suryanarayana, M. H. (1991), "Is PDS Urban Biased and Pro Rich? An Evaluation" *Economic and Political Weekly*, Vol.26, No, 41.

Majumdar, N A. (2007), *Inclusive Growth: Development Perspective,* Academic Foundation, New Delhi, p.108-115

Paul , D. K. (1997), 'Rainfed Farming System Development in India: Retrospect and Prospect'. In Katyal, J. C. and Farrington, J. (eds) Research for Rainfed Farming , ICAR, New Delhi.

Rai, Mangala (2006), "Green Revolution- II, Agricultural Research and Education" Paper presented during *ASSOCHAM Summit on Green Revolution- II, Delhi*

Raju, K.V. et al. (2004), "Water Resources" Vol. 3, States of Indian Farmers- A Millennium Study, Academic Foundation, New Delhi.

Renfro, R. Z. (2005), "The Value of Participation in Development-Relevance to Soil and Water Conservation." Internet site http://www.adbi.org.

Rhoades, R.E., and Elliot, T.S. (2000), "Participatory Watershed Research and Management: Where the Shadow Falls." Gatekeeper Series No. 81, London: International Institute for Economic Development.

Sachs, J. (2006), Interview with Jeffry Sachs, Times of India, February 06, 2006.

Shah, Amita (1997), "Watershed Development Programme in India: Emerging Issues for Environment–Development Perspective" Paper presented as workshop on Environment and Agriculture, Delhi School of Economics, December.

Shah, Amita (2001), "Who Benefits from Participatory Watershed Developments? Lessons from Gujarat, India", Gatekeeper, Series No 97, London,: International Institute for Economic Development.

Sharma, S.(2005), "Rethinking Watershed Development in India: Strategy for the Twenty-first Century". In M. Achouri, L. Tennyson, K. Upadhyay and R. White, eds. *Preparing for the Next Generation of Watershed Management Programmes and Projects.* Proceedings of the Asian Workshop, Kathmandu, 11 to 13 September 2003.

Singh, A. J., Joshi, A.S., Singh R.P. and Ravi Gupta (1991), "An Economic Appraisal of Kandi Watershed and Area Development Project in Punjab", *Indian Journal of Agriculture Economics,* Volume 46(3), July-September, pp287-93.

Singh, Manmohan (2005), "Second Green Revolution in Indian Agriculture", Inaugural Address at the Agricultural Summit, Organised by FICCI and Ministry of Agriculture, New Delhi, April 09,2005; *Economic Development in India,* Vol.89, Academic Foundation, New Delhi, p.21.

SRISTI-(2005), "Rethinking Policy Options for Watershed Management by Local Communities: Combining Equity, Efficiency and Ecological- Economic Viability." Society for Research and Initiative for Sustainable Technologies and Institution

Swaminathan, Madhura (1998), "Understanding the Costs of Food Corporation of India", *Economic and Political Weekly,* Vol..34, No. 52.

Wani, S. P.., Singh, H. P., Sreedevi, T K., Pathak, P., Rego, T. J., Shiferaw, B. and Iyer, S. R. (2005), *"Farmer-Participatory Integrated Watershed Management: Adarsha Watershed, Kothapally India An Innovative and Upscalable Approach"*.Case-7 in Para-3 Case Example Series, ICRISAT, India, 2005

——(2004), World Bank, *Managing Watershed Externalities in India,* Washington DC.: World Bank.

CHAPTER–15

WATERSHED MANAGEMENT FOR LIVELIHOOD SUSTAINABILITY IN INDIA

S.S.P. Sharma

INTRODUCTION

With the widening of international development goals from merely increasing food production to include poverty reduction and environmental sustainability, to protect the environment is a big challenge for a country like India, and greater emphasis should be given to check the exploitation of the natural resources base. Soil erosion and land degradation coupled with declining per capita availability of land and freshwater are posing serious threat to environment. This is becoming more intense with the burgeoning population causing food security problems in developing countries. Hence careful and concerted efforts are needed for efficient and effective management of natural resources for increased productivity of the soils.

Several government and non- government agencies have launched watershed development projects to tackle some of these generic problems with the objectives of soil conservation, improving the land productivity and promoting appropriate technologies for efficient and sustainable use of natural resources. However, many watershed projects around the world have not performed well because of the poor community participation (Johnson et al., 2001). The key to the success of any watershed project and its sustainability depends on people's participation. For achieving the desired participation of people, the roles of community organizations, groups and other stakeholders are crucial. Local people must play an active role starting from project design, moving to implementation and the project maintenance. In this context, a participatory watershed management approach is considered as the ideal for achieving food security and sustainability.

HISTORY OF WATERSHED DEVELOPMENT IN INDIA

The development of ideas on sustainable livelihoods was witnessed during 1990s. These grew from awareness that rural development approaches based purely on agricultural production were insufficient to meet the livelihood needs of the rural and landless poor. Agricultural land and livestock frequently generate only a portion of rural livelihoods, which are *not* primarily agrarian or land-based. Other forms of income generation, perhaps derived from migration, part-time trade or handicraft production may make a large contribution to an individual's or a household's livelihood. Instead of considering land or water and its potential for development, attention was given instead to people's needs and their priorities for development, which is challenging for land-based development projects, such as the watershed development program.

A watershed is a logical, natural planning unit for sustainable agricultural research and development particularly when environmental considerations are emphasized. Hydro logically, watershed could be defined as an area from which the runoff drains through a particular point in the drainage system. India began to look at the watershed development programs in the 1970s for increasing land controlling land degradation and increasing the productivity of soils. In the 1970s, watershed development held no special significance for the development community in India, however by the end of the 1980s the situation changed radically. Initially watershed projects were concentrating on soil and water conservation issues. A decade later, it became apparent that technical and physical works alone would not lead to the desired objectives of watershed development and it must also take into account the social, financial and institutional aspects of rural development. Watershed programs have been established over a diverse range of rain-fed agro eco-regions in India. Watersheds in India are broadly grouped into five agro-climatic zones:

(i) Trans-Gangetic Plain zone
(ii) Western Himalayan zone
(iii) Western Plateau and Hill zone
(iv) Gujarat Plains and Hill zone
(v) Southern zone.

Due to inherent heterogeneity of agro-climatic characteristics over different regions, they have divergent potentials and opportunities.

Depending upon the size of the watersheds, these are broadly divided into micro and macro watersheds. Watersheds with areas up to 1250 hectares were classified as micro watersheds, whereas the macro-watersheds were those, of greater area.

In 1994, the Ministry of Rural Development (MoRD) of the GoI produced a set of guidelines for implementing its watershed programmes, which aimed to tackle the concerns related to the realisation of the full benefits of watershed work. This progressive policy was essentially people-centred and it incorporated good practice from NGO and government policy, such as awareness raising, bottom-up planning, partnerships with NGOs, and community participation. Since 1994-95 Ministry of rural areas and employment, government of India has spent over US $3.5 billion and implemented nearly 10000 watersheds. Currently about US $200 million is allocating annually for watershed development in India.

WEAKNESSES IN THE CONVENTIONAL APPROACH

The traditional system of natural resource use in rural communities has significantly evolved over the years. In the past, priority of watershed management was given to the Biophysical frame work of watershed which is often based on top-down approach (Rhoades and Elliot, 2000). However in the traditional system, local people were not often consulted in the design of top-down approach, which resulted in failure of projects in achieving the project goals. Watershed projects are more efficient and effective when users are given a role in managing their own watershed resources (Johnson et. al, 2001).

User participation has a lot of implications for watershed management and research. There was hardly any scope for learning in the traditional approach and there would be tendency towards giving priority to the biophysical frame work of watersheds justified a top-down planning approach. Planning in the traditional system was often based on the capacity of land rather than needs and capacities of local people (Rhoades and Elliot, 2000). This produced a mismatch between local population and outside watershed project managers and no flow of information between land users and other key actors such as researchers, planners and policy makers etc.

A major challenge in the traditional watershed management approach was the assumption of technology transfer instead of development of technology on peoples land and their surroundings. Another important weakness was regarding the training and research where the major responsibility for training has been given to agricultural research institutions and agricultural universities, which are sound in technical aspect of watershed but are weak in social science aspects of the institution building as well as forging links with non-farm sector to generate value added products from watersheds (SRISTI, 2005).

Another key weakness is ignoring local knowledge on local soil types and conditions for suitability of technology to the specific soil while designing and implementation of the projects. It would be better to adopt on-farm research trails for watershed projects designed and implemented jointly by users, scientists and other stakeholders. Farmer participation in the on-farm research will provide an interactive mode so that both scientists and farmers can decide on the conduct of trials and technology to be tested, and active participation of stakeholders in the research that is important for successful adoption of technology.

In the conventional approach people's participation often limited to project implementation stage and no focus on institutional building for long term collective management of resources (Joy et. al, 2004). In many watersheds excessive emphasis on engineering structures, soil and water conservation measures. *Paradigm shift:* Earlier resources were allocated by the central and state governments for watershed development and which are supply driven. This top-down approach was not conducive for including the stakeholder's participation in designing the programs that are targeted to their improvement. There was lot of mismatch between the needs of the stakeholders and the activities for implementation of watershed development. Such watershed projects often failed to achieve the intended targets in the absence of peoples' participation. Realizing this, participatory watershed management has emerged as a new paradigm for watershed development in India. This paradigm shift was expected to contribute towards more decentralized governance and increased participatory approaches to natural resource management that will rise to face the new challenges by strengthening the capacity of local people.

PARTICIPATORY WATERSHED MANAGEMENT AND ITS EVOLUTION

Participatory watershed management has emerged as a new paradigm for sustainable rural livelihoods and it occupied the central-stage of rural development in the fragile and semiarid environments of the developing nations. The concept of participatory watershed management emphasizes an inter-disciplinary, inter-sectoral and multiinstitutional mechanism (Rhoades and Elliot). Participatory watershed management has been defined as a process "which aims to create a self-supporting system, which is essential for sustainability" (Wani et al, 2005). Participatory watershed management provides opportunities to the stakeholders to jointly negotiate their interests, set priorities, evaluate opportunities, implement and monitor the outcomes. This concept came widely into practice in late 1980s and over the time peoples' institutions, like zilla parishads (district revenue administrative units), self help groups, and watershed-implementing committees were gradually involved in the project management system. With allocation of more funds for watershed development, several non-governmental organizations came forward to aggressively participate in implementing the watershed programs.

In India, participatory watershed management has roots in the non-government sector that go back nearly as far as the government programs. The seeds of the participatory watershed management can be traced to a small village called Ralegan siddhi in Maharshtra state of India. Anna Hazare, a local leader was responsible for bringing many social changes in the village particularly soil and water conservation measures besides family planning, a ban on alcohol, protection of non arable lands against open grazing and felling of trees and voluntary labor for community welfare and other measures which helped in restoring natural resources base of the village (Kerr et al, 2002). This ultimately led to people participation in watershed management and the evolution of participatory watershed management looking beyond just the biophysical aspects to also focus on social and institutional aspects following a bottom up approach. It is now widely accepted that the communities must participate to enhance the productivity of natural resources in a sustainable fashion (Turton et al, 1998).

MANAGEMENT AND INSTITUTIONAL SET UP

The management structure and the institutional setup appears to be complex and it is better to look at the institutional arrangements in implementing participatory watershed development program for understanding the impact of participatory watershed management better. The series of steps followed for forming watershed committees are presented below.

Management of watershed development in India evolved significantly over the past there decades. During the 1970s to early 1980s, the main concentration was largely on biophysical criteria. In late 1980s there were some significant changes looking beyond soil and water conservation to include improving the productivity of natural resources. In 1994-95 Ministry of Rural Areas and Employment, Government of India came up with strict guidelines to achieve multiple objectives including productive, social, ecological/ environmental and equity issues to achieve optimum utilization of the watershed's natural resources; employment generation and development of other economic resources in the village; easy and affordable solutions and social condition of the resource poor, respectively. The present guidelines outline the various implementation stages of the watershed development projects, the operational procedures and provide sufficient operational flexibility at State, District and Project levels to enable them to respond to differing situations and aspirations of the village community.

The 1994 Guidelines assumed new arrangements for allocating funds and managing projects. The District Rural Development Agency (DRDA) or *Zilla Parishad* (ZP—district level council) was made responsible for the overall responsibility for program implementation in the concerned district. They appoint watershed Development

Advisory Committee to advise on issues like selection of villages, training and monitoring. PIAs (Project Implementation Agencies) are selected by the DRDA and the programs requires formation of Watershed Development Teams (WDT) of technical experts like civil or agriculture engineers, agronomists, soil scientists etc. to assist watershed committees. The WDT works closely with the rural communities in planning and implementing the watershed program. Each WDT is expected to handle 10 micro watersheds. The Watershed Association (WA) represents all members of the community who are directly or indirectly associated with the watershed. The WA appoints a watershed committee (WC) consisting of representatives of user groups, self help groups, the *gram panchayat* (elected village assembly) and the WDT. Secretary from each committee is responsible for maintaining accounts and records. Funds flow directly from central Government and state government to the DRDA/ZP.

Partnership based community participation is central to the watershed program and the guidelines lay down a detailed planning process. The guidelines also encourage the involvement of users groups (UGs) and self help groups (SHGs). Each team is expected to conduct a participatory rural appraisal to identify potential programs and concerned user groups. This leads to the development of a watershed development plan, containing details of various activities, lists of user groups, funding requirements and users' contributions. The plan is approved by the WA and then submitted to the DRDA through the PIA. These new guidelines also aim to promote up-gradation and adoption of low cost local technologies and materials and emphasize the importance of people's participation in the programs and the need to improve technical as well as management skills of project staff and the village community.

ANALYSIS OF THE IMPACT OF PARTICIPATORY WATERSHED MANAGEMENT

In recent years, many developing countries have adopted watershed development approach as part of their rural development strategy. For example the Government of

India with the help of external donors, extensively undertaking the watershed development programs in the dry and semi-arid regions as a means of addressing soil erosion, drought rural unemployment and poverty. It was anticipated that watershed programs would augment farm income, raise agricultural productivity and conserve soil and water resources through the process of participatory watershed management.

Watershed programs were initiated over a wide range of agro eco-regions of India. These watershed programs are supported by National governments and also by some international donors. As Rhoades and Elliot noted funding participatory watershed projects was one of the most popular investments by development agencies and international donors in the post-Earth summit years. The new paradigm shift in watershed development focused on achieving the overall goal of enhancing sustainable rural livelihoods for reducing the incidence of rural poverty. Most of the watershed projects were launched for the following purposes:

- Raising farm income
- Enhancing agricultural productivity
- Soil and water conservation
- Generating rural employment
- Reducing risk by diversifying crops in rain fed areas

Several useful studies have been conducted to assess the contribution of participatory watershed programs (Turton et. al, 1998, Kerr et. al, 2002, Wani et. al, 2005, Joshi et al, 2003 and Reddy et al., 2004) and the results from these studies are discussed here.

Many studies revealed that participatory watershed projects had a positive impact on crop productivity. Due to increased irrigated area under watershed area helped in increasing crop productivity (shah, 2001). Productivity gains were reported to be greater in case of rain-fed crops. Average yields of rain-fed crops (e.g. soybeans and legumes) increased by as much as by 280% (Renfro, 2005).

This information suggests that participatory watershed management programs made significant impact in terms of productivity gains in rain-fed areas which contributes to increased farm income and better livelihoods of the poor in fragile and high risk environments. The watershed programs have also helped in improving soil moisture content. Many farmers in the watershed development area reported an increase in soil moisture level (shah, 2001). This improved soil moisture will open new opportunities for diversifying farming activities in rain-fed areas. Due to the watershed programs cropping intensity will be increased significantly and it is observed that cropping intensity is increased by 13-25% (Renfro, 2005).

Another important impact of watershed development was its impact on controlling soil erosion. Many studies have revealed that watershed development interventions were successful in controlling soil erosion. (Kerr et. Al, 2002) This effect was more significant in case of rain-fed areas as dry lands are more prone to erosion compared to the irrigated lands. Soil and water conservation measures adopted in the watershed development projects were helpful in augmenting water storage capacity and improving local water resources by reducing the rate of runoff, and increasing the ground water recharge. (Butterworth et. al, 2001).

Watershed development projects have greater potential to generate employment opportunities to the rural people. This was due to the increased availability of water resources, diversified cropping pattern including cultivation of labor intensive vegetable crops and other horticultural crops (Reddy et al, 2001). This additional employment generation from a watershed program varies across regions depending on the cropping intensity, and the labor intensive crops grown in that region. This additional employment generation in the villages led to minimizing migration of landless and other labor. Thus watershed programs also contributed towards checking migration of rural people to the urban areas. This migration has greater concern for planning and devising rural development strategies.

CASE STUDIES

There were several studies on examining the impact of participatory watershed management programs. We have selected three important case studies and the important results are presented below.

CASE 1: FARMER-PARTICIPATORY INTEGRATED WATERSHED MANAGEMENT–CONSORTIUM MODEL

This case describes a novel approach that International Crops Research Institute for the Semi-Arid Tropics (ICRISAT) has developed to address the issue of efficient use of natural resources in rain fed areas. The NRM team at ICRISAT led by Dr Wani adopted the participatory consortium model which is a unique model extended to their flagship watershed management project. This model has been adopted with great success in one of the ICRISAT's water shed project at Kothapally village of Andhra Pradesh in India. Consortium approach was an innovative model with a consortium of institutions (local, national and international research and development institutions for providing all the technical support to the NGO's and farmers) was formed for project implementation.

In this approach, all the government authorities were involved in the consortium from the beginning. Participation of local community was central to this approach and community participation will be encouraged by various communities. The important element of the model was using 'users pay' principle without giving any subsidies for investments on individual's farm for technologies, inputs and conservation measures.

Impact of Consortium Watershed Model:

- Sustainable increase in the productivity of crops
- Intensive avenue plantation has come up in wastelands of the project area
- Gliricidia saplings planted on bunds were generating Nitrogen rich organic matter
- Worm farming was helpful to women in generating income
- Significant reduction in runoff and soil loss
- Ground water levels were improved and additional lands were irrigated with additional ground water recharge.
- Crop productivity was optimized by adopting integrated soil, water, crop and nutrient management in the watershed
- Vegetation cover was increased form 129 ha to 200 ha
- With improved technologies farmers obtained high crop yields, particularly in dry lands
- Net returns on rain-fed cereal crops have more than doubled

- Watershed projects contributed towards capacity development of local people
- Finally this consortium watershed modal also contributed towards poverty reduction by increasing average household income. (for complete details see Wani et al, 2005)

CASE 2: IMPACT OF WATERSHED PROGRAM AND PEOPLE'S PARTICIPATION USING META ANALYSIS APPROACH

An important study by Joshi et al was useful and note worthy to mention here.

This study was based on the meta-analysis and the authors made an attempt to evaluate the watershed programs and people's participation, some important results of this study are presented in Table 1. (For complete details see Joshi et al, 2003).

It can be observed from the table that the mean benefit-cost-ratio of watershed program was 2.14 which indicate that the returns for investments in rain-fed areas are quite impressive. The mean internal rate of return on watershed investments was 22 percent. Another important result from this study is about creating additional annual employment generation in watershed areas was about 181 man days per hectare.

CASE3: SUSTAINABLE RURAL LIVELIHOODS FRAME WORK FOR ASSESSING THE IMPACT OF PARTICIPATORY WATERSHED DEVELOPMENT

This case study was based on the work by Reddy et al, (2004). This was an interesting study and the authors have adopted sustainable rural livelihoods frame work for assessing the impact of watershed program on the five capital assets. Any watershed development will have implications for all these five capital assets which are measured in different terms.

Physical Capital— through increase in durable assets such as house, machinery, livestock and irrigation facilities

Table 1
Summary of Benefits from the Sample Watershed Studies

Indicator	*Particulars*	*Unit*	*No. of Studies*	*Mean*	*Mode*	*Median*	*Min*	*Max*	*t-value*
Efficiency	B/C ratio	Ratio	128	2.14	1.7	1.81	0.82	7.06	21.25
Equity	Employment	Mandays/ha/yr	39	181.5	75	127	11	900	6.74
Sustainability	Irrigated area	percent	97	33.56	52	26	1.37	156	11.77
	Cropping intensity	percent	11.5	63.51	80	41	10	200	12.65
	Rate of runoff	percent	36	-13	-33	-11	-1.3	-50	6.78
	Soil loss	Tonnes/ha/yr	51	-0.82	-0.91	-0.88	0.11	-0.99	39.29

Source: Joshi et al. 2003.

Natural Capital— through changes in access to or improvements in land, water and other common pool resources (CPRs)

Human Capital— through changes in education, capacity building activities

Social Capital— through formation of watershed committees and self help groups, women's participation in decision-making process

Financial Capital— through savings and other income generating activities

The impact of watershed programs on each capital is presented below.

Physical Capital— There was a positive impact on physical capital in terms of enhanced availability of irrigation in the study area.

Natural Capital— Impact on this capital asset also was positive. The value of land assets has gone up in all the villages of the study area. There was also improvement in the terms of fodder availability in three of the four sample villages studied. Another improvement in the form of increased availability of drinking water that was greater in case of poor households. The proportion of area under irrigation has also increased marginally among all the households in the sample villages.

Human Capital— Impact on this capital asset was little and the expenditure on education was reported to be increased significantly.

Social Capital— Since the social development is a complex and long process, the study attempted to assess the social impact in terms of migration and gender. It was reported that migration of people was less during the implementation period of water shed which created additional employment in the villages. The other positive impact was strengthening the self help groups (SHG) through better employment and wages for women.

Financial Capital— Impact on this capital asset was positive in terms increased land productivity, increased employment in villages and significant increase in household income. (for complete details see Reddy et al, 2004)

The case studies described above provided sufficient evidence that participatory watershed management program met the desired the objectives towards creating sustainable rural livelihoods in India.

CONCLUSIONS

The participatory watershed management is a critical area of rural development that could support rural people in many ways. India's watershed development project is seen as flagship project of Ministry of Rural development, Government of India. Watershed management in India has undergone dramatic change to include greater stakeholder's participation for management of natural resources in a sustainable way. It is increasingly recognized that community participation was central to watershed development. More participatory approaches have achieved greater success in enhancing livelihoods in an equitable fashion (Kerr and Pangare, 2002).

It has been noted that participatory watershed management projects have been raising income, agricultural productivity, generating employment and conserving soil and water resources. Evidence from the three case studies and other general impact studies suggests that watershed development brought several positive trends including diversification of the rural economy, development of new institutions, increasing cropping intensity, Increasing cropping intensity, improved fodder production, increased availability of drinking water with rising ground water table, capacity development of the community etc. Based on the evidence found, it has been suggested that participatory watershed management could be a viable strategy of rural development for achieving sustainable rural livelihoods in India.

REFERENCES

Butterworth, J, Reddy, M.Y.V, and Batchelor, C. (2005), "Addressing Water Needs of the Poor in Watershed Management".

Johnson, N, Ravnborg, H.M, Westerman, O, and Probst, K. (2001), "User Participation in Watershed Management and Research", working paper No.19, CAPRi, IFPRI, Washington, D.C.

Joshi, P.K., Tewari, L., Jha, A.K. and Shiyani, R.L. (2003), "Impact of Watershed Program and People's Participation". National Centre for Agricultural Economics and Policy Research, (NCAP), New Delhi, India.

Joy, K.J, Paranjape, S, and Shah, A. (2004), "Scaling up Watershed Development Projects in India: Learning from the First Generation Projects", Forum for Watershed Research and Policy Dialogue, Bangalore, India.

Kerr, J., G. Pangare and V.L. Pangare (2002), Watershed Development Projects in India: An Evaluation. Washington, DC: International Food Policy Research Institute (IFPRI).

Reddy, V.R., Reddy, M.G., Galab, S., Soussan, J., Baginski, O.S. (2004), "Participatory Watershed Development in India: Can It Sustain Rural Livelihoods"?
Development and Change 35(2): 297-326.

Renfro, R. Z. (2005), "The Value of Participation in Development-Relevance to Soil and Water Conservation".

Rhoades, R.E, and Elliot, T.S. (2000), "Participatory Watershed Research and Management: Where the Shadow Falls". Gatekeeper Series No.81, London: International institute for Economic Development (IIED).

Shah, A. (2001) "Who Benefits from Participatory Watershed Development? Lessons from Gujarat, India". Gatekeeper series no.97, London: International institute for Economic Development (IIED).

Society for Research and Initiatives for Sustainable Technologies and Institution (SRISTI, 2005). "Rethinking Policy Options for Watershed Management by Local

Communities: Combining Equity, Efficiency and Ecological-Economic Viability".

Turton, C., Coulter, J., Shah, A. and Farrington, J. (1998), "Watershed Development in India: Impact of the 1994 Guidelines". A Report Prepared for Government of India (GOI) and DFID (New Delhi). London: ODI.

Wani, S. P., Singh, H.P., Sreedevi, T.K., Pathak, P., Rego, T.J., Shiferaw, B., and Iyer, S.R. (2005), (part3/case examples/ case 7)."*Farmer-Participatory Integrated watershed Management: Adarsha Watershed, Kothapally India. An Innovative and Upscalable Approach*". Case 7 in part 3 case example series, ICRISAT , India.

CHAPTER–16

Institutions, Equity and Different Stakeholders' Participation in Watershed Development: Some Evidences

U. Hemanth Kumar

INTRODUCTION

Resource degradation is found to have an adverse impact on human welfare. Enhancement of productivity in agriculture and sustainable maintenance of resources have already made significant impacts on poverty reduction in the country with proper policy doses. However, this has not been the case for many areas where the resource degradation is taking place. Rural poverty is mostly associated with recurrent occurrences of drought, poor maintenance and degradation of natural resources. In the recent past, several interventions have been made to reduce poverty through drought proofing technologies. Several partners are involved in designing new methodologies to tackle different constraints in the dryland areas. These include community-based watershed management and innovative institutional arrangements (Reddy 2000; Kerr 2001; Shiferaw and Bantilan 2004) to improve the productivity and sustainability of resources especially development of common property resource base in degraded areas.

World Bank's water Resource Management Policy (1993) also recognises user participation as a key element: "Participation is a process in which stakeholders influence policy formulation, alternative designs, investment choices, and management decisions affecting their communities and establish the necessary sense of ownership. As communities increase their participation in managing water resources, project selection, service delivery, and cost recovery are likely to be improved.

The paper looks into the primary stakeholders' participation and its impact on their livelihoods in the process, and management of watershed development. We have selected two states and two districts each in Andhra Pradesh and Rajasthan, namely, Medak and Prakasam in Andhra Pradesh and Bhilwara and Udaipur in Rajasthan. Two watersheds, completed and on-going were selected in each district based on groundwater recharge potential, common property resource management and involvement of landless include women, marginal and small farmers in the decision-making process and management of watersheds. The paper also seeks to highlight the significance of stakeholder participation in development of watersheds. It also aims at to assess the potential of participatory watershed development in ensuring livelihood security for the rural poor. Other aspects of participatory watershed development like the different dimensions and levels of participation by the stakeholder groups, and the role of external agencies etc. have also been looked at. An attempt has been made to present a comparative picture based on the findings from the two states.

REVIEW OF LITERATURE

Collective resources management occurs when individuals voluntarily cooperate as a group to coordinate their behavior to solve a shared problem. This requires formulating and enforcing rules that govern their interactions as a group to achieve a common goal. Property rights are defined as the capacity to call upon the collective to stand behind one's claim to a benefit stream (Bromely 1991). Since Harding's (the article on the tragedy of the commons (Harding 1968), extensive work has been made in the past on collective resource maintenance and property rights institutions in relation to management of common property resources (eg. development of community forestry, grazing lands, fishery) (Runge 1986; Jodha 1986; Ostrom 1990; Baland and Platteau 1996 Agrawal 2001). The focus is now shifting towards the broader natural resource management (NRM) and poverty issues in the country and how community as well as collective maintenance of resources and property rights institutions contributes to this effort (Meinzen-Dick et al. 2002). Along these developments, another approach to resource management –community –based integrated watershed management has evolved as a viable strategy for soil and water conservation as well as improvement of rural livelihoods in drought-prone areas. This approach focuses on a community in a given hydrological unit with emphasis on sustainable interventions that improve their livelihoods, and diverges substantially from the old focus on individual farmers, their plots and on soil and water conservation per se.

Farmer managed (cooperatives) resources are common in many regions especially in Europe (Nilsson, 2001), their performance accounts in relation to poverty reduction and provision of essential services to the rural poor has not been exemplary (Lele 1981; Hussi et al. 1993; Akwabi-Ameyaw 1997). Many of the cooperatives in the past under centralized planning were established by the state to replace private commercial activities in the provision of essential services to the rural poor sector (including credit and inputs). Hence, they functioned primarily as 'service cooperatives' supported by governments rather than as business enterprises owned and managed by the members. With structural adjustment and economic reforms, many of the service cooperatives lost this special protection from the state, further reducing their viability in the competitive economic environment (Lele 1981). The World Bank Study of these cooperatives and other rural organizations in many African countries indicates that cooperatives and other farmer organizations have often failed to develop in to viable and self-managed organizations capable of extending efficient services to their members (Hussi et al. 1993). This analysis showed that lack of independent and high degree of political interference was the main reasons for the failure of these organizations.

Community participation in watershed management has the potential to provide benefits to the poor. Watershed management contributes to enhancing resource productivity and sustainability. Social benefits can be maximized when the activity is carried out collectively. This collective action allows smallholder farmers to jointly invest in management practices that provide collective benefits to all members. When property rights to collectively held resources and investments are clearly defined and all beneficiaries respect the rules of collective action, farmers in drought-prone areas can benefit from increased availability of drinking and irrigation water, improved availability of fodder for livestock, reduced soil erosion, enhanced sustainability and improved environmental quality (Kerr et al. 2002; Farrington et al. 1999). This collective effect of the joint NRM investments and private production practices improves the productivity of available resources of the poor and reduces vulnerabilities to drought and other production risks.

Various kinds of interventions can be used to enhance awareness of the potentials of collective action and facilitate its emergence. While informal institutions of local cooperation commonly exist in the developing world (Bardhan 1993). The other external agencies of one or the other type facilitated the emergence of formal institutions of collective action in many documented case studies. The success of collective action in a given situation once it evolves depends upon several factors. The classic impediments of collective action are group size and inequality. A number of factors, either internal or external to the group, are identified as important determinants for the success of collective efforts in managing commons. These include clearly defined boundaries, monitoring, mechanisms for conflict resolution, and recognition of rights to organize and presence of graduated sanctions to penalize violators (Ostrom 1990). Some of the factors identified to the success of collective efforts of farmer organizations include homogeneity, size, choice of services, commercial activities, self-reliance and autonomy, finance, skills and education, participation, organizational structure and governance, legislation and focus. (Stockbridge, et al. 2003). It is anticipated that many of these factors will be relevant for issues related to collective participation in watershed management.

RESEARCH GAPS

The studies discussed did not give much importance to the role of stakeholder participation in development of watersheds. Some studies had noted the benefits from stakeholder participation in management of common property resources, i.e., enhancing resource productivity and sustainability of resources. Others stressed on the conflict resolutions through clearly defined property rights over common property resources. But inequalities in terms of asset endowments and social diversity (gender, caste, religion) among resource users raise issues regarding equitable access to allocation of water. The conflict potential over access to and utilization of water cannot be overlooked. This suggests the need for inter-community participation in management and development of watersheds. This also suggests that clear assignment of property rights would reduce conflicts among stakeholders and lead to equitable sharing of costs and benefits.

EMERGING ISSUES

1. Does community-based watershed management enhance equity? How does it affect the landless, marginal and small farmers and women?
2. What are the determinants of different stakeholder participation?
3. Whether the decision-making is participatory?

RESEARCH OBJECTIVES

In view of the above, the objectives set of the study is;

- To study the role of different stakeholders in the *process* of watershed implementation.

- To assess the impact of watershed development on *livelihood security.*

HYPOTHESIS OF THE STUDY

- The people-centred approach positively impacts on the livelihood security of rural poor
- Proper assignment of rules and norms within the watershed area would lead to better management of watersheds.
- Closeness of PIAs to different stakeholder groups at watershed level have helped to gain confidence as well as capacity building measures among watershed committee and user groups.

METHODOLOGY

This study was carried out at theoretical as well as empirical levels. As a first step, a through policy (guidelines) on participatory development and collective action in the context Watershed development/management in general and stakeholders' participation in particular was carried out. As a second step, the empirical analyses were used to verify the hypotheses and develop a more generalized and practicable framework for stakeholders' participation and equity distribution. The data were collected at two levels -i.e. village/ user group and household level through structured questionnaires. In order to identify the level of participation and to assess the impacts, property right regime, poverty and livelihoods, a set of indicators of participation watershed management have been developed. The sample includes women, landless, marginal and small farmers in watershed areas. For the purpose of assessing the impact of watershed development programme on different category of farmers we have adopted the method before and after watershed framework. Impact assessment is carried out using the village and household level information on various socio-economic aspects. At the empirical level, our approach was to study the problem extensively as well as intensively. At the extensive level a sample of 7 watersheds were selected from four districts (two watersheds, one is completed another is on going in each district) in two states (Table 1). A detailed Village watershed schedule was canvassed among these 7 watersheds in order to examine their structure and functioning. In all, 140 farmers include landless and women were studied in two states using the survey method with the help of a detailed household level schedule. The selection was purposive to cover the marginal, small, medium and large farmers and also landless, from each watershed a sample of twenty farmers, representing different size-class and socio-economic sections of the community was drawn using the probability proportionate sampling method for an in-depth survey. Prior to the sample survey Participatory Rural Appraisal (PRA) exercises were conducted in the sample villages in order to draw qualitative inferences about the village community. PRA was also helpful in designing the questionnaire. Besides, focus group interviews were held with the office bearers of the WC/WA and MDT and PIA officials.

GENERAL FEATURES OF THE SAMPLE WATERSHEDS

The general features of the sample watersheds, we have dealt with the critical aspects of land use pattern and physical characteristics of the watershed. The total areas under sample watersheds are uniform in almost all the sample watersheds except Ganeshpura (three Gram Panchayats were merged) is a major watershed where the area treated under watershed is about 12, 250 acres (see Table 1.2). The area under forest has been treated very low in our sample watersheds except Penchikalapadu of Prakasam district in Andhra Pradesh and Amargarh of Bhilwara district of Rajasthan. The cultivated area under watershed treated was not uniform. However, Ganeshpura watershed has more area under cultivation when compared to other selected sample watersheds. Since agriculture is a land intensive activity, the primary source of land increase or development is from increase in cropping intensity. Hence the importance of cropping intensity and how much area is not under cultivation, how much land available for cultivation and finally how much land available for

Table 1
Details of Sample Selection of the Village Watershed/ Households

State	*District*	*Mandal*	*Name of the Village/Watershed*	*Scheme*	*No. of Households Selected by Location of their Land in Watershed*				
					Marginal	*Small*	*Medium and Large*	*Land less and Women*	*Total Sample house-holds*
Andhra Pradesh	Medak	Kohir	Gottigar Palli	DPAP (Completed)	8	5	3	4	20
	Prakasam	Besthavaripet	Penchikalapadu	APRLP (Completed)	7	5	4	4	20
		Tangutur	Konizedu	DPAP (on-going)	6	4	8	2	20
Rajasthan	Bhilwara	Mandal	Ganeshpura	IWDP(Final Year)	6	4	6	4	20
		Jahazpur	Amargarh	IWDP (on-going)	6	7	4	3	20
	Udaipur	Gogunda	Palidana	DDP (Completed)	11	4	3	2	20
		Gogunda	Suwatian Ka Guda	DDP (on-going)	8	6	2	4	20

Note: Figures in brackets are the actual number of households in the respective size-class. Selection of Households within the marginal, small medium and large and landless was based on the proportion of number of farmers in the respective size-class to the total number of farmers in the respective watershed in the Village.

common property resources are important. If we see in the Table 2, area not available for cultivation, which comprises barren land/cultivable waste Ganeshpura watershed has having more area followed by Suwatian Ka Guda and penchikalapadu watersheds. This means that the present implementation of land augment technologies in these districts through watershed development programmes is inevitable. The area under permanent pastures and grazing lands (common property lands) is very marginal in Suwatian Ka Guda and Palidana in Udaipur district and Amargarh of Bhilwara district watersheds when compared to Ganeshpura and Gottigarpalli watersheds. One of the priorities of the watershed selection is as the area under Common Property Resources treatment under watershed, where the livelihood security of the marginal as well as landless (who is dependent upon on CPR more) was analysed.

In the physical characteristics, rainfall and type of soil are important aspects for treatment of land augmenting technologies under watershed. Our sample watersheds, the average annual rainfall were ranges between 600mm to 950mm (see Table 1.3). Penchikalapadu and Konizedu watersheds of Prakasam district in Andhra Pradesh were having high average annual rainfall when compared to other sample watersheds. The scanty rainfall in watershed areas reflects the one of the priorities of the selection of sample watersheds. The soil type is uniform in almost all the sample watersheds. The treatment of water and soil is varies across sample watersheds. Most of the treatment of soil and water bodies is Percolation Tanks, Farm Ponds, Check Walls, Bunding with Plantation and Renovation of Wells and Horticultural Plantations on Individual lands, Masonry Check Dams (drainage line Treatment), Vegetative Barriers, V-ditches, Stone Wall Fencing and CPR Development. Another feature of conflict resolution and equity mechanism is nature of dependency over resources under watershed, where our sample watersheds the nature of dependency over resources or right over resources is mostly by hereditary and Government assigned land.

EXISTING POLICY AND IMPACT

In view of the mixture of policy guidelines, the study looked at the watershed implementation is based on performance criteria. The selection of watershed is clouded by political influences. The structure of PIA is directly or indirectly influences the watershed. For example, the IWDP watershed projects (Ganeshpura), the structure between PIA and WC is complex. Where PIA is Block Development Officer, who has looking after more or less 50 other/priority works than the watershed activities. Hence, delay in decision-making process in the watersheds is observed. Moreover, there is a gap between WC and PIA is also observed. The technical assistance mostly gets from watershed development team members who are expertise in watershed related areas by PIA in Amargarh where as in Ganesh pura PIA gets technical assistance from assistant engineers. Where as in DDP (Palidana and Suwatian ka Guda) projects the structure is simple and there is no gap between PIA and primary stakeholders. Hence, the capacity as well as confidence building measures was established among different stakeholders. The narrowed gap between PIA and primary stakeholders is helped the high level peoples' participation in the areas of CPR management, SHGs performance, crop diversification and institutional strengthening especially Palidhana and Suawatian ka Guda Watersheds. The Hariyali guidelines are almost in mission mode and it is not just like government programmes. The major observation was made here is that panchayat sarpanch/secretary and BDOs were not performing their administrative duties due to shortage of time and political pressures. The efforts made so far have shown mixed results. Nevertheless, the policy guidelines of IWDP, DPAP and DDP have helped the formation of Self-Help Groups (SHGs) mode of empowerment of women and sustainable livelihood security was taken place. The Present study and other impact assessment studies also revealed that green vegetative cover has improved in desert areas and having a positive impact in checking soil erosion by water and wind. And also indicated that the availability of fodder and fuel wood has also improved live stock and supported livelihood security in program areas. But in some of the sample watershed areas, the PIA and the villagers/farmers (User Groups and WC) did not achieve desired benefits due to widened gap between them and lack of political will and commitment.

ROLE OF STAKEHOLDERS' AT DIFFERENT LEVELS IN WATERSHED

The government of India and the respective administrative departments at the State level has undertaken Participatory Watershed Development programmes in order to facilitate sustainable and equitable utilization of resources through Community- Based Natural Resource Management. Common resources have diverse and often conflicting uses, and hence, the characteristics of the resource and its use play an important role in the process of natural resource. In addition most of the natural resource activities have a long gestation period. Consequently, community accruing benefits, whether by protecting and enhancing the livelihood needs of the people or from the commercial value of the produce, can be envisaged only in the long run. With these factors, the community based management of natural resources under watershed programmes stipulate management of Common Property Resources (CPR) by groups consisting of community members who are users of the existing resource. Apart from the equitable benefit sharing, such an arrangement also means more convenient management of resources that are spread over a large land area. In the context of Watershed Programmes, CBOs such as user groups are entrusted with the management and utilization/benefit sharing of assets developed on common land and selected CPRs. The various categories of rights over the natural resources are vested with different stakeholders. Typically, the rights to ownership and making decisions regarding the resources rest with the respective government authorities at different levels. Usufruct and management rights over the resources are devolved through various policy and legal instruments to the appropriate local level institution, such as the Panchayat Raj Institutions or User groups.

KEY DEVELOPMENT IN PARTICIPATORY RESEARCH: INSTITUTIONAL STAKEHOLDERS

There are wide differences in implementing agencies. NGOs have more experience in participatory research and development (Hemantha Kumar. U, 2005 and Reddy, V. Ratna and Hemantha Kumar. U, 2006), their localised and often personalized experience limits their scale of operation. GOs are in contrast to the wider reach of state institutions and the ability of the state to create favourable policy environments. State institutions therefore have a valuable role in 'scaling up' such experience (e.g. Wells, 1995; Farrington and Lobo, 1997; Alsop and Farrington, 1998; Turton and Farrington, 1998). Government institutions, NGOs and farmer organisations have different objectives and motives for their work and there can be communication difficulties between the different organisations. To analyse the reasons for participation, the capabilities of the different stakeholders and what each wants to get out of the process. Another feature is that participation has been better integrated into the early stages of the research cycle, than into the later stages (Farrington, 1997). In other words, problem appraisal—through such methods as participatory rural appraisal (PRA)—is more likely to involve farmers than monitoring and evaluation (M&E). Stakeholders are usually defined as those who can affect or may be affected by a particular activity; there remains a grey area over the extent to which individuals can be lumped into groups for practical purposes (Grimble and Wellard, 1997). This contrasts with an actor-oriented approach, which argues against agglomeration into groups (based on criteria such as ethnicity or gender).

The homogeneity within each stakeholder group's archetype is assumed to be greater than the variability between groups, i.e. that aggregation into stakeholder groups of essentially similar strategies (CPR benefits sharing based, fishing based, sharecropping based, etc.) is a valid assumption. This was observed in sample district of Udaipur Watersheds. The purpose of the research is to understand patterns of access to, and use of, natural resources by different social actors so that future development can avoid benefiting some groups at the expense of others.

EQUITY

In the composition of watershed committee, landless/asset less, women and other socially or economically disadvantaged persons (SC/STs) were considerably involved so as to minimize inequalities and social conflicts (see Table 2). As size-class wise composition also some equity was maintained. Considerable composition of marginal and small farmers was involved in watershed development. Each SHG was given an amount as revolving fund which they could use for providing loans at mutually agreed rate of interest to their members. Repayment and the interest earned were recycled for giving loans to the remaining un serviced members. This kind of practice were emerged in APRLP and DDP watersheds (Penchikalapadu of Besthavaripet mandal of Prakasam district and Gottigar palli of Medak district in Andhra Pradersh and Suwatian ka Guda in Gogunda block of Udaipur district in Rajasthan). They also set up micro-enterprises to provide supporting services for agriculture, livestock, poultry or piggery rearing or even for setting up grocery shops, tailoring and any other activities.

CONFLICTS

Any alternative development process involving communities of different interests, social, economic and political groups is expected to manage inherent contradictions by adequately designed resolution mechanisms. This same was influenced in our sample watersheds also.

Major players in the watershed development process at the state and central level are Ministry of Agriculture, Ministry of Rural Development and other small initiatives including donors and NGOs. The Ministry of Rural Development enforced relatively better participation by issuing very comprehensive and well-meaning guidelines in 1994. However, Ministry of Agriculture took another eight years to internalize fully a typical participatory process by accepting

Table 2

Institutional and Economic Environment of the Watershed

	Andhra Pradesh			*Rajasthan*			
	Prakasam District		*Medak District*	*Bhilwara*		*Udaipur*	
Name of the Watershed/ Institutional Arrangements	*Penchikalapadu*	*Konizedu*	*Gottigar Palli*	*Ganeshpura (Four Villages)*	*Amargarh (Three villages)*	*Palidhana*	*Suwatin ka Guda*
Composition of Watershed Committee							
Social Composition (in Totals)							
SC/STs	1	2	4	5	5	4	5
BCs	7	2	3	4	2	3	2
Others	6	7	4	2	2	2	4
Out of Total Members					2	4	2
Landless	5	3	3	2	2	2	4
Women	14 (all are Women)	2	2	2			
Size-Class Composition in Watershed area (Totals)							
Marginal	43	45	35	828	120	179	153
Small	15	75	20	420	103	60	65
Medium and Large	13	140	5	238	75	16	07
Arrangements for conflict resolution	Through gram Sabha and MDT Members involvement	Through Gram sabha	By conducting meeting and mutually agreed rules and regulations	Meeting with Watershed CommitteeAnd other User Committees	Forest officials involvement and Watershed Committee	By formulation of Mutually agreed rules and regulations	By formulation of Mutually agreed rules and regulations

Contd.

Selection procedure	Democratic	Mostly influenced by political pressures	Through Gram Sabha, Based on acute problems facing families given priority	Democratic but mostly elders are playing major role	Democratic But Forest officials involvement is there	Democratic	Democratic
Priority of Watershed	Drinking Water, fodder and fuel Sustainable alternative income generate activities through SHGs		Drinking water and protective irrigation through Groundwater recharge, Horticulture and Afforstation	Crop productivity enhancement, Common property resource development Fodder and fuel development	Common Property Resource Development, fodder and fuel	Crop productivity enhancement, Groundwater recharge, CPR Development and fodder and fuel	Crop productivity enhancement, Groundwater recharge, CPR Development and fodder and fuel

common guidelines. Earlier approach of Ministry of Agriculture was mostly designed for the landowners with a larger emphasis on production for meeting requirements of food for large population. Ministry of Rural Development on the other hand concentrated more on poverty reduction; employment generation and goals of the two ministries were quite contrasting and conflicting in the implementation process (see as mentioned in Table 2).

Both the ministries still claim that the entire watershed activity should be allocated to them. After a lot of discussions they at least agreed to adopt common guidelines in 2002, which have again been modified by the Ministry of Rural Development in January 2003 (Haryali) by assigning greater role to the democratically elected village institutions of Panchayats. The watershed approach calls upon treatment from ridge to valley by the PIA and whenever there is a forest in a part of the watershed the foresters do not allow other agencies to operate in the forest area and insist to implement that part themselves.

In some of the states development funds provided by Central government were diverted towards non-productive expenditures like payment of the salaries, etc. As mentioned earlier Chief Secretaries of the states were bypassed and Central funds were remitted directly to the district level by Rural Development Ministry for ensuring prompt delivery of the finances for quicker implementation of development process. However, this conflict could be resolved by engaging them in a constant dialogue and sensitization process.

There are following two competing centres of power at the district level which is a basic administrative and development unit:

(i) District Collector/Commissioner/Magistrate representing bureaucracy with a well-established hierarchy, command and control system of an organized service.

(ii) Zila Parishad: They are elected representatives and represent the powerful political stream of grassroots level contacts.

Both these centres of power are struggling to exercise the control over the development funds received from the state or Central government. In some of the states elected representative (Zila Parishad- Rajasthan) have upper hand while in others the organized services operates all levers of public administration. In some other places the relative upper hand of these two powers keeps on changing depending upon which of the political party is ruling. The organized services exercised most of the administrative and financial powers in the past and are feeling threatened with the dilution of their authority, command and control structure. Zila Parishad, on the other hand, view that they are public representatives, have come up through the process of election and know ground realities more intimately and can provide better solutions. It is, therefore, necessary to internalize relative strengths of the two centres of power so as to complement overall development process by minimizing conflicts.

Panchayati Raj (elected) institutions, of late, complained that watershed associations are not statutory institutions for taking up the development activities. Elected institutions also argued that the 73rd and 74th amendments of the Constitution have allocated watershed management business to the Panchayats and they should have upper hand in the implementation process. The Ministry of Rural Development, which administered the Panchayati Raj institution, had already obliged elected institutions declaring them PIA to handle development funds. The watershed boundaries being a natural geo-hydrological unit may not coincide with the administrative boundaries and many a times a watershed may fall into two Panchayats which inhibit treatment from ridge to valley as envisaged scientifically.

Another aspect is in the past NGOs were mostly active in the area of health, education, social services, etc. and their role in natural resource management became significant after 1995. On the other hand well-established government departments have been implementing projects in the past and they did not like competition from the alternative institutions of NGOs. (as it was in present APRLP and District Water Management

Agency structure in Andhra Pradesh. But in Rajasthan, in most of the cases Government machinery was involved.). As a result of that there was a lot of dogmatism and unhealthy competition between the GOs and NGOs, which was expressed in many ways. As on today NGOs are relatively better equipped or experienced to handle socio-economic and capacity building issues and are not very strong in technical matters. GOs on the other hand have technically highly experienced or trained manpower and are more competitive to implement biophysical aspects of the development process. A conflict resolution mechanism should aim at harmonizing relative strengths of the GOs and NGOs so as to internalize their complementarities to convert conflicts into opportunities.

The present sample watersheds the resolution of conflicts were mostly at lower stages (at Gram Panchayat/Watershed Committee with the help of AEs/JEs and WDT/MDT) by mutually agreed rules and regulations (see Table 3.1). The selection procedure of beneficiary is mostly democratic but some of the places it was clouded by political influences.

TRANSPARENCY

PIA opened and operated joint account with the office bearers of WA as co-signatories to all the financial transactions. Cash book and other records were maintained and kept with the Secretary of the WA in the village, which could be examined by any watershed resident. Details of the budget and funds received were displayed prominently on the display boards. Collective decision-making process with the participation of all stakeholders irrespective of social groups, gender and economic status was also a key element of removing misgivings or apprehensions. Most of the cases our sample watersheds this practice was went on smoothly. There were no complaints against mismanagement of funds.

ENTRY POINT ACTIVITIES

About 3 percent of the budget was earmarked to take up any activity in the watershed, which was most appreciated by the majority of the people. It could be de-silting of a community pond, installing a hand pump for drinking water or repairing a religious structure so as to establish credentials by striking the most effective social chord. The whole idea was to create an impression of a service provider and gain confidence with villagers. The whole process was designed to mobilize community participation without any opposition, conflict or resistance. This activity proved very effective for ensuring participation of majority of the communities by building bridges of mutual trust and confidence. This was so effective in sample watersheds of Palidana and Suwatian Ka Guda of Udaipur district, Amargarh of Bhilwara district and Penchikalapadu of Prakasam district.

EXIT PROTOCOL

The active intervention period of most of the projects is about five years after which the PIA is expected to withdraw and move to other watersheds/areas. Maintenance of the created infrastructure was a serious handicap prior to the concept of people's participation. All contributions mentioned previously were kept into a separate account called Watershed Development Fund (WDF). This account was also in the name of watershed associations and was to be operated upon generally after the exit of the PIA. Wherever participants could be convinced about the philosophy of cost sharing, overall contribution per watershed went up beyond the 5-10 percent of the stipulations since it was meant for welfare of the community and maintenance of the infrastructure being created under the watershed program. After several guidelines, this aspect was not dealt properly still date. Hence, most of our sample watersheds the WDF was not utilised remain unspent. The changes/replacement of political /elected representatives in local bodies and lack of proper guidance to Watershed Committees this account was remain at present PIA.

COMMUNITY CONTRIBUTIONS

As far as user contributions are concerned, 10 percent contribution in cash or kind for activities or investment on private land was envisaged. The rate was scaled down to 5 percent for socially disadvantaged participants. The contribution rate was also 5 percent for the activities to be taken up on open access or community owned resources and activities. The idea was to induce a thinking process in the minds of participants of evaluating pros and cons of activities since their investments were also involved. If an activity was totally financed from the public funds they would normally demand anything without keeping in mind ultimate utility. Contributions in the form of labour or material (in kind) were generally monetised in the records. Sharing of cost inculcated sense of belongings and sustainability of the development process. These contributions constituted a corpus fund for the future use of the WA. Our field data shows that except Konizedu, Ganeshpura and Amargarh other sample watershed beneficiaries were contribute both in cash as well as in kind. It was observed that the nature of contributions is associated with interaction with the people and the PIA. If PIA is close to the Watershed committee and other beneficiaries the understanding of the watershed concept is also positive.impact over contributions by the beneficiaries.

USER GROUPS (UG) AND WATERSHED COMMITTEE (WC): TIME SPENT

Time spent by the user groups and watershed committee in watershed area is also one of the positive indicators of the sustainability of watersheds. Our field observations revealed that the stakeholder processes especially by PIAs of the watershed helped the UGs and WCs for maintenance and attending meetings whenever necessary. Our sample APRLP watershed (Penchikala padu) the composition of Watershed Committee is all women members due to stringent efforts were taken by the PIA as well as multi disciplinary team the confidence and capacity building measures were established among women members. This helped them that they were spent time and watching/looking and development of watershed activity whenever it necessary. The same was observed in our sample watersheds in Udaipur district and Gottigar palli in Medak District. But our sample watersheds of Bhilwara district and Konizedu watershed in Prakasam district due to lack of institutional strength looking/watching after the watershed development activities/structures/ plantations/fodder/fuel in common property resources by the panchayat/watershed committee is lacking.

EQUITY AND REHABILITATION PROCESS

Equitable sharing of the benefits among all the intended population of the watershed remains a major challenge. The very best projects help the poorest and socially backward community members negotiate with other members to ensure that everyone benefits, but this remains an area where all projects need to pay special attention. The role of livestock and Self-help group mode of loan facility as watershed-based livelihood strategies of landless, poor women and men needs further articulation as well as research and policy support. During the rehabilitation process of watershed, our field data shows that almost all the sample watersheds regarding maintenance of CPR resources rules and regulations were set by the Watershed committee an some of the watersheds priority and need based also. But actually in some of sample watersheds political dominance is taken place (see Table 3). As far as encroachment of the watershed /CPR area the data shows that there was no such encroachment problem in almost all the sample watersheds. Access to landless and women and protection of traditional rights were maintained but most of the watersheds these rights were strengthened by certain rules and regulations. Access was also strengthened after watershed development through formation of SHGs providing revolving fund. Resource flows and productivity enhanced through land augmenting technologies helped the farmers for additional area brought under cultivation. After initiation of watershed the nature of dependency over resources especially CPR reduced and alternative sources like live stock, watershed based self help mode of entrepreneurship were increased.

As far as user's knowledge is concerned all most all the sample watersheds are lacking but in homogeneous watersheds and small group size of watersheds the

Table 3
Equity of the Rehabilitation Process

	Andhra Pradesh			*Rajasthan*			
	Prakasam District		*Medak District*	*Bhilwara*		*Udaipur*	
Name of the Watershed/ Institutional Arrangements	*Besthavaripet*	*Konizedu*	*Gottigar Palli*	*Ganeshpura (Four Villages)*	*Amargarh (Three villages)*	*Palidhana*	*Suwatin ka Guda*
Control over CPR	No CPR land	Rules and regulations set by the Watershed committee but actually some political dominance is taken place	Priority Basis and need Based	Set up of User Groups and rules and regulations	Set up by rules and regulations	By Gram Panchayat-rules and regulations	By WC and Gram sabha
Encroach Problems	No	Yes	No	No	No	No	No
Protection of Traditional users rights (Dependents over CPR)	No	There is no as such Watershed Committee is not empowered	No CPR Land	Yes	Yes	Yes but Rules and regulations	Yes
Access to landless and poor (Before and After Watershed)	Yes	Status quo	Access made after watershed development through Formation of SHG providing revolving fund	Yes	Yes (forest department official involvement is more)	Yes	Self sustained through formation of SHGs

Contd.

Clarity of boundaries	Yes	yes	Clarity of boundaries is maintained	Yes	Yes	Yes	Yes
Resource Flows and productivity	Increased especially Strengthening of SHG mode of development	Land augmenting measures helped the farmers for additional area brought under cultivation	increased	Increased	Increased	Increased	Increased
Nature of Dependency	No	Landless are depend upon Common property Resources	No response	There is a gap between PIA (BDO) and WC	Yes For fuel and fodder	No	No
UsersmKnowledge	Localised Training	Involvement of MDT	Through localized training, awareness		Very low		Very high Through Training
Any other(related)	APRLP mode of Development of watershed ensures the sustainability of the income	This village is heterogeneous social pattern	Follow up of entire guidelines is itself quite effective in meeting the challenges		This Watershed is under control of Forest Department So flexibility of WC is very low	Homogeneous Watershed and size of the group is also very small Empowerment of WC is very high	The Group size and committed WC helped the watershed activities efficient implementation

empowerment of WC through participation and making people aware of potential benefits of collective action in conserving and managing natural resources, including demand driven activities in the watershed program, empowering people in planning, implementing and managing watershed programs and expecting high private economic benefits are observed especially in Palidana and Suwatian ka Guda sample Watersheds in Udaipur districts.

As far as membership in the Watershed Committee our sample data shows that except sample watersheds of Konizedu, Ganeshpura and Amargarh, the remaining sample watersheds covered respondents who are having membership in the Watershed Committee was more than 40 per cent (see Table 4). These respondents were expressed that the decision-making in the committee is widely acceptable and some sort of equity was emerged among user groups in the watershed area. Majority of respondents also expressed that formation of watershed committee was positive indication for development of watershed related structures and CPR development. This positive trend was highly influenced by the committed PIAs and other stakeholders who are involved in the watershed. The initiation of watershed activities in the sample watersheds has also improved access to CPR and other socio-economic developments among sample respondents. There was significant improvement in food security, level of indebtedness and access to and benefits accrued by the user groups. This was mainly attributed to the PIA and other supportive staff of the watershed in sample Watersheds of Gogunda Watersheds (Palidana and Suwatian Ka Guda) and APRLP Watershed of Penchikala Padu in Prakasam district and Gottigar Palli of Medak district. These sample watersheds have experienced and committed PIAs, MDT/WDT and AEs/JEs staff was involved . The average number of visits to CPR area is also reduced in different seasons after initiation of Watershed Committees/User Groups. Hence, sustainability of watershed development was mostly influenced by stakeholder processes, where efficiently deliver goods/services in time during watershed implementation.

Table 4
Equity and Distributional Aspects of Watershed Development

Name of the Watershed/Institutional Arrangements	*Andhra Pradesh*					
	Prakasam District				*Medak District*	
	Besthavaripet		*Konizedu*		*Gottigar Palli*	
	YES	*NO*	*YES*	*NO*	*YES*	*NO*
Membership in Watershed	40	60	10	90	40	70
Regularity of meetings	40	60	6	94	40	70
Involvement of decision-making process	40	60	10	90	70	30
Opinion about present functioning of Watershed	85	15	45	55	90	10
Access to meeting minutes	40	60	10	90	70	30
Opinion about Watershed committee decisions	70	30	50	50	90	10
Opinion about formation of Watershed Committee and strengthening of Watershed Development activity	90	10	50	50	90	10
Formation of Watershed Committee and Changes/developments in watershed area	90	10	60	40	90	10

(Figures in parenthesis are percentages to the total respondents in the sample watersheds)

Contd.

Name of the Watershed/Institutional Arrangements	*Rajasthan*							
	Bhilwara				*Udaipur*			
	Ganeshpura		*Amargarh*		*Palidana*		*Suwatin ka Guda*	
	YES	*NO*	*YES*	*NO*	*YES*	*NO*	*YES*	*NO*
Membership in Watershed	20	80	15	85	70	30	70	30
Regularity of meetings	20	80	10	90	70	30	70	30
Involvement of decision-making process	40	60	25	75	70	30	80	20
Opinion about present functioning of Watershed	65	35	50	50	90	10	100	-
Access to meeting minutes	60	40	60	40	70	30	90	10
Opinion about Watershed committee decisions	75	25	50	50	90	10	90	10
Opinion about formation of Watershed Committee and strengthening of Watershed Development activity	60	40	50	50	90	10	95	05
Formation of Watershed Committee and Changes/ developments in watershed area	70	30	60	40	90	10	95	05

(Figures in parenthesis are percentages to the total respondents in the sample watersheds)

There was tremendous changes occurred after initiation of watersheds activities on CPR lands. Regeneration and vegetation have developed positively almost all the sample watersheds. The rules and regulations were framed for grazing and fodder collection in some of the sample districts (Palidana and Suwatian ka Guda), the collection of fodder was on contract basis (through Gram Sabha by User Committee) accordingly, a lump sum amount was fixed by the committee and the same was credited to Watershed Development Fund. Household basis arrangement was also made by the some of the sample watersheds. Some of the financial arrangements were also made as 50 per cent of income was paid to Choukidar as salary to monitor the CPR area for guarding.

During the implementation of watershed, various stakeholders involvement and their abilities especially the quality of PIA's work /WC and commitment is revealed clearly in the perceptions of the farmers/beneficiaries. As far as farmers are concerned, the continuation of watershed programme in the long run as well as PIA is not withdrawn from the watershed –almost all the sample watershed beneficiaries expressed the same (see Table 5). Same order is followed in the case of the increased sense of ownership of watershed activities and benefited from the common assets of watershed activity. However, such wide variations are not observed when the perceptions of the beneficiaries on violating watershed rules, serious losses due to watershed and gets official wage rate if beneficiaries work in watershed related works. The process of implementation of watershed and involvement of different stakeholders is directly influenced by the kind of PIA implementing the watershed programme. As we have seen here, unless the PIA has long term vision and commitment it unlikely that the PIA will follow a truly participatory approach that would sustain in the long run. In most of the cases, as we observed, the implementation is followed in mechanistic way without any emphasis on social capital development. Despite the well-designed guidelines, as observed and also data shows in Gogunda watersheds (Palidana and Suwatian Ka Guda in Udaipur district) that only

Table 5
Perceptions on Participatory Watershed Programme

Name of the Watershed	*Andhra Pradesh*					
	Prakasam District				*Medak District*	
	Besthavaripet		*Konizedu*		*Gottigar Palli*	
	YES	NO	YES	NO	YES	NO
Have you ever been fined for violating rules	-	100	-	100	-	100
Are there any serious losses due to watershed	-	100	-	100	-	100
If you worked any watershed related work, did you get official wage rate?	40	-	05	-	24	-
Have you benefited from any common assets of watershed activity	60	-	15	-	75	-
Have you ever taken loan from SHG/WDF	45	55	-	100	12	88
Do you feel an increased sense of ownership of local watershed development activities	70	-	25	-	80	-
Have your Watershed been protected at the cost of another land/resource damage	-	100	-	100	-	100
Do you feel that Watershed Programme will continue in the long run	65	-	80	-	88	-
Do you feel that PIA should totally withdrawn from Watershed		98	12	88	14	86

(Figures in parenthesis are percentages to the respective total respondents in the sample watersheds)

Contd.

Name of the Watershed	*Rajasthan*							
	BhilwaraUdaipur							
	Ganeshpura		*Amargarh*		*Palidana*		*Suwatin ka Guda*	
	YES	*NO*	*YES*	*NO*	*YES*	*NO*	*YES*	*NO*
Have you ever been fined for violating rules	-	100	-	100	-	100	-	100
Are there any serious losses due to watershed	-	100	-	100	-	100	-	100
If you worked any watershed related work, did u get official wage rate?	30	-	40	-	60	-	34	-
Have you benefited from any common assets of watershed activity	45	-	60	-	80	-	95	-
Have you ever taken loan from SHG/WDF	-	100	-	100	10	90	55	45
Do you feel an increased sense of ownership of local watershed development activities	30	-	44	-	90	-	100	-
Have your Watershed been protected at the cost of another land/resource damage	-	100	-	100	-	100	-	100
Do you feel that Watershed Programme will continue in the long run	70	-	80	-	95	-	100	-
Do you feel that PIA should totally withdrawn from Watershed	-	98	-	86	14	86	-	75

(Figures in parenthesis are percentages to the respective total respondents in the sample watersheds) those PIAs with commitment can enhance the much-needed social capital in the rural communities as well as sustainability of watersheds even after exit protocol.

PARTICIPATION AND CAPACITY BUILDING OF DIFFERENT STAKEHOLDERS IN SAMPLE WATER-SHEDS

Capacity building is a process by which groups, institutions and individuals increase their ability to understand and address their development needs in a sustainable manner. Ultimately, development takes place through organizations and institutions. As it is a continuous process, it should be undertaken at all stages of watershed development, viz., planning, and implementation and monitoring. Capacity building could be done through imparting training to the target groups, arranging exposure visits and making them more participatory in the whole gamut of implementation of watershed development programs. Empowerment of human resources is an important component in watershed development program. Different people have different roles and responsibilities in project implementation and there is a need to train all the people involved. Training and exposure visits enhance knowledge, skill, attitude and human relationships. Though, a number of measures have been taken for strengthening of training at various levels, the experiences show that the training programmes should aim at: (I) strengthening those processes, skills and knowledge that help in the delivery of various watershed development activities; (ii) improving the quality and content of the subject matter; and (iii) providing more number of relevant trainings involving more community participation particularly rural women (Palanisami. K and Suresh Kumar D, 2005). Therefore, it is essential to examine in depth the whole gamut of training towards capability building among the various clientele groups operating in watershed.

In view of the above, our field data shows in the sample district watersheds, the low level of capacity building as well as confidence building measures coupled with the gap between the PIA and Watershed committee (primary stakeholders) have led to insufficient management of watershed structures and CPR management, especially in Konizedu and Ganesh pura watersheds. It reflects negatively the sustainability of watersheds. If we look at the financial allocation and expenditure incurred under these watersheds for capacity building, only 1.5 per cent of the total funds allocated/ expenditure was incurred for training and exposure visits (see Table 6). As part of Training programme and exposure visits, Gottigar palli watershed of Medak District and Palidana and Suwatian ka Guda watersheds in Gogunda block of Udaipur District, the Watershed Committees, WDT, PIAs and Self Help Groups (SHG) were trained at different places. For capacity building of these groups were trained at within the village and outside locations like MYRADA in Gulbarga district Kamalapur Training Centre , in Krishi Vignan Kendras, Relegoan siddi, Mt. Abu, Ram Devra, Ajmer, Jodhpur and Jaisalmer in different fields and improved skills and knowledge.

CONCLUSION AND POLICY IMPLICATIONS

In the context of people's participatory approach advocated by the different watershed guidelines right from 1994-95, it is expected that it would make a dent as far as enhancing the livelihood security is concerned. Our analysis of seven selective watersheds in two states of Andhra Pradesh and Rajasthan though indicates the potential of watershed development in enhancing livelihoods; it brings out clearly the importance of different stakeholders involvement in the processes of watershed implementation. Based on the preceding analysis coupled with our wider field observations, we discuss here some of the emerging important issues regarding the role of different stakeholders viz., Watershed Committee, User Groups, Self-help Groups, Sarpanch, Gram Panchayat, Gram Sabha, Multi-disciplinary Team/Watershed Development Team and PIA to achieve effective and sustainable implementation of the watershed development programme.

Table 6
Capacity building Measures

Level of Training /Exposure Visits	*Name of the Watershed (After Watershed)- Andhra Pradesh*		
	Prakasam		*Medak*
	Besthavari pet (oneyear due)	*Konizedu (two year due)*	*Gottigar pally (Completed Water shed)*
Training outside watershed (exposure visits)	Addakula L. Kota	no	KVK, ICRISAT,Relegoansiddi ,MYRADA and SangaReddy
Number of Days	4 days (total)	-	46 (days total)
Number of persons			
WC	14		11
WA	-		15
WDT	3		-
Others (SHG and farmers)	7	-	70
Training within the village (including demonstrations) (in different dates)	Monthly once by PIA and MDT members	-	Weekly once by PIA and WDT members

Contd.

Level of Training /Exposure Visits	*Name of the Watershed (After Watershed)*			
	Bhilwara		*Udaipur*	
	Ganesh Pura (Two year due)	*Amargarh (one year due)*	*Palidhana (Completed Water shed)*	*Suawatian ka Guda on-going)*
Training outside watershed (exposure visits)	No	Jaipur	K.V.K	Ram Devra, Mt. Abu, K.V.K, Ajmer, Jodhpur and Jaisalmer
Number of Days	No	6 days (total)	12 days (total)	32 days (total)
Number of persons				
WC	-	11	9	9
WA	-	2	9	30
WDT	-	-	4	4
Others	-	-	10	80
Training within the village (including demonstrations) (in different dates)	2 weeks	2 weeks	5 weeks	9 weeks

- The foregoing analysis of stakeholder processes draw conclusions at three levels: (I) stakeholder analysis for improving the quality of inter-institution interaction in planning; (ii) adoption of stakeholder approaches in subsequent phases of the watershed processes and corrections at different phases, and (iii) stakeholder analysis as a generic tool for the evaluation of watershed programmes. Diverse institutions from different sectors as a multi-agency Disciplinary team to plan, and then participate in, to improve integrated watershed development. During the stakeholder processes an important factor in this first stage is discovering each other's strengths, abilities and motivations. The use of the stakeholder matrix as a preliminary step, which elicited some of this information, helped build the capacity and confidence building measures. As a result, it was observed in our sample watersheds, that participatory planning with the farmers for deciding the location of the water ponds, check dams, vegetative barriers and development of CPR land was found highly beneficial.
- When come to the sustained livelihood security, no doubt, our field data shows that initiation of participatory watershed development activities in our sample watershed villages have helped the beneficiaries to strengthen their livelihood security. The increase of cropping pattern as well as cropping intensity, regeneration of fodder and fuel availability in common resources area, rise in groundwater levels coupled with additional employment generation in watershed area and sustained income generation activities through self-help groups have indicated positive impact.
- Bringing together heterogeneous groups into one umbrella is a crucial task. As our sample watershed villages especially Udaipur watersheds of Palidan and Suwatian ka Guda, it reflects constructive experience

in watershed development, the results shows the immediate and positive impact of bringing together institutional stakeholders and involve in developmental activity. The policy implication of stakeholders' processes is the extent to which an analysis of power relations (involvement of /stake of political leaders). This aspect is concerned seriously as our filed observations reveal that involvement of locally dominated political parties in the decision-making and stakeholder processes. So that parallel exercises of powers both by Watershed committee in one hand and the sarpanch and other ward members (Gram Panchayat) in another will be minimised.

- The gap between PIA and Watershed Committee at the watershed level appears to be critical in the whole process. Some of our sample watersheds (Ganesh pura, Konizedu, and Amargarh) there was a huge gap between PIA and WCs, The PIAs mostly hails from line department where PIA is Block Development Officer, who has looking after more or less 50 other/ priority works than the watershed activities. Hence, delay in decision-making process in the watersheds is observed. As a result, capacity building as well as confidence building measure among User Groups, Watershed Committee and Self-help Groups is lacking.
- In context of Exit Protocol, maintenance of the created infrastructure was a serious handicap prior to the concept of people's participation. All contributions mentioned previously were kept into a separate account called Watershed Development Fund (WDF). This account was also in the name of watershed associations and was to be operated upon generally after the exit of the PIA. Wherever participants could be convinced about the philosophy of cost sharing, overall contribution per watershed went up beyond the 5-10 percent of the stipulations since it was meant for welfare of the community and maintenance of the

infrastructure being created under the watershed program. After several guidelines, this aspect was not dealt properly still date. Hence, most of our sample watersheds the WDF was not utilised remain unspent. The changes/replacement of political /elected representatives in local bodies and lack of proper guidance to Watershed Committees this account was remain unutilised and kept with PIA.

- In the context of user contributions, 10 percent contribution in cash or kind for activities or investment on private land was envisaged. The rate was scaled down to 5 percent for socially disadvantaged participants. The contribution rate was also 5 percent for the activities to be taken up on open access or community owned resources and activities. The idea was to induce a thinking process in the minds of participants of evaluating pros and cons of activities since their investments were also involved. As our field data shows that a few watersheds (Penchikalapdu, Gottigar palli, Palidana and Suwatian ka Guda) were successfully sharing of cost inculcated sense of belongings and sustainability of the development process. But remaining other watersheds (Konizedu, Ganeshpura and Amargarh) the kind of cost sharing/contributions by beneficiaries is lacking. It was observed that the nature of contributions is associated with interaction with the people and the PIA. If PIA is close to the Watershed committee and other user groups/beneficiaries the understanding of the watershed concept is also positive impact over contributions by the beneficiaries.
- As far as looking/watching and visits by user groups in the watershed and CPR area is usually limited to supervising the works in his field as well as in watershed area. This aspect has to be strengthened further. Regarding repairs to the structures, most of the cases the repairs were not carryout. This is mainly attributed to the concept of revolving fund is not

properly evolved. There is no mechanism to continue this fund through user contributions. Where there is a good understanding between PIA and other stakeholders in the watershed area, the mechanism of user contributions are maintained.

- Establishment of capacity and confidence building measures between different stakeholders is necessary for sustainable development of watershed. Our field data shows in some of the sample watershed districts, the low level of capacity building as well as confidence building measures coupled with the gap between the PIA and Watershed committee (primary stakeholders) have led to insufficient management of watershed structures and CPR management, especially in Konizedu and Ganesh pura watersheds. It reflects negatively the sustainability of watersheds. If we look at the financial allocation and expenditure incurred under these watersheds for capacity building, only 1.5 per cent of the total funds allocated/ expenditure was incurred for training and exposure visits. But, our field data also shows in other sample watershed districts as part of training programme and exposure visits, Gottigar palli watershed of Medak District and Palidana and Suwatian ka Guda watersheds in Gogunda block of Udaipur District, the Watershed Committees, WDT, PIAs and Self Help Groups (SHG) were trained at different places. This helped them strengthening of their livelihood security.

REFERENCES

Akwabi-Ameyaw K. (1997), "Producer Cooperative Resettlement Projects in Zimbabwe: Lessons from a failed agricultural development strategy" *World Development*, 25 (3): 437-456.

Agrawal A. (2001), "Common Property Institutions and Sustainable Governance of Resources". *World Development* 29 (10): 1623-1648.

Alsop, R. and Farrington, J. (1998), "Nests, Nodes and Niches: A System for Process Monitoring, Information Exchange and Decision Making for Multiple Stakeholders". *World Development*. Vol. 26, No. 2, pp.249-260.

Anna Lawrence, Julian Barr and Graham Haylor (1999), "Stakeholder Approaches to Planning Participation Research by Multi-institution Groups", AgREN, Net Work Paper No 91.

Baland J-M and Platteau J-P. (1996), *Halting Degradation of Natural Resources: Is there a Role for Rural Communities?* Oxford, U K : Clarendon Press.

Bardhan P. (1993), "Analysis of the Institutions of Informal Cooperation in Rural Development". *World Development*, 21 (4) 633-639.

Bharat R. Sharma, J.S. Sharma, C. A. Scott and Suhas P. Wani (2005), *Watershed Management Challenges: Improving Productivity Resources and Livelihoods*, IWMI, Colombo, Srilanka.

Bromely DW. (1991), *Environment and Economy: Property Rights and Public Policy*. Cambridge, Mass. Basil Blackwell, Inc.

Farrington, J. (1997), 'Farmers' Participation in Agricultural Research and Extension: Lessons from the Last Decade'. *Biotechnology and Development Monitor*. Vol. 30, pp.12-15.

Farrington, J. and Lobo, C. (1997), 'Scaling up Participatory Watershed Development in India: Lessons from the Indo-German Watershed Development Programme'. *Natural Resource Perspectives* No. 17. London: ODI.

Farrington J, Turton C and James AJ (eds.) (1999), *Participatory Watershed Development: Challenges for the Twenty-first Century*. New Delhi, India: Oxford University Press.

Grimble, R. and Wellard, K. (1997), 'Stakeholder methodologies in natural resource management: A review of principles, contexts, experiences and opportunities'. *Agricultural Systems*. Vol. 55, No. 2, pp.173-193.

Government of India (1994), "Guidelines for Watershed Development", Ministry of Rural Development, New Delhi.

Hanumantha, Rao, C.H. (2000), "Watershed Development in India: Recent experiences and emerging issues." *Economic and Political Weekly*, XXXV(45): 3943-3947.

Harding G. (1968), The Tragedy of the Commons. *Science* 162: 1243-1248.

Harsh Mitter (2005), HARIYALI- *Planned Investment in Watershed Development*, Ministry of Rural Development, Govt. of India, New Delhi, India

Hemantha Kumar.U. (2005), "Capacity Building for Enhanced Women's Participation in Watershed Development: Some empirical observations", *Afro-Asian Journal of Rural Development*, Vol. xxxviii, No.2 July-December, 2005, pp. 65-82

Hussi P, Murphy J, Lindberg O and Brenneman L. (1993), "The development of cooperatives and other rural organizations". World Bank Technical Paper No. 199. The World Bank.

Jodha N S. (1986), "Common Property resources and the rural poor in dry regions of India." *Economic and Political Weekly* 21: 1169-1181.

Johnson N and Ravnborg HM, Westermann O and Probst K. (2002), "User Participation in Watershed Management and Research." *Water Policy* 3 (6): 507-520.

Joshi, P.K., Tewari, L., Jha, A.K. and Shiyani, R.L.(2000), "Meta Analysis to Assess Impact of Watershed.", Proceedings Workshop on Institutions for Greater Impact of Technologies, National Centre for Agriculture Economics and Policy Research (ICAR), New Delhi, India.

Joshi, P.K., Pangare, V., Shiferaw, B., Wani, S.P., Bouma, J. and Scott, C.A. (2004), "Socio-economic and Policy research on watershed management in India: Synthesis of past experiences and needs for future research", *Global Theme on Agro-ecosystem*, Report No. 7, International Crops Research Institute for Semi-Arid Tropics, Patancheru, India.

Joy, K.J., Parnjpe, Suhas, Shah, Amita, Badigar, Shrinivas and Lele, Sharachchandra (2005), "Scaling up of watershed development projects in India: learning from the first generation projects." Fourth IWMI-Tata Annual Partners Meet, International Water Management Institute, Anand, India. pp.133-134.

Kerr, J. (2002), "Watershed development, environmental services and poverty alleviation in India". *World Development*, 30(8): 1387-1400.

Kerr, John., Pangare, Ganesh and Pangare, Vasudha (2004), "Watershed Development Projects in India: An Evaluation". *Research Report* 127, International Food Policy Research Institute, Washington, DC, USA.

Kerr J. (2001), "Watershed project performance in India: Conservation, productivity, and equity". *American Journal of Agricultural Economics* 83 (5) 1223-1230.

Kerr J, Pangare G and Lokur V. (2002), "Watershed development projects in India". *Research Report* 127. IFPRI. Washington DC.

Knox A and Gupta S. (2000), "CAPRI technical workshop on watershed management institutions: A summary paper.", CAPRI working paper No. 8 IFPRI. Washington, DC.

Knox A and Meinzen-Dick R. (1999), "Property rights collective action and technologies for natural resource management" Policy Brief No. 1. CAPRI.

Lele U. (1981), "Cooperatives and the poor: a comparative perspective". *World Development* 9: 55-72.

Meinzen-Dick R, Knox A, Place F and Swallow B (eds.) (2002), *Innovation in natural resource management. The role of property rights and collective action in developing countries.* The John Hopkins University Press for the IFPRI, Baltimore and London.

Nilsson J. (2001), "Organisational principles for co-operative firms". *Scandinavian Journal of Management* 17: 329-356.

Ostrom E. (1990), *Governing the Commons: the evaluation of institutions for collective action.* Cambridge, UK: Cambridge University Press.

Palanisami, K., Suresh Kumar, D. and Chandrasekharan, B. (Eds.). (2002), *Watershed Management: Issues and Policies for 21st Century.* Associated Publishing Company, P.O. Box No. 2679, New Delhi, India. 341 pp.

Palanisamy. K and Suresh Kumar D, (2005), "Leapfrogging the Watershed Mission: Building Capacity of Farmers, Professionals and Institutions" in (eds.,), Bharat R. Sharma, J.S. Sharma, C. A. Scott and Suhas P. Wani, 2005, *Watershed Management Challenges: Improving Productivity Resources and Livelihoods,* IWMI, Colombo, Srilanka.

Reddy V. Ratna, Hemantha Kumar. U and Mohana Rao D., (2006), "Participatory Watershed Development and the Role of Project Implementing Agency (PIA): The Experience of Andhra Pradesh" *Journal of Rural Development,* Vol 25, No 3, July-Sept,

Reddy V. Ratna (2000), "Watershed development for sustainable agriculture: need for an institutional approach". *Economic and Political weekly* 35: (38): 3435-3444.

Runge C.F. (1986), "Common Property and Collective Action in Economic Development". *World Development.* 14 (5): 623-635.

Shiferaw B and Bantilan C. (2004), "Rural poverty and natural resource management in less favoured areas: revisiting challenges and conceptual issues.", *Journal of Food, Agriculture and Environment* 2(1): 328-339.

Stockbridge M, Dorward A and Kydd J. (2003), *Farmer organizations for market access. Brief paper. Centre for Development and Poverty Reduction,* Imperial College London.

Swallow BM, Garrity DP and van Noordwijk M. (202). "The effects of scales, flows and filters on property rights and collective action in watershed management". *Water Policy* 3(6): 457-474.

Turton, C. and Farrington, J. (1998), "Enhancing rural livelihoods through participatory watershed development in India". *Natural Resource Perspectives* No. 34. London: ODI.

Wells, M.P. (1995), "Bio-diversity conservation and local people's development aspirations: New priorities for the 1990s", *Rural Development Forestry,* Network Paper 18.

CHAPTER–17

DYNAMICS OF WATERSHED DEVELOPMENT: THE CASE OF THE PANCHAYATS IN WEST BENGAL

Dilip Kumar Ghosh

In response to all round crises, the conservation of water becomes a widely discussed issue in the present day affairs. Commonly a watershed is defined as an area in which all water drains to a common point. In dry land areas where rainfall is normally low and availability of water for use is very much limited, watershed projects widen the scope for enhancement of water availability through on-site soil and moisture conservation, infiltration into aquifers, and safe run off into surface ponds. The importance of watershed development needs no elaboration. The Report (1994) of the Technical Committee on Drought Prone Areas Programme and Desert development Programme constituted by the Ministry of Rural Development, Govt. of India laid down in the preface the purpose of watershed development. To quote:

"The Drought Prone Areas programme (DPAP) and the Desert Development Programme (DDP) have been designed to retore ecological balance through soil and moisture conservation on watershed basis within the framework of area development plans. In practice, however, these programmes have been implememted in a fragmented manner by different departments through rigid guidelines without well-designed plans prepared on watershed basis by involving the inhabitants."

These remarks of the Technical Committee prompt to take up the present study with its specific objective to portray what the panchayats can do in watershed development, and what the panchayats are doing at the grassroots levels. With the effect of the Constitution (Seventy Third Amendment) Act,1992 the panchayats at three tiers, namely district, blocks, and villages have been given the responsibility for making plans for their local area and implementation of programmes for ensuring economic development and social justice in their respective jurisdiction. The present study explains the case of the panchayats in watershed development through West Bengal example. West Bengal is considered because in this State, the panchayats have well placed themselves in the rural areas since the year 1978 when the first election to the panchayat bodies at districts, blocks and villages were organized by the State government soon after its coming into powering 1977. This is a matter of more than 30 years back. Since very inception of the journey of the elected panchayats in 1978, the State government fully patronizes the panchayats for development of the rural areas – the panchayats in all three tiers have the authority to prepare development plans (both perspective and annual) for their respective jurisdiction and implement different programmes of both the Union and the State governments. So far as watershed development is concerned, in West Bengal there are no outstanding examples like Ralegaon Sidhi and Adgaon in Maharashtra, tribal areas of Panchmahal in Gujarat, Mittemari in Karnataka, and Jhabua in undivided Madhya Pradesh.

In studying dynamics of watershed development it is needless to say that the progress of the programme in West Bengal is very much lagging due to multiplicity of the agencies in the arena of implementation and the absence of lead role by the panchayats. The present paper discusses in details the different provisions of the West Bengal Panchayat Act, 1973 where the panchayats have been entrusted with the authority and responsibilities to implement programmes for the benefits of the local people in order to ensure economic development and social justice. Establishing equity in getting the benefits of water and participation of local people in the planning process and implementation are the two essentials for achieving any success in watershed development programme. Even after consolidation of the panchayats in the rural Bengal ,it is no denying that each village is unique and has its own standard of what is fair and workable. Participation of local people in a watershed project is very crucial as any externally imposed standard has every possibility of being inoperative. In the framework of the West Bengal Panchayat Act, 1973 the Government of West Bengal created different platforms for people's participation in panchayats' activities. But all these ventures have very little impact in terms of drawing people to the public meetings. These aspects are adequately addressed in this paper to depict the state of people's participation in the affairs of the panchayats who are supposed to act for the people according to the vision of the State government.

Apart from the introductory section, the present paper has three sections. Section 1 deals with the provisions of the guiding Act i.e. the West Bengal Panchayat Act, 1973 relating to the roles and responsibilities of the panchayats and the process of decision making within the legal frame-work. People's participation, mainly reflected through their attendance in the meetings of gram sansad and gram sabha is the matter of discussion in the section 2. The role of gram unnayan samitis in the planning and implementation of different programmes is also presented in this section as these samitis formed at each and every village constituency are sources of many interactions and rivalries in framing village level plans and implementation of the programmes as well. Section 3 discusses the equity and other aspects of watershed development affecting the livelihoods of the local people. In a watershed development it shall be the prerogative to protect the interests of the poor and marginalized – this is crucial because the use of and access to water conserved can disturb the equity and tranquility in the local area if not appropriately distributed. The panchayats have the responsibility to take care of such issues.

SECTION 1

In the recently published Common Guidelines for Watershed Development Projects (2008) by the Ministry of Rural Development, Government of India, a network of institutional arrangements has been prescribed. It is laid down that for having 'a unified perspective by all ministries' these guidelines are framed in coordination with the Planning Commission of Government of India. In the guiding principles of the common guidelines, decentralization and centrality of community participation are two areas where the panchayats have definitive role – "involvement of primary stakeholders is at the centre of planning, budgeting, implementation, and management of watershed projects". The West Bengal panchayats in three tiers have already been entrusted with the responsibilities of planning and implementation of various rural development programmes. For analyzing the role of the panchayats in watershed development it will be appropriate to present the institutional arrangements within the legal framework of the panchayats.

73rd Amendment to the Constitution of India not only conferred Constitutional recognition to the panchayats but also specified their tasks through enlistment of 29 subjects in the Eleventh schedule of the Constitution where minor irrigation is a subject. In West Bengal for adopting decentralization in the function of the gram panchayats, the State Government introduced a Section 32A in the West Bengal Panchayat Act, 1973 through an amendment of the Act in 1997. The purpose was to delegate power to the sub-committees comprising of the members of the gram panchayat. The section was again amended in 2003 for delegating additional powers to the sub-committees and specifying their functions distinctly in the Act and Rules framed thereunder. The section 32A made the provision that subject to direction as may be issued by the State Government in this behalf, a gram panchayat shall as soon as may be within three months from the first meeting of the gram panchayat (that is constitution of a gram panchayat after the panchayt general election), forms upa-samitis (sub-committees). Presently the State Government has approved constitution of following five upa-samitis:

(i) Artha-O-Parikalpana upa-samiti (Finance and Planning Sub Committee);

(ii) Krishi-O-Pranisampad Bikas upa-samiti (Agriculture and Animal Resource Development Sub Committee);

(iii) Siksha-O-Janasasthya upa-samiti (Education and Public Health Sub Committee);

(iv) Nari, Sishu Unnayan-O-Samaj Kalyan upa-samiti (Women, Child Development and Social Welfare Sub Committee);and

(v) Shilpa-O-Parikathama upa-samiti (Industry and Infrastructure Sub Committee).

Sub section 3 of section 32A, specifies the provision regarding formation of sub-committees. The pradhan and the upa pradhan shall be the ex-officio members of all upa-samitis. Every upa-samiti shall consist of members ranging from 1 to 3 depending on the size of the gram panchayat. Only exception is the Artha-O-Parikalpana upa samiti where the heads of other upa-samitis shall be the members. The head of a upa-samiti is known as Sanchalak (coordinator). Apart from the gram panchayat members in upa-samitis, the West Bengal Panchayat Act has the provision to include members appointed by the State Government by any general order or special order. The West Bengal Panchayat Act mentions two categories of persons from whom the State Government can make the appointment.

These Two Categories are:

(a) from among the officials of the panchayat bodies having jurisdiction, the State Government or any Statutory Board, Corporation or Organisation or any individual official receiving grant, financial assistance or remuneration from the State Exchequer, and

(b) any person having any specialized knowledge about the locality or any area of activity.

By a general order issued in the month of September 2004, the State Government made the appointment of different village level officials of functional departments to the upa-samitis. For example, two key employees of a gram panchayat, namely, the Executive Assistant and the Secretary have been appointed as members in Artha-O-Parikalpana upa-samiti. This upa-samiti is responsible for preparation of the budget and formulation of perspective and annual plans of the gram panchayat. In this way the State Government makes an endeavour to team up people's representatives and officials for development of local areas. A provision in the West Bengal Panchayat Act, 1973 is there to select one convenor (sanchalak) for each sub-committee - "members of such upa samiti shall elect one member from among themselves in such manner as may be prescribed to act as sanchalak for such upa samiti". Within the framework of law, the sanchalak is responsible for convening the meetings of upa-samiti and coordinating function of members of the concerned upa-samiti. Every upa-samiti has been empowered by the State Government to prepare schemes and perform the functions of the gram panchayat in relation to the subjects allotted to the upa-samiti within the budgetary provisions of the gram panchayat. To this effect, the sanchalak has the responsibility to prepare and place report of actions taken or proposed to be taken relating to the upa-samiti, to the pradhan and the gram panchayat. This is a continuous process. The idea behind constitution of upa-samitis is that the gram panchayat as a body will discharge its responsibilities through the upa-samitis. Under Rule 66 of the West Bengal Panchayat (Gram Panchayat Administration) Rules, 2004, the subject matters on which the upa-samiti of a gram panchayat shall deliberate upon and deal with are specified against each upa-samiti. Watershed development falls within the domain of Agriculture and Animal Resource Development Sub Committee. At the village level the planning as a concept is not all clear to the persons/agencies involved. By plan, they only mean the listing of beneficiaries and schemes. That too is also limited within a few. In politicized panchayats, decisions are mostly taken outside the panchayat structure and placed in the panchayat meetings for ratification. Obviously the party having majority dominates the process.

In every panchayat samiti and zilla parishad there are ten standing committees (sthayee samitis) to look after different subjects of development. Sections 124 and 171 of the West Bengal Panchayat Act, 1973 (and subsequent amendments) make provisions for constitution of these standing committees.

The list is here under:

(i) Artha, Sanstha, Unnayan o Parikalpana (Finance, Establishment, Development and Planning),

(ii) Janasasthya o Paribesh (Public health and Environment),

(iii) Purta Karya o Paribahan (Public works and Transport),

(iv) Krishi,Sech o Samabaya (Agriculture,Irrigation and Cooperation),

(v) Siksha,Sanskriti,Tathya o Krira (Education, Culture, Information and Sports),

(vi) Sishu o Nari unnayan, Janakalyan o Tran (Child and women development, Social welfare and Relief),

(vii) Bon o Bhumi sanskar (Forest and Land reform),

(viii) Matsya o Prani sampad bikash (Fishery and Animal resources development),

(ix) Khadya o Sarbaraha (Food and Supplies),

(x) Khudra shilpa, Bidyut o Achiracharit shakti (Small industry, Electricity and Non-conventional energy).

More or less all 29 subjects under the Eleventh Schedule are covered within these standing committees where the Artha ,Sanstha ,Unnayan o Parikalpana takes the prime role. According to the provisions of the West Bengal Panchayat Act, each sthayee samiti has the responsibility for the financial and executive administration of the schemes and programmes under the purview and control of the sthayee samiti within the budgetary provisions of the panchayat samiti. For proper coordination the chairperson of the panchayat samiti or the zilla parishad has been made the head of the Finance, Establishment, Development and Planning standing committee. In addition, the heads of all other sthayee samitis have been made the members of this standing committee for monitoring and reviewing of implementation of programmes. This provision of the West Bengal Panchayat Act incorporated through an amendment in the year 2003 enables to maintain a controlled guidance of decision making and functioning at sthayee samiti level. In the same amendment the State Government created the space for representation of opposition in the Finance,Establishment, Development and Planning standing committee. The provision goes like this: "leader of the recognised political party in opposition having largest number of members in the Panchayat Samiti in comparison with other recognized political parties in opposition shall be a member of the Artha, Sanstha ,Unnayan o Parikalpana sthayee samiti." Similar provision has been made for the zilla parishad. In this particular amendment (2003) of the West Bengal Panchayat Act, a provision of inclusion of opposition members in other sthayee samitis was also made: "one member from each recognised political party in opposition shall be selected to be a member of each of the sthayee samitis." The purpose of such amendment was to ensure representation of opposition in the decision making process and implementation of various programmes by the panchayat samitis and zilla prishads. This democratic practice can assure transparency in the activities of the panchayats which is taken to be an important yardstick of good governance.

In West Bengal, the planning process in rural areas originates from the gram sansad. Generally in the month of November meeting of the gram sansad the demands are placed, discussed and recommended to the gram panchayat for consideration in gram panchayat plan. Through a memorandum dated 7th July 2003, the State Government in the Department of Panchayats and Rural Development applied the principles of subsidiarity for guiding the distribution of functions among three tiers of the panchayat structure. In the words of the memorandum, "this principle demands that in the matter of assignment of responsibilities, the functions that can be done by the Panchayat body at a particular level should be done at that level and should not be assigned to the

Panchayat body at a higher level." For example, the memorandum specifically prohibited the zilla parishad from taking up earth work schemes (except those linked to capital intensive projects such as metal roads or building). In case of individual beneficiary oriented schemes it becomes mandatory that 'identification of the beneficiaries will be initiated at the Gram Sansad level and finalized at the GP level.'On the basis of the principle of subsidiarity, projects and activities which can be implemented at the gram panchayat level should be included in gram panchayat plan. From the gram sansad, only the lists of names of schemes for different programmes and locations are raised. In case of individual benefit oriented programmes like Indira Awas Yojana for house construction and augmentation of existing houses of the rural poor, the gram sansad prepares lists for the prospective beneficiaries. The West Bengal Panchayat Act in the sub section (3) of section 19 makes it obligatory on the part of the gram panchayat to accept the recommendation of a gram sansad, if it is not other wise impossible.

The provision of subsection 1 of section 19 of the West Bengal Panchayat Act, 1973 delineates the functions of the gram panchayats in clear terms. The relevant extract is given below:

"A Gram Panchayat shall function as a unit of self-government and in order to achieve economic development and secure social justice for all, shall, subject to such conditions as may be prescribed or such directions as may be given by the State Government, -

(a) prepare a development plan for the five year term of the office of the members and revise and update it as and when necessary with regard to the resource available;

(b) prepare an annual plan for each year by the month of October of the preceding year for development of human resources, infrastructure and civic-amenities in the area;

(c) implement schemes for economic development and social justice as may be drawn up by, or entrusted upon it."

Preparation of perspective plan and annual plan is the obligatory duty of a gram panchayat. In practice the gram panchayats in general do not prepare perspective plan for five years. In course of dialogue with the pradhans, it becomes quite clear that majority of them are not aware of this provision.The story does not end here. The employees of the gram panchayats, in particular the executive assistants and the secretaries also are not fully aware of the provision that by law it is obligatory for the gram panchayats to prepare a five year perspective plan. The provisions of five-year perspective plan have been made as the tenure of a gram panchayat is for five years. For preparing a perspective plan it is essential that the party holding the majority in a gram panchayat should have a vision. This vision is practically lacking among the panchayat members. Obviously, it is desirable that this vision would not come from the field level bureaucracy or the district authority. It should emerge from the panchayat members themselves. Due to lack of this vision, they simply are engaged in spending money received from the State Government through different channels. This money is very much tied in nature and the panchayats have to spend according to the directives of the funding authority and the programme guidelines. The local priorities and people's agenda take a back seat in the process. Whatever resource is given to the gram panchayats in the form of untied fund is also tied by a lot of instructions from the State Government. Thus the untied fund is not purely untied in nature. The panchayats prepare plans only for such shemes which are very much conversant to them. The importance of watershed development is not at all intheir agenda even in the districts like Purulia, Bankura, and some areas of Paschim Medinipur (Jhargram sub-division) where rainfall is low.

The panchayats being a political entity, it is expected that the persons within these bodies shall posses a minimum level of knowledge to realise the inner dynamics of the system. It is not sufficient to know the guidelines of the programmes; rather it is necessary to know how a system functions in close association with political and social contents. Because of this gap even with so much of investments, everywhere deficits, distortion and dys-functionalities are the common features. This is something different from the picture of ideal democratic state. One more prevalent practice in West Bengal is that the local political leaders dictate the panchayats and the bureaucracy in different tiers making the panchayats overburdened with dictates,orders and guidelines. Practically, none of them truly guide the panchayat members with care and sympathy–this creates confusion and in-coordination. The participation of local people in the different phases of watershed development is urgency. The next section throws light on the people's participation in the panchayats as they are responsible for planning and implementation of all types of rural development.

SECTION 2

People's participation does not mean only enlistment of the support of the masses: but it expects their active involvement in different stages of formulation and implementation of plans and programmes. The Report of the Team for the Study of Community Projects and National Extension Service (under the chairmanship of Balvantray G. Mehta) addressed the concept of people's participation. The Report of the Study Team (November, 1957) observed that "generally, the more prosperous sections of the village community have participated in community works less than others; and when they did, it was more by contributions in cash or kind than by actual physical labour". The suggestion of the Report for making participation worthy was that "it (participation) should be widespread, should be fairly similar for all participants and should not call for disproportionately large sacrifice from the weaker sections of the community."

Through an amendment of the West Bengal Panchayat Act in the year 1994, the State Government brought in the concept of gram sansad. According to the definition of the West Bengal Panchayat Act, gram sansad means a body consisting of persons registered at any time in the electoral rolls pertaining to a constituency of a gram panchayat. West Bengal's gram sansad is just like gram sabha as defined in the 73rd Amendment of the Constitution. This means that all voters in a constituency of a gram panchayat are the members of a gram sansad. In respect of the meetings of gram sansad, the Act in section 16A makes two provisions: (i) every gram panchayat shall hold within its local limits an annual and a half yearly meeting for each gram sansad at such place, on such date and at such hour as may be fixed by the gram panchayat; and (ii) the annual meeting of the gram sansad shall be held ordinarily in the month of May and the half-yearly meeting of the gram sansad shall be held ordinarily in the month of November every year. The essence of the importance of gram sansads can be viewed from the Annual Administrative Report, 2003-04 of the Department of Panchayats and Rural Development, Government of West Bengal:

"The main function of Gram Sansad is to guide and advice the gram panchayat in regard to the schemes for economic development and social justice, identification of beneficiaries for various poverty alleviation and food security programmes, constitution of one or more beneficiary committees for ensuring active participation of people in implementation, maintenance and equitable distribution of benefits of one or more schemes in its area. A Gram Sansad may raise objection to action of Pradhan or any other member of gram panchayat for failure to implement any development work properly. Further, it is mandatory for a gram panchayat to place in the meetings of Gram Sansad, the budget and audit report of the accounts of Gram Panchayat for deliberation, recommendation and suggestion of Gram Sansad".

Section 16 B of the The West Bengal Panchayat Act makes the provision for holding the gram sabha meeting in every gram panchayat. All members of the gram sansads in a gram panchayat are the members of the gram sabha. The provision of the law is that every gram panchayat shall hold within its local limits an annual meeting, ordinarily in the month of December every year, of the gram sabha after completion of the half-yearly meeting of the gram sansads in November. In many cases the gram panchayat cannot complete the gram sansad meetings within November; then the gram sabha meeting has to be deferred to January or even to February. Attendance of one twentieth of the total number of members shall form a quorum for a meeting of a gram sabha.

Provision of the law is that a gram sabha shall deliberate upon, recommend, and adopt resolution on the matters discussed in different gram sansads. In practice, a gram sabha meeting in a gram panchayat is merely a routine affair to satisfy the directives. This meeting simply endorses the proceedings and decisions taken in the constituent gram sansads of a gram panchayat. Attendance in gram sabha meetings also hovers around the minimum stipulated attendance of 5 percent of the electors. In discussions with the people, it would come out that if there were any shortfall, the members and their followers went to the houses for taking signatures of the electors in villages. The proceedings of the meetings are not written in details. People normally do not interact with the panchayats even if there are forums created by the State government for deliberation. The patron- client relationship is very dominant in the rural areas even after more than 30 years of the panchayati raj in West Bengal.

For attaching importance to the gram sansad meetings, the State Government through an amendment in the West Bengal Panchayat Act in the year 2003 has made it obligatory on the part of a gram panchayat to act upon any recommendation of a gram sansad relating to prioritization of beneficiaries for assistance under a programme or regarding a scheme which will be of importance for the gram sansad. If a gram panchayat has to take decision that recommendations of a gram sansad cannot be implemented or are not acceptable under the framework of the law, this decision has to be placed by the gram panchayat in the next meeting of the concerned gram sansad. For strengthening gram sansads, the State Government places enormous weightage on convening these meetings with wide publicity among the public. The purpose is to bring all sections of people in these meetings and to deliberate freely. It is expected that these measures can boost up the process of functioning at local level toward holistic development of the area.

Field experiences often lead to the feeling that in course of discharging their functions, the panchayat representatives who in general are very near to the people, are accruing bureaucratic vices. Browsing through the average attendance of people in the gram sansad meetings over the years since 1996, their unwillingness to participate in the affairs of panchayats can be realised.

Table 1
Average Attendance in Gram Sansad and Gram Sabha Meetings: West Bengal

Year	*Gram Sansad (May)*	*Gram Sansad (November)*	*Gram Sabha*
1996	11	18	5
1997	15	18	5.1
1998	11	16	5.3
1999	12	13	5.5
2000	12	13	5
2001	12	11	9
2002	12	12	5
2003	12	11.7	7
2004	13	14.2	6
2005	13.5	14	6
2006	14.6	13.9	6.8
2007	14.8	15.1	6.5

Source: *Annual Administrative Report of Department of Panchayats &* Rural Development, Govt. of West Bengal for different years.
Note: All figures are in percentage.

From the Table 1 it can be seen that the attendance in the meetings of gram sansad and gram sabha are bare minimum required for validation of the meetings. The provision of the Act (sub section 4A of section 16A) states that one tenth of the total number of members shall form the quorum for a meeting of a gram sansad i.e. there should be a mandatory presence of 10 percent of the members of gram sansad to validate the meeting. The common practice was that the panchayats made very little efforts to mobilise people for the adjourned meetings. To do away with such practice, the State Government through an amendment in the Act in the year 2003, made it obligatory for the adjourned meetings to secure quorum. The quorum to be achieved in an adjourned meeting is the attendance of at least one-twentieth of the total number of members of a gram sansad as against the first meeting quorum of one tenth of the total members. The attendance of women in gram sansad meetings or gram sabha meetings in West Bengal is very low. It does not differ substantially even if there is a woman panchayat member in any gram sansad. The crux of the problem is that people in general do not take any interest in the affairs of the panchayats. Only during the election they go to the polling booths for casting their votes. On an average, in the panchayat elections around 85 to 90 percent of the total votes are polled. During a gram sansad meeting only 10 to 12 percent of these voters come to attend the meeting. This indicates the aversion of the common people towards these meetings.

For strengthening decentralization and involvement of people in the process of development, the State Government by an amendment of the West Bengal Panchayat Act in the year 2003 took decision to constitute a Gram Unnayan Samiti (GUS) in each gram sansad. As specified in the Act, a gram unnayan samiti shall ensure active participation of people in implementation; maintenance and equitable distribution of benefits with respect to such subjects as may be prescribed. In the Act it is provided that the gram unnayan samiti shall be accountable for its functions and decisions to the gram sansad in which it is constituted. The gram sansad in turn shall exercise its power and authority in this behalf in such manner, as may be prescribed by the State Government. For giving local people pre eminent importance, the Act makes the provision that a gram sansad shall guide and advise the gram panchayat in regard to the schemes for economic development and social justice undertaken or proposed to be undertaken in the gram panchayat area. Legal provisions are there, but adherence to them is starred with many potholes. Motivated failures on the part of the panchayats dominate. The panchayats in majority cases do not have the tolerance to interact with the people and opposition. This is a major source of all disturbances.

SECTION 3

Equity question seems to be very vital in any watershed development programme. At the outset it will be appropriate to conceptualize the term in the context of the panchayats' functioning as well as outcome of watershed projects. Equity is a difficult concept, with a history of different interpretations, varying by country and academic discipline. In this study, no such attempts are made, however. In the West Bengal Panchayat Act, 1973 the concept of ensuring social justice in the respective jurisdiction of the panchayats is very much ingrained. Practice by the panchayats in three tiers of the panchayat structure does not conform to this concept – at least examples from West Bengal may corroborate it. The common denominator of many views on equality relates to fairness and transparency in activities. So far as watershed development is concerned this is something lacking. First instance is the watershed development committees at the grassroots level. The case of Purulia district in West Bengal has many examples to reflect that the panchayats are not at all interested in formation of watershed committees, mainly because they do not get their persons in the watershed areas. The gram unnayan samitis (GUS) at the village constituencies are predominantly occupied with the government sponsored programmes where funds are available with the gram panchayats, such as National Rural Employment Guarantee Scheme, National Old Age Pension Scheme etc. The long term vision is peculiarly absent among them. Watershed development requires this. In contrast to this familiar scenario in watershed development, involvement of the panchayats in rigorous way can be visible in case of Sishu Siksha Karmasuchi (SSK). Under this scheme, Sishu Siksha Kendras are set up in a village where at least there are 20 eligible children not having access to the formal education system. This alternative elementary education system is directly managed and supervised by the local people and the panchayats. The field reality is that these centres are becoming very popular to the local people as they accept them as their own institution. Teachers are appointed on contract by the gram panchayats and one of the conditions is that the teachers should be from the locality. This stipulation is made to develop effective bondage with both the children and local community. As a consequence, SSK becomes a supportive effort to universalization of primary education. The added dimension of SSK is that the teachers (known as sahayika) are mostly women and there is a very little intervention from the State Government department except giving funds for honorarium of the teachers, contingency expenditures and construction of centres where necessary. As the teachers are appointed on contract basis by the managing committee comprised of local people, their accountability is unquestionable. The villagers pay more attention to the immediate gains than to the long term benefits. This priority has very strong influence in selection of the schemes / programmes. Watershed development gives long term benefits, but sustainable also. Realizing this fact is still distant, both among the panchayat people and the commoners. For removing this blockage wide publicity is also needed. This aspect is not getting appropriate care and affection from the departments as well as the field level functionaries. The example of Purulia district proves this contention. Due to hilly and undulating terrain in Purulia and insufficient soil and water conservation measures, the run-off of rain water during the short and irregular rainy season is very heavy. As a result, not only the water, but also the valuable topsoil with all its nutrients is lost. Again, Purulia district's soil is shallow and nutrient-poor. Due to loss of forest cover the rate of soil erosion has increased so rapidly that it is likely to reach crisis proportion soon unless effective action can be taken. Watershed development can give relief to the emerging situation; but the panchayats, the decision making authorities at different tiers of governance are not at all concerned with these maladies. As a consequence poverty has been endemic in Purulia over the ages. The bulk of the population is engaged in rain-fed paddy cultivation by traditional methods once a year. Though large numbers of livestock are reportedly present in the district, their monetary yield is small – negligible for all practical purposes. In spite of a shortage of fodder in the summer season, no initiative for fodder cultivation on a large scale can be taken up for non-availability of water during dry season. All these facts simply disturb the equity aspects and strengthen the exclusiveness within the village society. The poverty of the farmers prevents adequate investment in agricultural inputs like good quality seeds, balanced use of different kinds of fertilizers strictly in accordance with the need of the soil, use of the required quality and quantity of pesticides. Ensuring minimum quantity of water even when rainfall is scanty or irregular through watershed projects can bring some way out from the age old miseries. This becomes a vicious circle–with low value inputs resulting in low value outputs–leading, in turn, to repetition of low value inputs and consequent low value outputs – and a perpetuation of poverty.

Involving self help groups in the watershed development throughout West Bengal is still sporadic. According to the Common Guidelines, the watershed committees shall constitute self help groups in the watershed areas with the help of watershed team from amongst poor, small, and marginal farmer households, landless / asset less poor agricultural labourers, women, scheduled caste and scheduled tribe families. Preferably these groups shall be homogenous having common identity and interests. This indicates that watershed development projects do not create any inequity in the implementation areas. The grassroots experiences tell different stories. The gram panchayats keep everything in their hands– decentralization is talked about by everyone, but up to one's own level; not beyond that. In this way people's interests are lost in the cobweb of decentralized governance. The equity concept is also disturbed when the gram panchayats fail to facilitate the convergence of various projects/schemes to watershed development. Though the services of village level officials of many departments are placed with the gram panchayats, yet the convergence of programmes is missing in most of the cases. This is a major hindrance in the planning and implementation process of watershed development. Group membership and creation of enabling circumstances affect how one is treated by the institutions with which one normally interacts. The gram panchayats are such institutions at the village level. When they do not rise to the desired occasion, it is obvious that the outcome will be short of desired expectations. Ensuring social justice in the local area is bound to suffer. The criss-crossing of interests hampers most. From the angle of ensuring equity in watershed development projects, sustainable resource management together with broadening the livelihood options of the people living in the watershed is a major concern.

In view of the Department of Panchayats and Rural Development of the Government of West Bengal, "watershed development programme being a process intensive programme requires long term planning with active participation of the community throughout the entire stages of formulation, implementation of project components and also maintenance of the assets created." The discussions in the different sections not clearly reflect the fulfillment of the contentions made by the State Government. Within the grey zones there are some hopes of ray also. The initiatives of the villagers can change the scenario. The case of Jatgoria, a small village in Kanksa development block, in Burdwan district at least tells so. Relevant extracts from the case study are presented below.

" ... some of the villagers thought other ways. They are the members of water shed committee. Being enlightened with the idea of watershed development project they ventured to turn the area green. Those villagers who surrendered to the vagaries of nature agreed to toil to bring an end to this.

A nearby pond on vested land with an area of 2.2 acre, which remained dry almost throughout the year, was taken up for excavation. A piece of so called barren land was taken up for establishment of orchard with the help of gram panchayat while field bunding (aal bandhi) was done on some plots of barren land measuring 16.73 acre. In doing all these work involving an expenditure of Rs. 230485 they had generated 3660 mandays (824 were women). Miracle started to trickle. Nature was happy with their hard labour. The once dried up pond was now providing life saving irrigation to their kharif crop which was dependent on rain, thus ensuring a modest harvest. The pond and orchard were handed over to a SHG for its maintenance. The user charge collected from the irrigation water of pond was being invested in maintenance of the orchard. The orchard of mango, guava and lemon will start bearing within a year..." (Annual Administrative Report of the Department of Panchayats and Rural Development, 2006-07).

This experience is fair enough to pinpoint that vision of the gram panchayat is essential for bringing effective implementation of watershed development projects. Involvement of the local villagers is the other ingredient for success. In general these are predominantly missing. Though the panchayats are functioning in West Bengal for more than 30 years the rivalry for power between the ruling and the opposition parties becomes the stark reality. The very premise of decentralization on which the panchayat institutions have been contemplated is being challenged day by day. There is scope for further research on this aspect. In the rural polity of West Bengal, the practice of patronizing the ruling party's support base by use of funds allotted in different centrally sponsored programmes becomes more or less legitimized – even the parties not in majority in the State Assembly follow the same path of the ruling Left front in the panchayats where they have the majority. In the process, rural people are readily divided between two groups, one receiving the benefits and the other being discriminated against. These situations to a large extent hamper the process of decentralized development and decision making.

IN LIEU OF A CONCLUSION

From the discussions in the foregoing paragraphs, it is more or less clear that the panchayats in West Bengal are not that much interested in development of watersheds in the drought prone districts like Purulia, Bankura and some parts of Paschim Medinipore, even if there acute crisis of water. The simple fact that more irrigation water has meant greater output and income at the household level does not get the appropriate priority in the action plans designed at the gram panchayats. Primary reason is that everybody is interested in immediate benefits but not in long term benefits. Attitudinal change is urgent; but this requires training of the panchayat office bearers on sustained basis. This is not coming up, however. In the training curricula of the Department of Panchayats and Rural Development, Government of West Bengal, the matters of watershed development do not receive adequate attention. The basic tenets of the West Bengal Panchayat Act,1973 like ensuring economic development and social justice remain mostly unrecognized in the field of activities of the panchayats, irrespective of their tier. Democracy ideally means working in consultation with all and respecting voice and choice of the oppositions. In spite of being democratic institutions, the panchayats are yet to reach that height. Lack of this not only hampers the progress of development activities but also the basic needs of the villagers, for example the availability of water in dry regions which very much restricts the livelihood options also. In general political systems do not always assign equal weights to everyone's preferences. For watershed development some aberrations from this general trend is necessary as the programme is concerned with water. Percolation of this need to the grassroots level is not picking up. Only directions from above in the administrative hierarchy do not serve the purpose. Political will and instructions from the party-bosses is essential for making any substantial and sustainable change. At the villages the panchayats tend to become clientelistic and more inclined to make individual exchanges of patronage to their followers only. This again leads to many animosities at local levels. Ownership, inclusion, and consensus are still missing both at the planning and implementation stages. The dichotomy requires immediate attention of the political leaders at the state and district tiers followed by their effective directives for corrective actions at local levels. Otherwise the existing scenario will sustain for long. There are many acts and rules coupled with administrative orders; but their grounding is a real problem.

REFERENCES

Department of Panchayats and Rural Development (2006-07), Govt. of West Bengal, Annual Administrative Report.

Ministry of Rural Development, Govt. of India (1994) Report of the technical Committee on Drought Prone Areas Programme and Desert Development Programme.

Ministry of Rural Development, Govt. of India (2008), Common Guidelines for Watershed Development Projects, World Bank (2006), World Development Report, 2006.

INDEX

31

EMPOWERMENT OF WOMEN IN INDIA

*S. Sagaya Doss**

Indian constitution in its fundamental rights has provisions for equality Social justice and protection of women. These goals are yet to be realized. Women continue to be discriminated, exploited and exposed to inequalities at various levels. So the concept of empowerment as a goal of development projects and programmes has been gaining wider acceptance.

By empowerment, women would be able to develop self-esteem confidence, realize their potential and enhance their collective bargaining power. The draft National Policy on Empowerment of women envisages : (i) to set up councils at the national and state levels to review the implementations of the national and state commissions for women (ii) the center and state to draw – up time bound action plans to translate this policy in to concrete action in consultation with the central and state commissions for women, and (iii) every ministry at the center and in the state is obliged to ensure equal flow of benefits in physical and financial terms to women through different programmes and plans.

The need of the hour is to empower women so that they can become independent in all matters concerned with their own family and the society at large. Mahatma Gandhi, the father of our nation, believed that women's productive abilities and attitudes were essential forces that need to be allowed full and

* Lecturer in the Department of Economics, Sacred Heart College, Tirupattur, Vellore Dt. 635 601. Tamil Nadu, India.

free play for human and social development with justice and dignity. The process of development would be incomplete and lopsided, unless women are fully involved in it. Emancipation of women is an essential pre-requisite for economic development and social progress of the nation. Women must be recognized as a power in development and involved actively and productively in the developmental process.

EMPOWERMENT OF WOMEN THROUGH SHGS.

The formation of women's Self-Help Groups is one of the means of empowerment of women found by the central and State Government in India.

The empowerment of women through self-help groups would lead to benefit not only to the individual women and women groups but also for the family and community as a whole through collective action for development. Empowering women is not just for meeting their economic needs but also for more holistic social development.

THE SELF-HELP GROUPS

The concept of SHG serves to underline the principle 'for the people, by the people and of the people". The origin of SHG is from the brain child of Gramin Bank of Bangladesh, which was founded by the Prof. Mahammed Yaunus of Chittagong University in the year 1975. This was exclusively established for the poor.

Self-help group is a small economically homogeneous and affinity group of rural poor which voluntarily agrees to contribute to a common fund to be lend to its members as per group decision, which works for group solidarity, self and group awareness, social, economic and political empowerment in the way of democratic functioning.

SHGS AND WOMEN EMPOWERMENT

Empowerment can serve as a powerful instrument for women to achieve upward social and economic mobility and achieve power and status in society. It is a source of mobility, equality and emancipation, both at the individual and at the societal

-level. It is important to bring women into main stream of development so that society benefits from women empowerment. Women's empowerment is all the more important because of the special problem that women face today. Gender bias in social, educational, economical and political fields is still manifest in many civilized societies of the world. Empowerment of women can serve as an essential input in development.

The Self-Help Groups are a viable alternative to achieve the objectives of rural development and to get community participation in all rural development programmes. SHGs enhance the quality of status of women as participants, decision makers and beneficiaries in the democratic, economic, social and cultural spheres of life. In all stages of economic and social activities involvement of women becomes essential. SHGs encourage women to take active part in the socio economic progress of our nation.

Participation of women in SHGs makes a significant impact on their empowerment in social and economic and political aspects. The SHG program itself aimed at empowering women on the following aspect:

(a) Social Empowerment
(b) Economic Empowerment
(c) Political Empowerment

(a) Social Empowerment

Social empowerment is brought slowly by way of capacity building for women. The capacity of an individual may be built in the form of providing education and training. Education and training will go a long way in achieving the goal of participation in national development and help in raising the status of women, enable development of their potential as independent and equal partners. The purpose of providing education to women is to enable them to think critically, identify their strengths and take conscious informed decisions, empower them to play a positive role on their own in the development of the nation.

There are three major causes contributing to educational backwardness of rural women which are as follows:

1. *Social-Cultural Factors*

The low status of women in our society and the preference given to males at every level is a major cause of female illiteracy. Parents in rural areas fail to see why their daughter must be educated as her training in household work is considered more important. Another argument is that an educated girl would require an educated husband who as a result of his education would demand a higher dowry. Many parents do not like the idea of sending their daughters to co-educational schools, particularly at the middle and secondary levels. Moreover, parents find it more reasonable to spend on son's education rather than the daughter as it gives return. Girls are expected to be married in their teens. Early marriage is also an important reason for dropout rates among girls.

2. *Economic Factors*

The expenditure on education is higher even while education may be free up to the primary level. A majority of people, particularly in rural areas, simply cannot afford expenses on text books, stationary and so on. Girls in rural areas often assist the family by either working in the field or household or in looking after younger children. The family in such cases may be not in a position to send her to school.

3. *Factors related to Education*

Lack of facilities in close proximity is one of the important problems in the education of girls in rural areas. To send girls to far-off places for education is both economically impractical and socially unacceptable in such a context. In addition, dull teaching methods and lack of educational support at home lead to low performance. With regard to higher education, girls tend to opt for teacher training as opposed to boys who enroll in science courses. As an incentive scholarships may be provided to girls who enroll in science courses.

Education and training of women is important so as to increase their knowledge, skill, ability, value and motivation which may lead them for social empowerment. The SHG concept is focused on that area. The major objectives of training to SHG members are to equip them with better skills and enhance their knowledge so as to prepare them to face new challenges in the society.

The training in SHGs is to be addressed to update knowledge and skills in the areas of child care, nutrition, hygiene and house keeping. There is a need to allow women to break out of stereotyped roles. There is a trend to give equal opportunities for women at all education levels. Educational facilities and incentives are provided for Women's education. So that there is a hope that women will become socially empowered.

B. Economic Empowerment

Social empowerment can be achieved only through economic empowerment because our social status is actually influenced by our economic status when women are economically well-off then automatically they attain social status. So in order to make SHG women economical well-off the savings and credit system was introduced through micro credit programmers.

In India, many NGOs have promoted SHGs for collective action through periodic group based savings and credit. Often the savings and credit is used as a natural issue for group organization and empowerment. This leads to sharing of responsibility and assets in groups. In this, all the members of a group should have an amount fixed by the members themselves periodically (weekly/ monthly) as the case may be fixed by the members. Every month the president or the secretary of the group collects the money and gets it deposited in the nearest bank. This type of periodic cash savings and credit at the group level provides a very simple but powerful mechanism to enable groups to manage, control and own their institution nurtured around local savings and credit SHGs can make best use of their micro credit programmes for improving knowledge and capacity of women.

The proper functioning of self-help groups can create conditions for rural women to realize their role in development. The group can also promote progressive attitudes; awareness and support women in improving their status and conditions gradually the self-help groups and also promote linkages and solidarity with other women's group working on women's issues.

SHGS AND MICRO FINANCE

Micro finance refers to the entire range of financial and non-financial services, including skill up gradation and entrepreneurship development, rendered to the poor for enabling them to overcome poverty. Micro Finance as an effective credit delivery system seeks to achieve the following broad range and multifaceted objectives to meet the credit needs of the rural poor.

- To Support financial services to the rural poor, particularly women, who have not been able to secure the needed services from the formal financial system.
- To Provide lendable end capacity building funds in respect of SHGs and various types of cotton grass-roots level micro-finance institutions.
- To Support all initiatives of the SHG – bank linking programmes through thrift related backing activity.
- To Build up expertise in micro finance activities.

ADVANTAGES

Micro financing has turned out to be an effective strategy for formal financing agencies. Group lending minimizes transaction cost and at the same time the members of a group can avail small loans through that group. The chances of misutilisation are minimal and there are assured repayment because of peer monitoring by the group.

For the SHGs members, the system has been found beneficial because of minimal procedural formalities, access to institutional credit, full autonomy in the selection of activity and the availability of thrift for meeting urgent needs.

IMPACT OF MICRO FINANCE

- Micro Finance program are currently being promoted as a key strategy for simultaneously addressing both poverty alleviation and women's empowerment. This programme address the following impact.

- Increasing Women's income levels and control over income leading to greater levels of economic independence.
- Access networks and markets giving wider experience of the world outside the home, access to information and possibilities for development of other social and political roles.
- Enhancing perceptions of women's contribution to household income and family welfare.
- More general improvement in attitudes to women's role in the household and community.

Thus micro financing programmes targeting women has led to their empowerment in economic, social and political spheres and also empowerment, within the family.

The self-help groups are organized to manage their economic activities better and are gaining empowerment in directions, which are appropriate to their needs, interests and constraints. They gained confidence from an increase in their relative financial independence and security.

C. Political Empowerment

Political empowerment of women does not imply just a right to vote silently but to discuss, share politics by knowing its pros and cons and thereby to influence policies and decision making. In recent years there has been increased participation of women in politics. The members of SHG have access to government information such as rules and regulations, provisions available for women, policies, administrative and other services.

CONCLUSION

Women are organized to manage their economic activities better. They are empowered by increased financial position. The increase in literacy skill of the SHG members is another indicator of empowerment some of them learned to sign, to read and write and could do some simple arithmetic work. They got trained for this work by the NGOs with the help of Mahalir Thittam Officials.

Decision-making is the ultimate level of empowerment and equality. It signifies that women have started taking control of their lives and situations through attending group meetings, public functions, involvement in income generating activities, joining other women in social causes. The SHG members are sensitized in acquiring an attitude of protest against various abuses, knowledge about their rights and other social issues.

Better communication skills are an other indicator of empowerment. Most of the group members are attending the group meetings, and Grama Sabha meeting regularly. This develops their ability to interact and communicate with each other. Through this collective action with the ideology of empowerment SHGs are emerging as a movement in Tamil Nadu.

REFERENCE

Agnos Stephen, "SHGs and Micro Finance", *Social Welfare*, Vol. 52, No. 4, July 2005.

Murugan, Self Help Groups, Social Welfare, Vol. 47, No. 5, August 2000.

Bikram, Empowerment of Women and Rural Development", *Social Welfare*, Vol. 45, No. 10, October, 1997.

Leelamma Devasia, Social Development Issues in Self Help Groups, *Social Welfare*, Vol. 50, No. 10, January, 2004.

INDEX

[C]

[D]

[H]

[I]

[J]

[K]

[L]

[M]

[N]

[O]

[P]

[Q]

[R]

[S]